TEXT &
PRESENTAT
2015

D0671834

Text & Presentation, 2015

Edited by Graley Herren

The Comparative Drama Conference Series, 12

McFarland & Company, Inc., Publishers
Jefferson, North Carolina

ISSN 1054-724X • ISBN 978-1-4766-6334-0
ISBN 978-1-4766-2473-0 (ebook)

softcover : acid free paper ∞

Front cover: Becky Ann Baker, Frances McDormand, and Estelle
Parsons in the 2011 Manhattan Theatre Club production of *Good
People*. Photograph by Joan Marcus. Courtesy playwright David
Lindsay-Abaire, from his personal collection.

Printed in the United States of America

McFarland & Company, Inc., Publishers
  Box 611, Jefferson, North Carolina 28640
    www.mcfarlandpub.com

Acknowledgments

As editor of *Text & Presentation*, I follow in the footsteps of several inspirational predecessors: Karelisa Hartigan (1980–1993), Bill Free (1993–1998), Hanna Roisman (1998–1999), Stratos E. Constantinidis (1999–2008), and Kiki Gounaridou (2009–2011). I have been generously assisted each year by *T&P*'s associate editor, Kevin J. Wetmore, Jr., who served the Comparative Drama Conference magnificently as its director during the Los Angeles years. It has also been a pleasure to work with Jay Malarcher in his first year as book review editor. Our outgoing book review editor, Verna A. Foster, finished her marvelous run by moderating her final "Author Meets Critics" panel at the 2015 conference. Jay will assume the helm of that signature CDC series beginning in 2016. Kevin, Jay, and I serve at the pleasure of our esteemed colleagues on the CDC board, and our energetic director Laura Snyder, who organized another memorable conference this year on the sparkling Inner Harbor of Baltimore.

Like theatre itself, *Text & Presentation* is a collaborative effort that depends heavily upon many contributors behind the scenes. I wish to thank all those who participated in the 2015 conference, in particular those who submitted their work for possible publication in *Text & Presentation*. The number and caliber of submissions was high, making this year both a gratifying and a challenging one as editor. I wish to thank the editorial board for vetting the submissions, supplying thorough evaluations, and suggesting thoughtful avenues for revision to our authors. The high quality of the present volume is in large measure attributable to their scrupulous service: José I. Badeness, S.J. (Loyola Marymount University), William Boles (Rollins College), Miriam Chirico (Eastern Connecticut State University), Stratos E. Constantinidis (Ohio State University), Ellen Dolgin (Dominican College), Les Essif (University of Tennessee, Knoxville), Verna A. Foster (Loyola University Chicago), Yoshiko Fukushima (University of Hawaii, Hilo), Kiki Gounaridou (Smith College), Jan L. Hagens (Yale University), Karelisa Hartigan (University of Florida), William Hutchings (University of Alabama at Birmingham), Baron Kelly (University of Louisville), Jeffrey B. Loomis (Northwest Missouri State University), Ian Andrew MacDonald (Dickinson College), Jules Malarcher (West Virginia

University), Amy Muse (University of St. Thomas), Elizabeth Scharffenberger (Columbia University), Michael Schwartz (Indiana University Pennsylvania), Janna Segal (Mary Baldwin College), Laura Snyder (Stevenson University), Tony Stafford (University of Texas at El Paso), Kevin J. Wetmore, Jr. (Loyola Marymount University), and Kelly Younger (Loyola Marymount University).

Text & Presentation, 2015 contains several images, and I am very grateful to those who have permitted reproduction of those images. I am especially thankful to the playwright David Lindsay-Abaire for graciously permitting us to use a photo from his personal collection for the cover of the volume. The photo was taken by Joan Marcus and depicts Becky Ann Baker, Frances McDormand, and Estelle Parsons in the marvelous Manhattan Theatre Club production of his play *Good People*. I appreciate blueShadow Photography for permitting use of two production photos in Elizabeth Charlebois's essay. Davenne Essif's essay includes Giorgio de Chirico's *The Painter's Family*, owned by the Tate Gallery and reproduced here with the kind permission Artists Rights Society (ARS), New York / SIAE, Rome, and Tate, London / Art Resource, NY. Among the images included in Lurana Donnels O'Malley's essay, two are under copyright and are reprinted here with permission: *Ethiopia Awakening* by Meta Warrick Fuller appears with permission from the Art & Artifacts Division, Schomburg Center for Research in Black Culture, The New York Public Library, Astor, Lenox and Tilden Foundations; and "Ethiopia at the Bar of Justice" by James Lesesne Wells appears with permission from Crisis Publishing Company. I also thank Palgrave Macmillan for permitting reproduction of the cover image from J. Chris Westgate's book, *Staging the Slums, Slumming the Stage*, reviewed in this volume by William Hutchings. The image is *Slumming* (H. C. Miner Litho. Co., 1898) from the Library of Congress, Prints and Photographs Division.

The 39th Annual Comparative Drama Conference owes much of its success to the generous support of Stevenson University. We thank President Kevin Manning for once again leading off our keynote event and warmly welcoming the attendees. Heartfelt thanks go to Chelsea Dove and Brittany Proudfoot-Ginder, the magnificent assistants whose tireless efforts and boundless charm make us all feel so welcome to Baltimore each year. And no Acknowledgments section for *Text & Presentation* and the Comparative Drama Conference would be complete without expressing the deepest gratitude to our magnificent Conference Director Laura Snyder. Her dedication, hard work, organization, generosity, grace under pressure, and leadership made 2015 another banner year and make all of us look forward to returning to Baltimore each spring.

Finally, I offer my deepest thanks to my wife, Cathy, and our son, Dylan. You are the foundation on which all my work is built, and I depend deeply upon your love and support for everything I do.

Contents

Preface

The Comparative Drama Conference was founded in 1977 by Karelisa Hartigan at the University of Florida. The annual spring gathering has grown considerably over the years. In 2000 the conference moved from Gainesville to Columbus under the directorship of Stratos E. Constanidis (The Ohio State University). In 2005 Kevin J. Wetmore, Jr. (Loyola Marymount University), assumed the helm for a seven-year stint in Los Angeles. We began the latest leg of the journey in 2012 under the leadership of Laura Snyder (Stevenson University) at our new home base of Baltimore. The conference routinely attracts over some 200 total participants from across the country and around the globe.

Though the size and scope have expanded over the years, certain core principles have remained intact throughout the conference's history. From the start, Karelisa Hartigan fostered an environment of intellectual rigor combined with hospitality and support. The CDC has always facilitated generous exchanges across the entire career spectrum, from graduate students to the most senior experts in the field. The conference also brings together a refreshingly eclectic mix of scholars and practitioners from various disciplines, including Theatre, Classics, Literature, and Languages. In other words, the conference is truly *comparative*, not merely because papers often compare different plays, but primarily because we encourage comparative dialogue among drama devotees who don't often get the chance to compare notes. The CDC also stands apart as a theatre studies venue where texts are still taken seriously. We certainly acknowledge and appreciate approaches to theatre scholarship that emphasize performance. Indeed, we include staged readings of original plays as an important part of the conference, and we warmly receive any number of scholarly presentations each year that take performance-based approaches to studying drama. Nonetheless, in an academic environment where analyzing the language of plays is sometimes dismissed as pedantic or passé, the Comparative Drama Conference continues to value textual criticism as a vital scholarly pursuit. One of the surest signs of this ongoing commitment is the annual publication of our own text, aptly titled *Text & Presentation*.

This volume gathers some of the best work presented at the annual conference. Sponsored by Stevenson University, our sessions took place March 26–28, 2015, at the Pier 5 Hotel in Baltimore's Inner Harbor. There were numerous highlights among the sixty-nine panels and plenary sessions, and several deserve special mention. The weekend featured four staged readings of new plays: *The Mathematics of Being Human* by Michele Osherow and Manil Suri (directed by Michael Curry), *The Quickening* by Mark Scharf (directed by Chelsea Dove), *Dyskolos* adapted from Menander by Katherine B. Free (directed by Kevin J. Wetmore, Jr.), *Leah's Dybbuk* by Susan McCully (directed by Eve Munson). Each of these readings was expertly coordinated and moderated by our resident dramaturg Janna Segal (Mary Baldwin College). On Thursday we were both entertained and informed by "If Music Be the Food of Love, Play On," a special session on Shakespeare and song delightfully delivered from Brigitte Bogar and Christopher Innes (both of York University, Toronto). Thursday evening's highlight was a gripping performance of David Lindsay-Abaire's *Rabbit Hole* by the Vagabond Players in Fell's Point. Friday afternoon included CDC's signature "Author Meets Critic" plenary session. Each year the book review editor of *Text & Presentation* invites the author of a recent book in theatre studies to interact with two critics in the field. This year the spotlight was directed upon Katherine Weiss (East Tennessee State University), author of *The Plays of Samuel Beckett*. She had a lively exchange of ideas with Doug Phillips (University of St. Thomas) and William Hutchings (University of Alabama–Birmingham). At this session I also had the privilege of awarding the inaugural Anthony Ellis Prize for Best Paper by a Graduate Student to Giuseppe Sofo (University of Avignon; Università La Sapienza, Roma) for his 2014 paper, "Translating Tempests: A Reading of Aimé Césaire's *Une Tempête* in Translation." After such a thrilling night at *Rabbit Hole* on Thursday, the conference was buzzing with anticipation for Friday evening's keynote event with the playwright David Lindsay-Abaire. He engaged in a lively, provocative, funny, and very inspiration public conversation with Kelly Younger (Loyola Marymount University). Saturday afternoon featured "Visions of Tragedy in American Theater," a wideranging plenary discussion of eight major American playwrights. David Palmer (Massachusetts Maritime Academy) coordinated the event and J. Chris Westgate (California State University, Fullerton) presided over presentations on Eugene O'Neill by Jeffery Kennedy (Arizona State University), on Susan Glaspell by Sharon Friedman (New York University), on Thornton Wilder by Jackson R. Bryer (University of Maryland), on Tennessee Williams by Susan C. W. Abbotson (Rhode Island College), on Arthur Miller by Stephen A. Marino (St. Francis College), on Edward Albee by Natka Bianchini (Loyola University Maryland), on David Mamet by Brenda Murphy (University of

Connecticut), and on August Wilson by Sandra G. Shannon (Howard University).

All of the research papers contained in *Text & Presentation, 2015* began as relatively brief conference papers. Each was subsequently expanded and submitted for consideration before being double blind reviewed by experts in the field. The accepted essays were revised in response to reviewer suggestions. The final versions published here meet the highest standards of scholarship. Along with ten research papers, *Text & Presentation, 2015* also contains an interview transcript, a roundtable discussion compilation, and six book reviews. The broad range of subjects, methodologies, and perspectives contained between these covers should give anyone unfamiliar with the CDC an indication of our diverse spectrum of offerings every year.

We were honored to welcome David Lindsay-Abaire as our keynote speaker and to publish a transcript of his conversation with Kelly Martin Younger (Loyola Marymount University) as the first essay of this volume. Lindsay-Abaire impressed everyone with his wit, generosity, and affable approachability. I appreciate David Palmer for his coordinating efforts in arranging the plenary panel on American tragedy and in compiling the eight speakers' remarks into "Visions of Tragedy in American Theatre." It is also a great privilege to bestow our second annual Anthony Ellis Prize for Best Paper by a Graduate Student. The award is named in honor of our late friend Tony Ellis, who was not only a wonderful friend, colleague, and scholar, but was also a great supporter of work by graduate students. Tony would have been proud to know that this year's winner, Lydia Craig, is from his alma mater Loyola University Chicago. Her essay, "Politic Silence: Female Choruses in Lochhead's *Medea* and Wertenbaker's *The Love of the Nightingale*," is featured next.

"Gender, Democracy and the Justice of Athena's Vote to Acquit Orestes," by Jacqueline Long (Loyola University Chicago), interrogates Athena's intervention in Aeschylus' *Oresteia* and examines the jury verdict in light of social values. Then, Phillip Zapkin (West Virginia University) analyzes neoliberal ideology and Lacanian psychology in a South African context in "'Kill the Pity in Us': The Communal Crisis as Crisis of Individualism in David Greig's *Oedipus the Visionary*." In "With Rhyme and Reason: *Hip Hop Hamlet* in Prison," Elizabeth Charlebois (St. Mary's College of Maryland) reflects upon her innovative 2015 Shakespearean adaptation collaboratively composed and performed by inmates in the Northeastern Correctional Center of Bowling Green, Missouri.

Frequent *T&P* contributor Doug Phillips (University of St. Thomas) offers his latest philosophical meditation on the nature of theatrical experience in the provocative "Strange Interludes: Wallace Stevens and the Theatrical Event." Lurana Donnels O'Malley (University of Hawaii at Manoa) studies the rich history of depictions of Ethiopia in "Spirits in Black and White: Ethiopia as the Black Columbia in African American Pageantry." It is a pleasure to include the first publication by promising new scholar Davenne Essif (University of North Carolina at Chapel Hill). In "In Search of the Void: Metaphysical Theatricality in Giorgio de Chirico's *The Painter's Family* and Emptiness in the Arts," she applies notions of theatricality to shed light on de Chirico's late aesthetic achievements.

Another author familiar to *T&P* readers, Tennessee Williams expert Jeffrey B. Loomis (Northwest Missouri State University), offers an intriguing analysis of proto-*Menagerie* drafts in "Archives of an Ironic Film Fan: The 'Tony' Drafts of *The Glass Menagerie*." First-time *T&P* contributor Martha Johnson (University of East Anglia) was inspired by conversations with David Henry Hwang at CDC 2014 to write a comparative analysis of Hwang and Mamet in "'Bring Your Own Translator': Communication and Changing Business Paradigms in David Mamet's *Glengarry Glen Ross* and David Henry Hwang's *Chinglish*." The final research paper of the 2015 volume brings us full circle back to our keynoter, David Lindsay-Abaire. Amy Muse (University of St. Thomas) offers an original and illuminating comparative analysis with "Sympathetic Curiosity, Not Voyeurism: David Lindsay-Abaire Takes Up Joanna Baillie's Abandoned Grief Project." The volume ends with six book reviews of recent theatrical scholarship, ably coordinated by our new book review editor, Jay Malarcher (West Virginia University).

One more important feature of the Comparative Drama Conference which deserves special mention is the Philadelphia Constantinidis Essay in Critical Theory Award. This award is endowed by former conference director and long-time board member Stratos E. Constantinidis in memory of his late mother. Established in 2006 to encourage research and writing on Greek theatre and performance, the award recognizes the best comparative essay on Greek theatre published in the previous calendar year. Essays may address any aspect or period of Greek theatre, so long as the essay is comparative in nature and published (in English) in a journal or anthology (in any country). Essays and nominations should be emailed by December 31 to lsnyder4990@stevenson.edu. The 2015 winner of the award was Peter E. Pormann (University of Manchester) for his article, "Arabs and Aristophanes, Menander Among the Muslims: Greek Humour in the Medieval and Modern Middle East," *International Journal of the Classical Tradition* 21.1 (2014): 1–29.

The Comparative Drama Conference seeks original research papers investigating any facet of theatre and performance. Papers may be comparative across cultural, historical, disciplinary, and national boundaries, and may deal with any issue of theory, history, criticism, dramatic literature, historiography, translation, performance, or production. Information and updates are available on our website: http://comparativedramaconference.stevenson.edu. Only papers presented at the annual conference are eligible for consideration in that year's volume of *Text & Presentation*. On behalf of the executive board, I welcome all readers of this volume to come share your latest research with us at a future Comparative Drama Conference and to submit your work to *Text & Presentation*.

Graley Herren • *Xavier University*

A Conversation with David Lindsay-Abaire

Transcript of Keynote Panel: March 27, 2015
Presiding: Kelly Martin Younger

Abstract

The keynote panel at the 2015 Comparative Drama Conference was a conversation with David Lindsay-Abaire. His play Rabbit Hole *won the 2007 Pulitzer Prize and received five Tony Award nominations. His other plays include* Fuddy Meers, Kimberly Akimbo, Wonder of the World, A Devil Inside, *and* Good People. *He also wrote the book and lyrics for* Shrek the Musical *and the screenplay for* Rabbit Hole. *In this wideranging conversation Lindsay-Abaire discusses his writing process, the evolution of his drama, the autobiographical roots of his work, and his advice for getting plays written and produced. The interview was conducted by professor, scholar, and playwright Kelly Martin Younger (Loyola Marymount University).*

Kelly Martin Younger [KMY]: I want to begin by acknowledging that every play is different, but in some sense the craft is the same. Can you talk about some of the particular ways in which you craft your plays? I don't mean so much where you get your ideas, but once you have an idea, where do you begin?

David Lindsay-Abaire [DLA]: I have to say that I don't have a set way of crafting my plays. Pretty much all of them have been written in different ways. Generally the way the plays come to me, I have 12, 14, 16 ideas in my head that may or may not be a play. The ones that are most stubborn and don't go away, I start slamming together. I say, "Is this a play

7

David Lindsay-Abaire speaks to audience at the 2015 Comparative Drama Conference keynote event (photograph by Maximilian Franz, courtesy Stevenson University).

if I put these two or three things together?" But the crafting of every one is different.

For instance, I wrote *Fuddy Meers* at Juilliard. I had an idea for a play about a woman that has amnesia. Her memory is erased every night. That was the seed of the play. I had seen a report on "20/20" about a man who had that condition, and I thought what a great setup for a play. A woman wakes up and has to have explained, "Honey, I'm your husband, and this is your son, and you have this strange case of amnesia. Here's a book about all the details of your life that you'll need to know for the day." Then he goes into the shower. The second thing I thought of for the play was the very ending. What is it like for this family to lose this woman every night? She lives an entire life during the course of every day, but then she goes to sleep and wakes up again with no memory.

What I started with for that play was the bookends. At Juilliard I had to deliver ten pages every week, but other than having the end of the play I had no idea where I was going. The play was written in ten-page increments. If you read it, every ten pages there's a little cliffhanger or a big twist, and really that was designed to entertain my fellow students. The central image of that play turned out to be this funhouse mirror. The play felt like a funhouse ride or a rollercoaster. It went up and down and I had no idea where I was going. And the protagonist had no idea where she was going. So in turn the audience had no idea where they were going.

Another time, I was trying to write a play that I was desperately struggling with and just couldn't get off the ground. So I pushed it aside and decided to start a brand new play. I just started typing, "Lights up on a woman packing a suitcase." I didn't know who this woman was or where she was going. I knew nothing, but then the play revealed itself as I wrote it. That play was *Wonder of the World*.

The more plays I wrote, the more forethought I started to put into them, and the more structured they became. For plays like *Rabbit Hole* and *Good People*, I put in a lot more advance thought and they were more formed and charted out before I sat down and wrote them. That said, I followed my impulses and let the plays go where they wanted to go. But I had to develop my craft before I got to that point.

KMY: You say you saw an image of a woman with a suitcase. Do you find that, when you get that first image or idea, it becomes the first scene? Or does it land somewhere else in the play?

DLA: So far that's been the case. The way I generally start is just writing dialogue. If I have a theme I want to explore or some characters I think are interesting, it's never going to come out the way I plan it. The best thing for me is to sit down and start writing. I discover the play during the course of writing the dialogue and how characters interact with each other. I don't know who they are until they start talking. Once they do, I think, "Oh, now I see who these people are."

KMY: Speaking of talking, your characters have a very distinctive voice. So I would like to go back to Boston, to the beginning. Tell us about growing up in Southie. Tell us about being the scholarship kid who was taking the train out to Milton Academy. You've talked previously about feeling like you were in two different worlds.

DLA: For those of you who don't know, South Boston is very working-class, Irish—well, less so now than it was when I was growing up (now it's more gentrified)—but it was a predominantly Irish working-class neighborhood. When I was eleven years old, I got a scholarship through the Boys & Girls Club of America to attend a private academy in the suburbs of Boston. Every day I would get on the subway and go out to Milton. I would climb a mile up the hill to this amazing, tony campus and rub elbows with these kids that had a lot more money than I did. As an eleven-year-old coming from the poor neighborhood, I had no idea what I was doing there or how I fit in or how to "pass."

After a couple of years finding my footing there and getting an amazing education, I felt very different back at home. Now I had to do a similar sort of dance at home. God forbid I become "that fancy kid from the private school." I had to know my place in Southie and know my place at Milton. I was maneuvering my way through both environments all the time.

KMY: You've said that you felt like an "other," but that's what makes a writer: the quintessential other. Can you say more about this idea of the writer as outsider?

DLA: Maybe this isn't specific to writers; maybe everybody feels this way. But I just felt like I was assessing situations all the time, trying to figure out my place in whatever world I was in, whether it was back in Southie or at Milton. I don't think it's a coincidence that all my plays turn out to be about a person in an upside-down environment. They have no idea how they fit in or what their identity is within this new environment. How do they acclimate and figure it all out?

KMY: You've said that you wanted to wait until you were mature enough as a writer before you tackled writing about the neighborhood you grew up in and the people you grew up with. You also wanted a *good* reason—not just any reason—for writing about that subject. What was your "good reason" for writing *Good People*?

DLA: There were a few things going on, and it's attached to my entire career. Those early plays I wrote were mostly absurdist comedies. They were pretty ridiculous plays, but I liked them and I was lucky that many critics liked them, including the *New York Times*. But the people who didn't like those plays *really* didn't like them. That pissed me off, frankly. I would see these same critics writing about naturalistic or realistic plays in a totally different way. Whether the play was good or bad, their approach to the play was different. They would dig in a bit and at least try to figure out what the writer was talking about. The critics who disliked my comedies simply dismissed them out of hand: "Well this is silly nonsense." "People don't behave this way." "Why does Manhattan Theatre Club keep producing his plays?" So the spiteful part of me (which is very big) said, "I could write one of those damn naturalistic plays if I wanted to! You get a couch and some running water— how hard could that possibly be?" I said there are 12 or 14 ideas in the back of my head, and that was one of the ideas: I should write a naturalistic play one day.

Another thing had been at the back of my head since I was a student at Juilliard. I studied under Christopher Durang and Marsha Norman. One of my fellow students and I were having trouble coming up with an idea for a new play. Marsha said, "You know what always works best? Think of the thing that scares you more than anything else in the world. What is the thing that terrifies you to the core? Whatever that is write a play about it." When I was in my mid-twenties at the time, I didn't know what that was. Several years later after I became a parent, when my son Nick was around four or five, I heard two or three stories in quick succession about friends of friends who had children die very suddenly and unexpectedly. As a relatively new dad, I wondered what that would be like. In putting myself in the shoes of those parents, I experienced fear in a way I never had before. Feeling that terrible anxiety and that terror, I thought, "Oh, wait a minute—this is what Marsha was talking about." Now I knew what terrified me more than anything.

That's how *Rabbit Hole* came to be. I smashed it together with that naturalistic play I had thought maybe I should write. As an experiment, I decided to see what would happen. If I had only written the play out of spite, it wouldn't have done very well I don't think. I had to wait for an idea that I cared about, that I was passionate about and could invest in because it was connected to me. Only then could I actually write the play. The spite was still there a little bit, but it became smaller and smaller when I found something that I really cared about. This is all leading to *Good People*, I promise—

KMY:—I was going to say that writing out of fear and spite would definitely make you an Irish playwright! But let's talk about *Rabbit Hole*. I am interested in how both *Rabbit Hole* and *Good People* are such big departures from your early work.

DLA: The thing I learned from *Rabbit Hole* was that I could flex muscles I never knew I had before. After being a rather cocky know-it-all at Juilliard and thinking I didn't really care about naturalistic or realistic plays, or couches and sinks, I sort of began to think, "This isn't so bad. There's actually something to those sorts of plays that can still do things similar to what I want to do dramatically." I didn't know if I would ever write another naturalistic play again. But in writing *Rabbit Hole*, I found a whole tool box that I didn't know existed for me, that I could reach in and use when it seemed appropriate.

Now we're getting to the *Good People* part. There are a few reasons why *Good People* came about. First, I kept hearing that American playwrights never write about class. "Where are the new American plays about class? British playwrights write about it all the time. Why don't American playwrights do that?" I thought, "Is that true? Do we not write about class?" I think that's actually not true. We write about class all the time! I don't think we write didactic, soap-boxy plays, which is maybe what people are talking about. Maybe they're talking about plays that say Margaret Thatcher has destroyed the working class and shut down all these mines. Maybe they're talking about Clifford Odets. I'm not sure what they're talking about. But I know that playwrights write about people and their circumstances, and of course those circumstances will inform the story that they're telling. If somebody like Lucy Thurber or Annie Baker is writing a play about working-class people in Massachusetts, they're not overtly talking about class. But class informs everything that happens in all of those plays. So I decided that's not true, American playwrights *are* writing about class, all the time.

But I thought if I were to write a play about class, what would that be? This other thing I've been kicking around in my head for many years is I wanted to write about my old neighborhood of South Boston. I care about these people deeply. I think it's a rich environment full of stories, full of complicated things that I have been processing and will continue to process for all of my life. But I knew that I did not want to write about the people I knew and loved and respected who might be coming to see the play—in a way that someone could then write in the newspaper, "Well, this is just silly, because people don't really behave this way." Could I write an absurdist piece about Southie? I bet I could. But I didn't want to do it for *Good People*. I thought I had learned some things from *Rabbit Hole*, and I thought this one needs to be realistic or naturalistic, whatever that means.

That said, everything about me is informed by my upbringing in South Boston. Those working-class people, all of us, deal with our hardships through humor, almost exclusively. If things are awful—and this is very Irish, right?— no matter how dark things get, there's always room for laughter. In some ways that's all you've got.

KMY: Can you tell the story of when your mother came to see *Good People*, and how she left with a bruise?

DLA: I never write explicitly autobiographically. My sister might disagree, but I don't think I do. Writing *Good People* was the closest I got. I was tapping into people that I literally knew. I changed names and made amalgams. Still, my mother is very, very present in that play in a way that scared me. Talk about writing your fear! She came to see the play, and I thought, "Oh God, what is she going to think?" Afterwards I asked, "How was it?" She said, "I have a bruise on the side of my body." I asked why. She went to the play with her best friend Alice. For the entire play Alice kept doing like this [*makes jabbing motions with his elbow*], "That's you! That's you!" So she of course could see it, but it didn't bother her.

Also I'll say that, even with the early plays, which I never thought were autobiographical in any way—like *Fuddy Meers* and *Kimberly Akimbo*—my sister came to see those plays. I remember after one she said, "Do you think dad's going to be mad?" "What? Why would he be mad?" [*Makes pointing gestures*] "There. There. There. There." Holy cow! My mother would say, "Where do you come up with these crazy ideas?" I guess as writers we often have to put on these blinders and fool ourselves into thinking that we're not writing about ourselves. But inevitably you're always-always-always writing about yourself.

KMY: Moving into *Rabbit Hole* after what you just said about class, what stood out to me seeing the play again last night [by Vagabond Players in Baltimore] was the scene where Becca's mom talks about the Kennedys. There's a great moment where they're talking about this idealized American family and the "curse of the Kennedys." It got me thinking that we also have this very ordinary family here with your characters. How do you think about the family that you give us in *Rabbit Hole*? Are they an idealized family? Are they an Every-Family?

DLA: I think they are an Every-Family. Before the play starts I don't think they are. Becca comes from a working-class family. If you saw the relationship between the mother and daughter, you know that it's different than the relationship between Becca and her husband. Becca comes from a family that's actually very similar to my family, very salt of the earth. She's gone to college and been educated. She has constructed a very specific life for herself, an idealized life. Everything she's done with her life—she went to this college, married this guy, moved into this neighborhood, had a perfect job at Sotheby's until it was time to become a mother, then decided "Now I will become a mother." Her life has been highly constructed and deliberate and compartmentalized. That's the idealized life that you're talking about. But then things happen in life. This bomb was thrown in the center of her life. She was thrust into a world that was turned upside down, a world that challenged everything about her.

How do the Kennedys fit in? I won't get too much into the Greeks and hubris and that stuff talked about in the play. The Greeks are mentioned a few times in the play. Izzy says, "I think that's sad," and the mother says, "Of course it's sad: all those good-looking people falling out of the sky like that." There's some hubris in there. For the Greeks, the way theatre functioned was that there were rules. Whatever happened in your life was because of the gods. The gods were in charge of your fate and things were pretty clear, right? But in *Rabbit Hole* things aren't so clear for Becca. About that Kennedy curse, Nat says that people made it up because they "want things to make sense." About Aristotle Onassis, she mentions how he offered up a reward to anyone who could prove his son's plane was sabotaged. When something awful happens, we have this need for there to be a reason. If there's a reason, we can find comfort. But without the gods, or in Becca's case, God, the comfort can be hard to find.

KMY: I can't think of an audience that would get more excited about a play where they actually pull out a dictionary and look up the word "hubris." But I don't think of *Rabbit Hole* as a tragedy in that classical sense.

DLA: No.

KMY: Can you talk about this play being about the aftermath? The dramatic event of the play happens eight months prior to the first scene.

DLA: That's just what I was interested in as a writer. It would be so difficult to dramatize the day of or the day after. Instead I was interested in exploring the process of grief and how people grieve differently and how those processes can butt up against each other.

KMY: I want to bring in Amy Muse's excellent conference paper from this morning where she discussed this concept of "sympathetic curiosity." And I noted that in the *New York Times* they referred to *Rabbit Hole* as "meticulously mapped empathy." I wonder what your thoughts are on an audience's urge to watch people in distress.

DLA: It's distressing in a safe way.

KMY: In what way?

DLA: Well, in two hours you can leave the theater. I don't necessarily think of it as a voyeuristic thing. To take a step back: why do we go to the theater? I think we want to connect. For some people watching *Rabbit Hole*, it's experiencing something they're terrified of. They watch it and think, "Oh my God, I have children. This is unbearable. I'm glad that's not me." Sadly, other people have experienced it. I've gotten dozens of letters from parents who say, "Thank you for that play. That was my experience." Or "Here's how my experience was different." For other people it's just that "brick in the pocket" speech. They say, "I haven't lost a child. But my sister died, and that's my way into the play." We go because we want to feel less alone. We want to feel that we're in communion with the story and with the other people in the room. It's about connection. It's not necessarily about wanting to see how awful the characters' lives are. But maybe it is for some people.

KMY: It's a challenging thing to pull off in production. In your author's note you give very specific instructions regarding the tone. To quote you: "It's a sad play. Don't make it any sadder." You also say, "Don't ignore the jokes. They're your friends." What experiences in production or rehearsal prompted you to write those notes?

DLA: In particular there was one reading of the play involving a really brilliant actress who was crying from the first page. This can be a perfectly organic, legitimate choice to make. Someone is folding the clothes of their dead child? Yeah, she might cry.

That said, there is a structure to this play. This is a play about a woman who is *not* crying yet, actually. This is a play about a woman who has compartmentalized everything in her life, including her grief. And that has served her well. We see that in the play: she's folding things up and boxing things away. It's what gives her control over the situation.

In the scene with the kid, if it's been executed properly, she hasn't cried yet. She hasn't even quavered; her voice has not shaken. Then he tells that funny story about going to the prom. Hopefully what we see in that scene, if it's executed properly, is that here is a woman who has been able to deal with the loss of her 4-year-old son—but she has not even approached the idea of losing her 12-year-old son, or her 18-year-old son who would have gone to the prom, or the 28-year-old son who would have gotten married, or the 38-year-old son who would have given her grandchildren. That loss is *so* enormous she cannot put it into a box. It's the climax of the play. So if she cries before that, there's no dramatic event, no heart to the play. It's just a big swamp of people being *sad*.

This actress that I talked to after the reading said, "Well, you know, with this type of play I think it's going to be different every night, and I'll just go where my emotions take me." And I thought, "*No.* You can't do that, not in this play. This is a play about a woman who doesn't cry until page 94, so you don't cry until page 94. Sorry!" By the way, this was a brilliant actress who is incredibly smart. So I thought, if even she doesn't get it, I should put a little signpost to people, saying this is what I would like. Ignore it if you will, it's up to you. I've never put a note in any of my other plays, though I have many opinions about all of my plays. But this was one case where I thought it was really important because it's so central to the storytelling and the arc of the play.

KMY: I want to back up a bit to some of your earlier plays and this idea of a funhouse mirror. I'm thinking of *Fuddy Meers* (or "Funny Mirrors" without the speech impediment). Here you have a character with a rare form of amnesia who wakes up every morning with no recollection of what happened the night before. (And after many years at this conference, I have several colleagues who suffer from a similar predicament rooted in the James Joyce Pub!) Also with *Kimberly Akimbo* you have this 16-year-old character who has a rare disease where she ages too quickly. So you have one character who is a blank slate, and another character who's running out of the paper on which she's writing her life. I'm interested in those two protagonists in particular. As a playwright, you give a character a problem. But these are problems that are very askew, they're akimbo. In those early plays, why were you drawn to those types of characters?

DLA: Frankly, I think it was just my worldview. Again I think it's deeply rooted in South Boston and those people. My view of the world was in fact skewed. Everything sad to me was also incredibly funny. Those things could live side by side perfectly. It makes sense to me. As absurd as *Fuddy Meers* is—and it is—there is a very deep, dark secret at the heart of that play involving pain and abuse. That's true for *Kimberly* as well. As whimsical as the play is, ultimately it's a play about mortality. This is a 16-year-old girl who has possibly weeks to live, and she needs to live in the moment. For both of them I guess I wanted to literalize that metaphor of the funhouse mirror in a dark and absurd way.

KMY: You've also said that you deliberately write female protagonists.

DLA: Yes.

KMY: That's a very conscious choice, for which every actress in America says thank you! Talk to us about that choice.

DLA: Well, if I had a psychiatrist—

KMY:—I have a Ph.D. Tell me everything—

DLA:—I'm sure he would say it's all about my mother. No joke, though, my mother was the center of every family event. She's an incredibly funny, amazing storyteller. Really inappropriate in a funny way. So it makes sense that my plays would be peopled by those sorts of women. Second, I know a lot of amazing actresses, and most plays are written for men. When I write a play, I stop and say to myself, "Does it matter if the protagonist is a man or a woman?" If it doesn't, I make it a woman, to throw some more roles on the other side of the scales.

Remember when I said earlier that, no matter what, with every play you're

Kelly Martin Younger, left, poses a question to David Lindsay-Abaire (photograph by Maximilian Franz, courtesy Stevenson University).

writing about yourself, whether you know it or not? I think I'm just playing a game with myself in pretending that those protagonists aren't me. It's like, "Well, it's a woman, of course it's not me." But then watching *Rabbit Hole* last night, I thought, "God, Becca can be so unlikeable." And then I realized, "Oh, that's you." It's just another way of giving myself distance and pretending that I'm not writing about stuff that's going on inside my own head.

KMY: I would like to ask you about the new play that I know you're working on. The latest issue of *American Theatre* magazine has an article which rants against realism. You are a playwright who started out in a very anti-realistic genre. Then you went into a realistic, naturalistic genre. Your new play is going to be a return, also with two female leads. Can you talk to us a bit about that?

DLA: I did *Rabbit Hole* and *Good People* back to back, and they are relatively naturalistic plays. Some people have said to me, "Ah, I love those plays. But remember when you wrote comedies? *Those* were so great." Very backhanded compliment, right? One of those things stuck in my head is "Can I in fact still write one of those plays?" Can I? That's the big question. Or were those just the plays of a willful young man who didn't know what he was doing? So I thought, let me try that. Let me try to write in that spirit of a play, using what I hope is some of the craft I've acquired since *Kimberly Akimbo* and *Wonder of the World*.

I have now written that play. It's called *Ripcord* and will be premiering at the Manhattan Theatre Club in the fall. We're not even in rehearsals yet. But it does feel like two playwrights wrestling each other. It's not like, "Aha—he's back—*Fuddy Meers*!" It's like, "Wait, there's *Rabbit Hole* ... what's happening?" Tonally there are very naturalistic scenes, but then there are two old ladies skydiving. So I don't know if they'll work together or not.

The main thing is I wanted to write a part for Marylouise Burke. She is an amazing actress who was in all of those early plays. She was Kimberly in *Kimberly Akimbo*, she was Gertie in *Fuddy Meers*, and she was in *Wonder of the World*. I wanted to write a play for her. That was the other thing in my head: if I'm going to write one of these plays, then Marylouise Burke has to be in it.

KMY: I have a question about one of your early plays, *A Devil Inside*, which was your first New York play. In it you have a character who is a crazed academic and serial killer.

DLA: Mhmm.

KMY: So I guess what we'd all like to know is what the hell do you have against academics?

DLA: ...

KMY: I'll let you off. Here's my real question. You have a room full of academics here who are teachers, many who have taught or will teach your work after this. What would you like to say about teaching a David Lindsay-Abaire play?

DLA: You know what's been great about this conference? I'm so used to people responding to work in a very specific way, which is usually "This is what I liked, and this is what I didn't like, and here's why I didn't like it." Hearing you guys talk over the past couple days, what I'm hearing instead is "This is what I think the play did, and this is what it makes me think of." So instead of coming from a place where you don't like something because this wasn't in it, you come from a very generous place of recognizing what is in it and saying what you think about it. It makes me think, "Good Lord! Why can't critics write like that?" It only makes sense. Don't talk about what *isn't* there. Talk about what *is* there. I don't know if that's attached to the teaching question or not. But just digging in the way you guys dig in is refreshing.

KMY: That's actually the perfect segue to open it up to some questions about what is there.

[*Question from the audience about advice for first-time playwrights*]

DLA: First, make sure that you are writing about something you care about deeply. Second, make sure you're writing about something that other people might care about deeply. It sounds very basic. But it's not a bad idea to tell somebody, "I'm thinking of writing a play about this. Does that intrigue you at all?" If you're trying to write a sort of Aristotelian type of play, make sure you know what your character wants *every page*. I read a lot of plays by young writers in particular—and if they're writing something more experimental or Beckettian then this question doesn't come up—but I'm surprised how often the dialogue is just going on and on and on, and I have no idea what's at stake or what the character wants. It's very basic, but you'd be surprised how that can solve most of your problems. If you're having a problem with the scene, just ask, "What do these characters want? What's in their way?" It generally gets solved by answering those questions.

[*Question about differences in writing the stage play and screenplay for* Rabbit Hole, *particularly why Jason pursues the family in the stage play but Becca pursues Jason in the film*]

DLA: I did want to make her more active in the film. As far as the difference, I've seen a lot of plays adapted into film. When they fall down, it's generally because they haven't escaped their theatrical roots. Things that work on stage often don't work on film because they're two completely different animals. Film is a visual medium. You can't have twenty-minute scenes with people sitting on couches in a movie. What I had in my back pocket in *Rabbit Hole* was a pretty extensive off-stage life. Watching the play, a lot of scenes are described that you don't see, including the support group, the scene at the supermarket where Becca slaps a woman, the hint that Howie may or may not be having an affair. So when I was approached about the screenplay, I thought I could go to all of those places and dramatize all of those events instead of having characters talk about them. It's a completely different thing, but I was excited by the opportunity.

It's a funny thing, but in seeing these scenes with the support group and Howie's flirtations with Sandra Oh in the movie (the woman he may or may not be having an affair with), the movie shifted the story. The play is very much about a woman struggling with loss. The movie is about a couple. They're on parallel tracks and finding solace in two very different places. With her it's the boy, and with him it's the Sandra Oh character. The process for me was really letting go of the play, and letting it be different. Whether or not that was successful? If you ask my mother—

KMY:—This is the third time you've mentioned your mother.

DLA: That's how it is! The process was mostly not being precious about the play and allowing the film to be its own thing, for better or worse. I'm happy with that.

[*Question about* Crazy Eights *and the position of short plays in American theatre*]

DLA: Well, they're definitely not supported enough. Short plays are what they are. Not every writer should write a novel; there's beauty to a short story. And not every stage story belongs in a full-length play. *Crazy Eights* is a play in 35 pages because that's how long it took me to tell that story. I love those little bon-bons of plays. They are what they are, and they don't outstay their welcome. I wish there were more evenings like that. But it's hard to get theaters excited about producing short plays. I don't know why, but there you have it.

KMY: What do you wish were different about new play development?

DLA: That's really easy: I wish they would produce the plays. A couple generations of playwrights now are writing plays that work at music stands. Those plays don't always belong on a stage. You're trying to figure it out as a writer, especially a new writer. You don't know how it works. So you can write it and put it out in front of people with a reading, and people can give you notes. But not until it's given flesh and blood, and people are off book in front of an audience, do you know *what the play is*. I've had plays work at music stands that fall apart in front of an audience. But this generation of playwrights I'm talking about is never going to get any better if they're not allowed to get away from those music stands.

[*Question about deciding the gender of the protagonist and how a male lead differs from a female lead*]

DLA: I don't know because it hasn't happened yet! Again, back to those 14 ideas in my head, I do have a play in mind about two brothers. The reason they have to be men is because I have a brother, and I'm interested in writing about a bunch of stuff that I've not written about yet. But I don't know how that will change. I don't really think so much in terms of "This is a male character, and this is a female character. Therefore, I will approach it differently." I'm just trying to write three-dimensional characters regardless of the gender, and let's see what happens.

[*Questions about Becca's father and Howie's family, never directly addressed in* Rabbit Hole]

DLA: I actually didn't think much about Howie's family, so that answers that question. As for the father, there was a very clear idea in my head. When I've been a part of the rehearsal process for *Rabbit Hole* (and I wasn't for last night's production), this question always comes up. We've just got two little tidbits in the play. We know that Becca's brother was a drug addict and he hung himself. We also know that her sister Izzy has had a history of partying and drinking. Becca asks her, "Were you on anything?" And we know that her mother likes to drink a lot. So there's a lot of substance abuse, or at least a lot substances (whether abused or not). Anyway, I suspect that the father was not the nicest person. That much is said in the play. As to whether or not he was abusive, I leave it up to the actors to make those decisions. In my head I think Becca was escaping that family for a reason. She wanted to construct a life that was incredibly different than the life she had grown up in.

[*Question about career trajectory from studying at Juilliard to being produced at Manhattan Theatre Club*]

DLA: I don't think I can tell you how complicated it actually was, so I'll give you the slightly cleaned up version. [*To Kelly*] You know the real version.

Here's what I'll say about Juilliard. They were incredibly active in terms of making connections for their new playwrights' program. At the end of every year they have a scene night where they invite literary managers and artistic directors from theaters, and agents and managers. So your work was being put in front of the people who needed to see it. At Juilliard where I wrote *Fuddy Meers*, that's how I got my agent. He saw a few scenes and thought it was exciting. He actually didn't have any other clients. He was answering somebody else's phone at The Gersh Agency and said, "Can I sign this guy? I like him."

They said, "I don't really like him but go ahead." So that's how I got my agent, who eventually took over that department.

Manhattan Theatre Club. I submit my plays to every single theater and conference and development workshop—anybody who would take an unsolicited script, I would send it to them. I got *The Dramatists Sourcebook* and went page by page. At that time I had a full-time job at Dance Theater Workshop. I would use their postage meter and their supplies and mail out my plays everywhere. The way I got into Manhattan Theatre Club was that I submitted for a fellowship. They said they weren't giving me the fellowship, but they liked the play and put it on their reading series. It was called "Discovering the Next Generation." I think it's now called "5@5" or "6@6." They did a staged reading with their subscribers on Stage II. To this day it's the best reading of a play I've ever had. They said, "Oh, it went over really well. And our subscribers like it—they don't like anything! We're going to try and find you a slot next year."

Guess what? They didn't find me a slot. I thought, "What do you have to do? That's the best it could have gone." So I kept submitting my plays. It went to the National Playwrights Conference at the O'Neill, and we did it there. The new assistant literary manager at Manhattan Theatre Club came and saw it and went back and said, "Oh, I just saw this great play at the O'Neill. I know that Steppenwolf wants to do it and Hartford Stage wants to do it." Manhattan Theatre Club then said, "We want to do it!"

KMY: And did you change a word at that time?

DLA: I did not. It was the same play. So that's a slightly ugly story because I did everything I thought was right, and the audience liked it, but they weren't quite ready yet. Then other people wanted to do it, and I became more interesting. I don't fault the Manhattan Theatre Club for that. Nobody knew me from Adam. They were just trying to fill their bill and get plays people wanted to see. For whatever reason, that wasn't the right year. Then the next year it was.

Every single thing that has happened in my career has happened in that circuitous way. I've applied to something and not gotten it. But somebody was on the panel who passed it on to somebody else who liked it. Everything. I meet with new playwrights and they ask, "What should I do?" The only advice I have is to just put yourself out there. Keep casting the line because you never know when the fish is going to hit.

[Question about winning the Pulitzer and its impact]

DLA: It was awesome! Honestly, it was amazing of course, but it didn't change the fact that I had to get up the next day and write a play. It's more changed, ridiculously, people's perception of me. Take those comedies I was writing early on that were being dismissed. Now I read regional production reviews where they're being approached in a very different way because of the "P-word" at the front of my name.

KMY: In the tradition of Kevin Wetmore, we're going to conclude with rapid-fire questions like we're on a quiz show.

DLA: Oh God.

KMY: Are you ready?

DLA: Yes sir.

KMY: What play by another playwright do you wish you had written?

DLA: Well, look, I can only write the plays I can write. One of the most important plays for me was *House of Blue Leaves*. It's one of my favorite plays, and it's the play that made me want to be a playwright. I don't wish I had written it because I love John Guare so much. Just the other night I saw Stephen Adly Guirgis's play *Between Riverside and Crazy*. I guess I thought I wish I had written that play.

KMY: What actor or actress do you hope to work with in the future?

DLA: Marylouise Burke. Honestly, it's not a new actor. It's that lady. I would work with her a million times. There are a lot of actors I've worked with and have been very lucky. But Marylouise Burke is who I most want to work with.

KMY: If you could have dinner with one playwright from the past, who would it be?

DLA: O'Neill. Because we'd drink so well.

KMY: If you could have dinner with one theatre critic, what would you serve him or her?

DLA: It wouldn't be one it would be all of them. And I'd definitely serve humble pie.

KMY: If you were not a playwright, what would you be?

DLA: I'd be a teacher.

KMY: If a graduate student wrote a thesis on you, what would it be titled?

DLA: Judging from your program, it would have a very long title! I don't know. "Two Sides of the Mirror"? I don't even know what that means.

KMY: Someone is scribbling furiously back there. What was the first play you saw that had an impact on you?

DLA: It wasn't a good impact. I think I was only in first or second grade. We were brought to an opera of Babar the Elephant. It was so *abysmal*. I loved those story books, but I remember thinking, "This is awful! This is what theatre is?" Then luckily *House of Blue Leaves* came later.

KMY: Do you want to be best friends? [*big laugh from audience*]

DLA: You know that's not possible.... [*bigger laugh from audience*]

KMY: And finally, what is your favorite scholarly conference, David Lindsay-Abaire?

DLA: Well, I've only been to the one, so here we are.

Visions of Tragedy in American Theatre

Transcript of Plenary Panel: March 28, 2015
Coordinator: David Palmer

Abstract

The plenary round-table session at this year's Comparative Drama Conference, "Visions of Tragedy in American Theatre," was organized by David Palmer (Massachusetts Maritime Academy) of the Arthur Miller Society, in cooperation with other academic societies devoted to American dramatists. It was part of the Miller Society's celebration of the centennial of Arthur Miller's birth. The eight dramatists discussed were Eugene O'Neill, Susan Glaspell, Thornton Wilder, Tennessee Williams, Arthur Miller, Edward Albee, David Mamet, and August Wilson. The session moderator was J. Chris Westgate (California State University, Fullerton), vice president of the Eugene O'Neill Society. These eight short papers prompted group discussion around four questions: How is each dramatist's vision of tragedy distinctive? Is there a way in which all the authors' visions are similar? Is there a characteristically American vision of tragedy? What can be learned from these eight dramatists about the nature of tragedy in general? The dramatists are presented here roughly chronologically.

Eugene O'Neill (1888–1953)

Jeffery Kennedy, Arizona State University,
The Eugene O'Neill Society

"In any expression of tragic theory," Joseph P. O'Neill reminds us, "two facts should be kept clearly in mind: the basic concept of tragedy differs among various authors; and tragic expression has always preceded theory" (481). Playwright Eugene O'Neill is considered by scholars to be the first American to truly embrace the tragic form and to attempt to create an "American" version of it for the twentieth century. In his critical study of O'Neill, Sophus Winther wrote,

> In the final analysis, O'Neill's plays must be judged in the terms of tragedy. That is exactly what he wanted, for he held that whatever greatness a man may have his ultimate stature is measured in the terms of his ability to experience tragedy in his own life and in the life of man [Winther].

Winther posits that any analysis of the concept of tragedy as it finds expression in modern drama, particularly in O'Neill, must recognize that the traditional Aristotelian definition cannot be used. Though there are elements that would be considered tragic in O'Neill's plays prior to 1926, it was then that he set out to create what he called a "modern psychological drama using one of the old legend plots of Greek tragedy for its basic theme" (O'Neill to Commins). Joseph O'Neill writes that O'Neill's "immediate problem was to create a modern tragic interpretation of the Greek concept of fate without benefit of the Greek gods" (483). O'Neill set out a challenge to himself: "Is it possible to get modern psychological approximation of the Greek sense of fate into such a play, which an intelligent audience of today possessed of no belief in gods or supernatural retribution, but could accept and be moved by?" (Clark 530). His experiment to answer this question came two years later in *Mourning Becomes Electra*, a modern adaptation of the *Oresteia* set in New England at the end of the American Civil War.

It was clear to O'Neill that twentieth-century Americans did not have the close relationship between drama and life that existed in ancient Athens. However, because he fully realized this dissociation and, more especially, "the disintegration of life itself in a modern mechanized culture," he desired to create a modern counterpart of Greek theatre, "to reassert the socio-religious function of an imaginative truly vibrant theatre" (Clark 530). According to O'Neill, this should be:

> a theatre returned to its highest and sole significant function as a Temple where the religion of a poetical interpretation and symbolic celebration of life is communicated to human beings, starved in spirit by their soul-stifling daily struggle to exist as masks among masks of the living ["Memoranda" 166–67].

O'Neill's tragedies express the absolute futility of humans' struggles against themselves and those that have died before them. The juxtaposition of fate and free will establish a tension and balance, as they do in all good tragedy, making this essential to the tragic circumstances in his plays. While embracing elements of naturalism, O'Neill "passes beyond mere defiance and determinism in his development of fate and human responsibility" (J. O'Neill 493).

William Greene wrote, "The greatest Greek drama [...] rests on the interplay between fate and character, between what man cannot change and what remains within his power" (92). O'Neill was aware of this. In a letter to Arthur Quinn, written about a year before he began *Mourning Becomes Electra,* he explained,

> I'm always, always trying to interpret Life in terms of character. I'm always acutely conscious of the Force behind—(Fate, God, our biological past creating our present, whatever one calls it—Mystery certainly)—and the one eternal tragedy of Man in his glorious, self-destructive struggle to make the Force express him instead of being, as an animal is, an infinitesimal incident in its expression. And my proud conviction is that it is possible—or can be—to develop a tragic expression in terms of transfigured modern values and symbols [Quinn 199].

Winther believes that O'Neill's tragedy, "if it has universal appeal, deals with the fall of man from prosperity into adversity in a manner that is 'shocking' and through causes that lie within man himself in relation to the outward forces of his world" (Winther). From the beginning in O'Neill's plays, man is brought to disaster not so much by a fatal flaw as by forces more powerful than him. "The men and women of his world are victims of a cosmic trap, cold and impersonal as steel" (Winther). In *Long Day's Journey Into Night* Mary says to Edmund, "It's wrong to blame your brother. He can't help being what the past has made him. Any more than your father can. Or you. Or I" (64). Later when she knows that there is no escape, she thinks of her happiness as a student in the convent: "You were much happier," she says to herself. "If I could only find the faith I lost, so I could pray again." However, this could not and will not ever happen; O'Neill makes it clear that the forces of fate have sealed her in her place of despair. Instead, Tyrone asks her to "Forget the past." Her answer is, "How can I? The past is the present, isn't it? It's the future, too. We all try to lie about that, but life won't let us" (87). O'Neill tragedies, while not without moments of realization and learning, get progressively harsh and bald with the literal naming of the folly of "pipe dreams," most famously in *The Iceman Cometh.* Winther reminds us, "At the end of *The Iceman Cometh* there is no one left to summarize the story and give it meaning, for the meaning of life has been lost in Pipe Dreams. Kafka's Castle is visible on the hill, but there is no road through the tangled thicket that surrounds its base. This is the meaning of tragedy" (Winther).

Susan Glaspell (1876–1948)

Sharon Friedman, New York University,
The International Susan Glaspell Society

Several critics have pondered the "surprise" element in Glaspell's work: her twists on conventional plot lines and her range of styles and genres—the sentimental novel with unsentimental conclusions, character-driven plays with absent protagonists, farce, satire, expressionist theatre—even within the same play ("Woman Satirizes"). Most famously her one-act murder mystery *Trifles* turns into a "modernist revenge tragedy" (Makowsky 53) when two women discover that an isolated and silenced prairie farm wife has countered abuse. Glaspell draws on all these theatrical modes to dramatize conflicts that emerged with cultural and political shifts during the early decades of the twentieth century. We hear in her plays written for the experimental Provincetown Players (which I envision as a small civic theatre) the discourses of feminism, psychoanalysis, socialism, eugenics, and a retort to nativism and the heightening of American nationalism during the crisis period of World War I. As theorists have argued, tragic drama seems to emerge during periods of social upheaval (Wallace 8) that impel individuals to "draw [...] old relations into question" (Rosslyn 6) and, in some cases, to transgress the murky boundaries between freedom and necessity.

I argue that two of Glaspell's full-length plays—*The Verge* and *Inheritors*—weave in a "tragic mode" as Rita Felski has theorized this term. Acknowledging the "hybrid mixed qualities of genres," Felski resists defining tragedy as a "text's overall defining structure" as well as the generalizing "idea of the tragic [...] forged in the crucible of German Romanticism" with its claims to the "pathos and horror of human existence." Felski sees the "tragic mode" as denoting "a selective group of features" in texts of "various forms and guises" with "formal particulars" that she calls the "shape of suffering" (2, 14). Protagonists grapple with "the ineluctable power of social forces or unconscious desires," test "the limits of agency," encounter "the inevitability of conflict [or] the constant possibility of acting badly or wrongly," and confront "incompatible goods" (9, 12). Situating Glaspell's use of the tragic mode historically as well as aesthetically, I also take my cue from classicist Simon Goldhill who urges us to historicize the terms by which we define "the tragic" and to "pay due attention to the specific socio-political context of ancient drama [and later developments within the genre] [...] while recognizing the drive toward a transhistorical truth both in the plays' discourse and in the plays' reception" (61).

Clearly, Glaspell's drama in no way resembles Aristotelian form, and although her questing figures seem to evoke the "modern idea of the tragic [...] a painful and irrevocable schism between the individual and the world in which he finds himself stranded" (Felski 2), the world is very much with Glaspell's protagonists—mostly women. They struggle with a range of issues within and beyond the home (the home being the prevalent setting of modern American tragedy), and their actions resonate with the feminisms of the period as they deviate markedly from prescribed gender norms in plots that turn tragic as tensions within and between characters move toward catastrophic ends.

Claire Archer, the scientist/artist of *The Verge* (1921) is Glaspell's most radical character. The play begins as a comedy of manners surrounding a woman who slowly but surely turns the witty repartee into a debacle. The setting of the second and third acts morphs into an expressionist and symbolist rendering of her subjectivity as the psychically imprisoned Claire seeks both sexual and spiritual autonomy in her effort to smash existing forms in her botanical experiments and in her relationships. She spends much of the play in her greenhouse, which has become her home, though it has the aura of a laboratory, its temperatures carefully controlled, its atmosphere refined. When not in the greenhouse, she retreats to a tower, seeking escape from the demands of others—husband, sister, daughter, and lovers. Claire remains isolated and alienated, ultimately strangling the would-be soul mate who intercedes in her quest.

To be sure, many scholars note the European influences in this work, the Nietzschean or Dionysian rapture in Claire's exhortations (Carpentier 46, Bigsby 22, Ozieblo 186), or her debt to Strindberg (Bigsby 19, Gainor 144) and Maeterlinck (Ben-Zvi 96–97). I hear echoes of Ibsen's artist figures, Master Builder Solness, for example, in his pursuit of the creative will and the soaring imagination. Unlike Solness, however, Claire is devoid of a muse, and takes this journey alone as she suffers the consequences of her vision, lapsing into madness. If tragedy is determined not only by a protagonist's action but also by its effect upon the audience, we might note that members of the Heterodoxy Club, a radical women's discussion group, responded to *The Verge* with "collective fervor" (Gainor 167) that perhaps approximated catharsis.

My second example of Glaspell's "tragic mode" involves a reversal of fortune in the life of the young college student Madeline Fejevary of *Inheritors* (1921), a family-saga that becomes a problem play with tragic consequences. The scenario traces the three-generation trajectory of a family that in the spirit of inclusion has founded a college for the children of Midwestern farmers. The seemingly light-hearted but sensible Madeline, granddaughter of its founder, becomes the tragic protagonist when the play's action moves from local disturbances on the college campus to the ramifications of these incidents for state and nation. Madeline attempts to reclaim the college's democratic principles during the war years when heightened nationalism and repressive politics threatened freedom of expression for conscientious objectors and dissidents. We witness Madeline's labored decision to abandon her family, confront prison, and become an exile in her own country. In a chilling scene, Madeline inscribes with chalk the narrow dimensions of the prison cell that awaits her, walling herself up like a modern-day Antigone. However, if we situate her within twentieth-century American drama, Glaspell's young co-ed turned enemy of the people anticipates Arthur Miller's tragedy of the "common man" whose "revolutionary questioning of the [apparent] stable environment is what terrifies" (Miller 3). That Glaspell gives this tragic choice to a young woman raises the stakes for the community that silences her.

Thornton Wilder (1897–1975)

Jackson R. Bryer, University of Maryland,
The Thornton Wilder Society

In considering how to approach this topic, I have been struck by how difficult it is characterize Thornton Wilder or his work simply or definitively. Some examples, first one from his personal life. Wilder was seemingly the most sociable of men, with friends all over the world and from all walks of life. Yet, in May 1962, nine days after attending a White House dinner where he reveled in the company of the President and Mrs. Kennedy, as well as—among many others—Robert Penn Warren, Robert Lowell, Tennessee Williams, Isaac Stern, George Balanchine, Anne Morrow Lindbergh, and Saul Bellow, he got into his Thunderbird convertible, bound for the desert Southwest. At the top of a hill in Arizona, the car stalled at a sign that read "Douglas, Arizona"; whereupon Wilder spent the next twenty months in a town of 10,000 residents where he knew no one and where no one knew who he was (Niven 653–56).

With respect to his writing, Wilder's work frequently has been dismissed as the literary equivalent of Norman Rockwell's *Saturday Evening Post* covers, when, in fact, it was intended by its author to convey a far darker view of life, one that verges on tragedy. Sinclair Lewis, in accepting the 1930 Nobel Prize for Literature, praised Wilder for "dream[ing] of old loves [...] and eternal romances" (Wilder). F. O. Matthiessen criticized him for not struggling "with the actual" but rather turning "too gracefully away" (213). The misconception of Wilder that these observations suggest can be countered by looking directly at his work and his comments about it.

The one overt commentary on tragedy that I have been able to find among Wilder's writing is an essay on Sophocles' *Oedipus Rex*, written in 1939 as an Introduction to Francis Storr's translation but not published until 1955. In it, Wilder, who, it must be noted, was extraordinarily well-read and spoke French, German, Spanish, and Italian fluently, maintains that Sophocles' play "presents a number of aspects which were more impressive to the Greeks than they are to us," chief among these being "its religious force." By this he means what he describes as "the shudder and awe induced by the presence of the numinous, by the *tremendum* of religious experience" (*Collected Plays* 710–11). I take it that what Wilder is saying here is something that we have long acknowledged to be true: Greek audiences responded to these plays with a different set of assumptions about the forces that lay behind human behavior than modern audiences are willing to accept.

I want to turn now to two of Wilder's novels—and here I am taking some (I hope allowable) license with the announced topic of this session because unlike most other authors, Wilder had equally illustrious careers as a writer of fiction and of drama; he remains the only recipient of Pulitzer Prizes in both. Here also we see Wilder expressing this difference between modern audiences and the Greeks. In *The Bridge of San Luis Rey* (1927), certainly his most famous work of fiction, Wilder very deliberately juxtaposes the belief of Brother Juniper that the collapse of the bridge and the loss of five lives cannot be anything other than "a sheer Act of God" and that, in Russell Banks's words, "the apparently accidental collapse of a bridge" has "a divine purpose" (xii) against what the investigation of the five people killed reveals. Wilder believes, as Banks says, that "any one of us could have been on that bridge when it collapsed" (xiii). In Wilder's own words, "the central idea of the work [...] stems from friendly arguments with my father, a strict Calvinist" (Bryer 59). Wilder denies the "religious force" assumed by the Greeks and substitutes the inexplicable. Similarly, in his 1948 novel *The Ideas of March* he explained his intention in an epigram only slightly mistranslated from Goethe's *Faust*: "Out of man's recognition in fear and awe that there is an Unknowable comes all that is best in the explorations of his mind" (ix). For Wilder it is the unexplained and the unknowable that lie behind tragic occurrences in human lives.

I would further assert—and here I admit I am on somewhat shakier ground—that the mixture of comedy and seriousness, of dark and light, that characterizes Wilder's writing is based on this belief that, ultimately, there is no definitive explanation for human behavior and for the tragedies that befall us. How else can one reconcile the seemingly sunny tone of much of Wilder's work with his belief, expressed in a 1928 interview with André Maurois, that:

> all human beings are unhappy—in varying degrees [...]. They are solitary, they are consumed with desires which they dare not satisfy; and they wouldn't be happy if they did satisfy them, because they are too civilized [Bryer 14].

Or how can we reconcile the madcap doings in *The Skin of Our Teeth* with its author's assertion, in a 1962 interview, that its theme is Sabina's line, "This is a wicked world, and that's the God's truth" (Bryer 96). Even Emily's famous lines in *Our Town*, "Oh, earth, you're too wonderful for anybody to realize you" and "Do any human beings ever realize life while they live it?," usually read as positive comments, can just as easily be seen as negative ones (*Collected Plays* 207). In *The Matchmaker*, the farce is interrupted by Dolly's comment, "there comes a moment in everybody's life when he must decide whether to live among human beings or not—a fool among fools or a fool alone" (*Collected Plays* 363).

Yes, there certainly is a dark side to Thornton Wilder. He saw life and its tragedies clearly in all its complexity and resisted any simple explanation. Ultimately, he is far from an optimist, in the cliché understanding of that word. He prized the willingness of human beings to survive in a harsh and cruel world, as his nephew Tappan Wilder has described. He certainly was not unaware of the tragic.

Tennessee Williams (1911–83)
Susan C. W. Abbotson, Rhode Island College

While Williams only occasionally refers to any of his plays as tragedies, and several critics refuse to view him as capable of tragedy, I see a strong tragic aspect in his work. Despite Robert Heilman's insistence that Williams's characters lack tragic stature because they display "a limitedness or weakness that is not the raw material of tragic life" (34), Williams's tragic dimension draws powerfully on both ancient and modern considerations of tragedy. Offering a combination of Aristotelian unities with a desire for cathartic action through violence and large emotion, mixed with Arthur Miller's tragedies of the common man, Williams adds his own unique twist. His plays are filled with his own personal brand of tragic heroes, frequently balanced between guilt and/or insanity, and the main tragedy in their lives is not that they are nobly striving to correct a wrong, or that they have even committed a wrong, but that in a profoundly hostile world, they are largely unable to find the supportive kindness or love they need to simply survive.

While Williams's characters often echo mythical archetypes, they are contemporized by a deeper sense of humanity, and a far more muted possibility of triumph. The impact of Williams's problematic relationship with his sister Rose has been noted, and her ghostly presence haunts more plays than *The Glass Menagerie*. She is forever represented in those characters driven insane by the demands of a society that simply cannot accept them, and she becomes a cypher for Williams himself. Just like Oedipus, many of Williams's protagonists search for an uncomfortable truth. It will be a truth that destroys rather than uplifts, but it is a truth from which they cannot hide. A network of imagery runs throughout his work, much of it darkly violent, that depicts, as Henry Schvey has suggested, "sacrifice and martyrdom" (75). These two key elements of tragedy underpin what Schvey correctly identifies as Williams' "tragic conception of life" (74).

As I have written elsewhere, "Williams's life can be read as a romantic quest with himself at the center as the flawed and misunderstood hero" (Abbotson 39). Given his awareness of human nature and assessment of his own self, it is also a quest doomed to failure. The quest is to find comfort and acceptance in the world; but as Blanche famously intoned, "I have always depended on the kindness of strangers," and there lies the rub. A passing respite might come through the attentions of a stranger. But once fully known, the Williams hero will always be cruelly rejected because he or she is intrinsically rotten in the eyes of the larger society, and even more importantly, in his or her own eyes. John Clum points out the "connection between disease/ugliness and homosexual desire" in the short story "Hard Candy," and acknowledges the resonance of such homophobic imagery throughout Williams's work (232). Despite coming out of the closet, Williams, was never entirely comfortable with his own sexuality, always portraying his homosexual characters as predatory, self-hating, and doomed (think *Cat on a Hot Tin Roof, Suddenly Last Summer, Vieux Carré*, etc.).

The "goat-song" sacrifice of archetypal tragedy is the noble hero being martyred by the stern hands of fate. In contemporary tragedy, while the heroes may have less stature, they are nevertheless meant to be enviable on some level for a willingness to sacrifice themselves for something they see as greater than their individual lives. Williams offers us no characters whose sacrifice has that sense of greater good, and yet they still demand our interest and sympathy through a tragic vulnerability.

When Greeks initially conceived of "tragedy," a fundamental necessity seemed a belief in gods, fate, or at least some kind of divinity at the helm. Williams, partially raised and certainly supported by his Episcopal grandparents, maintains a dark thread of religious belief throughout his work, which feeds his self-rejection because of his indefensible (to him) homosexuality. In New Orleans, where Williams most likely had his first homosexual encounters, he explains how he "found the kind of freedom I had always needed. And the shock of it against the Puritanism of my nature has given me a theme, which I have never ceased exploiting" (Leverich 285). The tragedy of a man divided not against others, but against himself.

Arthur Miller (1915–2005)

Stephen A. Marino, St. Francis College, Arthur Miller Journal

Arthur Miller always found himself in the middle of controversy: sometimes on purpose, often inadvertently. Among the playwrights represented here, Miller arguably caused more trouble with one essay which challenged us to redefine tragedy for the modern era.

This was instigated by the critical reaction to *Death of a Salesman* immediately after its Broadway premiere on February 10, 1949. In the early criticism of *Salesman*, no topic dominated more than the consideration of the play as a tragedy. Critics argued over how it applied to our definitions of Greek and Aristotelian tragedy, Shakespearean tragedy, modern tragedy, or whether tragedy is even possible in twentieth-century American theatre. Consequently, consideration of Willy Loman spilled over into whether he possessed—or whether it was even possible for a modern character to possess—the qualities associated with a classical tragic hero.

Theatre critics began this argument in their reviews the weeks after the play's premiere. The chief drama critic of the *New York Times*, Brook Atkinson, was particularly influential in leading those who saw the play as a tragedy. In his review the morning after the premiere, he wrote that Miller "conveys this elusive tragedy in terms of simple things [...]. Chronicler of one frowsy corner of the American scene, he evokes a wraith-like tragedy out of it that spins through the many scenes of his play and gradually envelops the audience" (Atkinson 27). He described Lee J. Cobb's depiction of Willy Loman as a "tragic portrait of the defeated salesman" (27).

On February 27, 1949—not quite three weeks after *Salesman's* premiere— Miller threw himself in the middle of the critical debate by publishing a response in the *New York Times*. Entitled "Tragedy and the Common Man," this controversial essay remains one of the most important commentaries on the nature of the tragic hero in modern drama. Miller redefines the Aristotelian principles of tragedy. He first rejects the notion that tragedy is an archaic form in which high figures are central characters. He declares that the "common man is as apt a subject for tragedy in its highest sense as kings were" (Miller, "Tragedy and the Common Man" 3). He focuses, as Aristotle does in *The Poetics*, on the effect of the tragic hero's action on the audience. However, Miller does not focus on pity, fear, and *hamartia* that are germane to the *Poetics*. Rather, he posits, "The tragic feeling is evoked in us when we are in the presence of a character who is ready to lay down his life, if need be, to secure one thing—his sense of personal dignity" (4). He classifies great classical heroes such as Orestes, Hamlet, Medea, and Macbeth as "individuals attempting to gain [their] rightful position in his society" (4). Miller never mentions Willy Loman in this essay, but by implication, this certainly applies to him.

Miller further maintains that possession of a tragic flaw is not a trait that exists only in the lofty. He does not believe that the tragic flaw indicates a weakness of character; rather, a flaw exists only when a character is passive against a "challenge to his dignity" (4). Thus, tragedy is "the consequence of a man's total compulsion to evaluate himself justly" (4). Moreover, Miller rejects the notion that tragedy is pessimistic. He instead views a character's struggle to achieve his humanity and dignity as optimistic.

One month later on March 27, 1949, Miller further clarified his definition of tragedy in an essay that appeared in the *New York Herald Tribune*. He focused on the feelings that tragedies evoke in the audience, making a clear distinction between the tragic and the pathetic. To Miller, both tragedy and pathos stimulate "sadness, sympathy, identification and even fear, yet tragedy is distinguished by the requirement to deliver knowledge or enlightenment to the audience. And that knowledge pertains to the right way of living in the world" (Miller, "The Nature of Tragedy" 9). Thus, Miller declares, "tragedy is the most accurately balanced portrayal of the human being in his struggle for happiness" (11).

So which of the great tragic figures created by the playwrights represented in our discussion today is not ready to lay down his or her life against the challenge to his/her personal dignity? Who does not seek his/her rightful place in society? Who does not desire to evaluate himself/herself justly? Blanche Dubois? The four haunted Tyrones? Minnie Wright? Emily Webb? Troy Maxson? Shelly Levene? John Proctor? Eddie Carbone?

Edward Albee (1928–)

Natka Bianchini, Loyola University Maryland,
The Edward Albee Society

Compared to the works of several titans of American drama represented on this panel, Edward Albee's *oeuvre* is not a comfortable fit within the genre of tragedy. His work is most commonly identified as "Theatre of the Absurd." He was the sole American playwright to be labeled absurdist in Martin Esslin's landmark book, largely on the basis of his early plays *The Zoo Story* (1959) and *The American Dream* (1961). Despite the fact that Albee's plays traverse and transcend the boundaries of absurdist theatre, it remains the critical lens through which scholars and audiences consistently have analyzed them. Albee was quick to denounce the label, writing in the *New York Times* in 1962 that he was deeply offended by it: "I don't like labels; they can be facile and can lead to non-think on the part of the public" (Albee). But taxonomies can be stubborn in their persistence. This is one association Albee has never been able to avoid.

Along with the absurdist moniker, most of Albee's greatest plays, including *The Zoo Story*, *Who's Afraid of Virginia Woolf?*, *A Delicate Balance*, and *Seascape,* are considered comedies. Although they all contain tragic elements, none can be properly identified as a formal tragedy.

That all changed with the 2002 premiere of *The Goat or Who Is Sylvia?*, his first self-identified tragedy. *The Goat* focuses on the Gray family. Husband Martin is a fabulously successful architect who has just turned fifty. He is happily married to wife Stevie, and they share their immaculate New York City apartment with their teenage son, Billy. Within this perfect nuclear family, Albee's subtitle—*Notes Towards a Definition of Tragedy*—points toward the horror that awaits.

It is soon revealed that Martin is having sexual intercourse with a goat he has named Sylvia. What's more, Martin's congress with the animal is not merely Albee's coded attempt to compel audiences to examine their own prejudices about what is and is not morally reprobate. Martin confesses that he is deeply and spiritually in love with Sylvia, even while he insists that he continues to love Stevie. Emotionally shattered by this revelation, Stevie responds with the literal shattering of vases, plates, and other decorative items carefully placed throughout the couple's immaculately curated living room. At the end of the play, amidst piles of debris, shards of broken glass and clay, Stevie returns. She is covered in blood dragging Sylvia's slaughtered carcass behind her on a white sheet.

Albee is clearly inviting his audiences to identify the parallels between his play and classical Greek tragedy as set forth by Aristotle in *The Poetics*. The play conforms to all of Aristotle's main criteria. It observes the unities of time, place, and action—the setting is the family's living room, Stevie's murderous act takes place less than twenty-four hours after the affair is revealed. Martin, the play's tragic hero, is undone not by shame or guilt stemming from an inability to control his bestial desires. Martin's *hamartia* is that he does not comprehend *why* he should feel ashamed of his relationship with Sylvia. Much like Oedipus's unintentional incest, Martin does not understand why his behavior is taboo. The Greek prohibition against violence onstage is kept intact; Stevie murders Sylvia offstage, with only the gruesome aftermath presented for the audience's view. Finally, Albee's decision to make Sylvia a goat, as opposed to any other animal, is yet another classic reference. The word "tragedy" comes from the Greek *tragoidia*, or "goat-song." It is believed that perhaps a goat was sacrificed as part of the festival of Dionysius during which the original Greek plays were performed. Sylvia becomes our American ritual sacrifice in service of Albee's tragic vision.

What is Albee up to with this classically tragic play? Over four decades of playwriting, Albee has typically used humor, comedy, and yes, even absurdity, to represent the unrepresentable. Why now the sudden emphasis on tragedy? Many of the play's early critics assumed that Albee's use of bestiality was merely a metaphor for other acts of forbidden love, an ironic jab at what society condones and condemns in the bedroom. It was only after the play's debut that Albee added the subtitle, redirecting us to the play's true meaning. Might we not read this, then, as his attempt to finally and definitively shake free of the ill-fitting label "absurdist playwright" while presenting us with our own American tragedy?

David Mamet (1947–)

Brenda Murphy, University of Connecticut

Classical tragedy is not the first thing that comes to mind when David Mamet is mentioned. But Mamet has had a long-standing interest in tragedy, particularly as defined by Aristotle. He has written that the "purpose of theater, like magic, like religion—those three harness mates—is to inspire cleansing awe" (*Knife* 69). He believes that "tragedy is cleansing because it confronts us with [...] our humanity, with our capacity for evil" (Kane 181), but that fundamentally, it is based on human choice. Mamet has said that when a character is presented with what appear to be good and evil alternatives, tragedy says, "'choose which one you want to be. Whichever one you choose, you're going to be wrong, and, P. S., you never had a choice to begin with. You're just human.' And we leave shaken and perhaps better for the experience" (Kane 181). Time and again, Mamet has said that tragedy is fundamentally about revealing the truth. "Tragedy is about horrific things," he said in an interview. "It's about bringing the hidden to light so that one can grieve. And that's why tragedy, in the perfect form, is cleansing, because it enables us to deal with repression. [...] And as Freud would have said, instead of living a happy life, be more capable to live a life of ordinary misery" (Kane 209).

Perhaps because he sees revelation as central to tragedy, Mamet sees Aristotle's description of recognition and reversal at the heart of tragic structure. He has described his play *The Shawl* as "a twentieth century version of the idea that what the hero is following and what he ends up with may be two very different things, but they are nonetheless related in the subconscious. [...] What happens at the crucial moment, as Aristotle says, is that the protagonist undergoes both recognition of the situation and a reversal of the situation" (Kane 66).

Mamet has identified four of his plays as classical tragedies on the Aristotelian model: *American Buffalo, The Cryptogram, The Woods,* and *Oleanna.* In *American Buffalo,* he describes Donny the junk store owner as the protagonist. He is "trying to teach a lesson in how to behave like the excellent man to his young ward" (Kane 67). Tempted with money by Teach, he betrays his principles, finally allowing Teach to beat up Bobby. According to Mamet, Donny then undergoes [...] recognition in reversal—realizing that all this comes out of his vanity, that because he abdicated a moral position for one moment in favor of some momentary gain, he has let anarchy into his life and has come close to killing the thing he loves. And he realizes at the end of the play that he has made a huge mistake, that, rather than his young ward needing lessons in being an excellent man, it is he himself who needs those lessons. That is what *American Buffalo* is about [Kane 67].

Mamet describes *Oleanna* as "a tragedy about power" (Kane 125). He says that Carol and John are "two people with a lot to say to each other, with legitimate affection for each other. But protecting their positions becomes more important than pursuing their own best interests. And that leads them down the slippery slope to a point where, at the end of the play, they tear each other's throat out" (Kane 125). Aware of the controversy the play has stirred in audiences, he insists that he doesn't "personally take the side of one rather than the other. I think they're absolutely both wrong, and they're absolutely both, both right. And that's to the extent that the play aspires to—or achieves—the status of ... a tragedy" (Kane 144). In the context of *Oleanna*, he has said that tragedy is the most difficult form to write, "where the hero or heroine is going to his.... Aristotle tells us, come to the end of the play and realize that he or she is the cause of their own problems and undergo[es] a change of the situation at the last moment of the play ... such that the audience will say, 'Oh my God, now I understand. I've seen something that is both shocking and inevitable'" (Kane 145). He has described John as the play's protagonist, saying that "he undergoes absolute reversal of situation, absolute recognition at the last moment of the play. He realizes that perhaps he is the cause of the plague upon Thebes" (Kane 119).

The Cryptogram embodies Mamet's belief that "every tragedy's based on deception; that's the meaning of the, the tragic form ... something has been hidden and can only be uncovered, uncovered at great expense. And when it is uncovered we say, 'Oh, my gosh, it was in front of me the whole time'" (Kane 153). *The Cryptogram* is literally about solving puzzles, at many levels. The audience is simultaneously participating in the young protagonist John's attempts to understand the meaning of the adults' words and actions and reacting to their psychological effect on him, the "dynamics of a soul murder," as John Lahr has put it (73).

As committed as he is to Aristotle's description of tragedy, Mamet is aware of the dissonance that happens when applying it to modern life. This emerges in parodic form in his Wildean comedy of manners, *Boston Marriage*, where the characters frame their actions in literary references. When her machinations are exposed, Anna exclaims, "Oh, fate inexorable. Oh, fate misthought at first to be but circumstance, revealed at last as the minute operations of the gods. Oh fate but our own character congealed into a burning glass. Focus your cleansing light upon me, and I shall be cleansed" (*Boston Marriage* 51). Applying tragic discourse to Anna's pursuits at first seems to emphasize their triviality, but it also inspires a second look that suggests the tragic element embedded in this trivial comedy.

August Wilson (1945–2005)

Sandra Shannon, Howard University, The August Wilson Society

August Wilson begins his now-famous manifesto, *The Ground On Which I Stand* (1996), with a polite concession that the ground upon which he stands has been "pioneered by the Greek dramatists" (11). While he concedes his debt to the formal dramatic style outlined in Aristotle's rules of drama, he goes on to create the case for his focused and sustained efforts as a dramatist to affirm that "race matters—that it is the largest, most identifiable and most important part of our personality. [...] It is the one to which others in the world of men most respond." "Race," according to Wilson, "is also an important part of the American landscape, as America is made up of an amalgamation of races from all parts of the globe. Race is also the product of a shared gene pool that allows for group identification, and it is an organizing principle around which cultures are formed" (14).

While August Wilson's vision of tragedy does indeed bear the imprint of Aristotelian concepts delineated in the *Poetics*, many of his Pittsburgh Cycle plays call for another round of adjustments to this classic set of guidelines. In a manner reminiscent of Arthur Miller's 1949 defense of Willy Loman as "just as apt a subject for tragedy in its highest sense as kings were," August Wilson creates tragic figures whose race—not so much their economic status—is the largest determinant of their worth in America. In other words, race matters— to echo the title of public intellectual Cornell West's popular 1994 study on race relations in America. Wilson was convinced that tragedy results when all avenues to the mythic American Dream are blocked for African Americans.

But Wilson was adamant not to create tragic figures who are victims of fate or to cast them at the end of his plays as hopeless pariahs. Instead, his warriors, rebels, and spectacle characters such as Herald Loomis, Levee, King Hedley II, Troy Maxson, Ma Rainey, Boy Willie, and Hambone—like poet Claude McKay's men and women—do not concede defeat. Rather, they stand their ground while "pressed to the wall, dying, but fighting back!" (McKay). They rail against injustice and demand their due from a system that essentially has shut them out. Though death looms large among them, end of life for Wilson's reconstructed tragedians often signals new beginnings and cause for celebration along with reconciliation and reunion. Wilson's tragic figures go beyond the very basic pleas for the acceptance of one's humanity that is so reminiscent in the current "Black Lives Matter" international movement against violence. His tragedies elevate the focus upon black life to increase self-awareness and accountability as well as to embrace the cultural traditions that have sustained them.

August Wilson's concept of tragedy also owes a debt to Yoruban cosmology and theory, especially in his tendency toward evoking ritual, and envisioning both metaphysical and spiritual worlds. Several scholars (e.g., Harry Elam, Paul Carter Harrison, Kim Pereira, and Sandra Richards) have begun to explore the extent to which Yoruban cosmology informs the actions of some of his most enigmatic characters. Reading his plays through this pertinent lens will likely prevent possible misinterpretations of his works when the Aristotelian model is applied arbitrarily or awkwardly. Essential to understanding the dynamics of Wilson's tragic mode is the work of Nigerian theorist and playwright Wole Soyinka, whose landmark essay, "The Fourth Stage," theorizes Yoruban theater as well as Yoruban philosophy. Soyinka argues that traditional Yoruba tragedy acts out the suffering caused by the gulfs in existence and by the painful acts of will or assertion performed to bridge them. He has sought to develop a contemporary African theatre that would not only be drama in the Western, secular sense of the term, but also ritual in the Yoruba sense of tragedy. In "The Fourth Stage," Soyinka weaves African myth into the idea of tragedy, with important implications for the task of the modern African playwright. Knowledge of Yoruban deities, such as Ogun, whom Soyinka acknowledges as the divine patron of Yoruban drama, can enrich our understanding of both nuanced and quite obvious differences in Wilson's brand of Africanist inspired tragedy. Read through this lens, plays such as *Gem of the Ocean, Joe Turner's Come and Gone, The Piano Lesson, King Hedley II, Fences, Seven Guitars,* and *Ma Rainey's Black Bottom,* for example, take on more pertinent new meaning.

One has to wonder what kind of plays a 70-year-old August Wilson would have written for the present decade. When considering the recent findings of the National Urban League in its annual report on the State of Black America, the tragic mode most likely would have been his choice to best convey these troubling findings that African Americans still fare worse than whites and other demographic groups in terms of education and income and that justice for African Americans was challenged on every front in the past year—especially in terms of accountability for police misconduct, erosion of voting rights, and widening economic gaps (National Urban League). Given these and other alarming results from this report's findings, it stands to reason that August Wilson could have been motivated to write a second ten-play cycle that would add to an already-long list of tragedians who stand their ground while, for example, seeking atonement for misdeeds, journeying to find a starting place, holding out for their Coca-Cola, arguing their case for a 125-year-old piano, wrestling with Death, demanding their promised ham, and fighting against insurmountable and fateful odds to avenge a father's death.

WORKS CITED

Abbotson, Susan C. W. "Tennessee Williams on America." *Critical Insights: Tennessee Williams*. Ed. Brenda Murphy. Hackensack, NJ: Salem, 2010. 38–57.

Albee, Edward. "Which Theatre is the Absurd One?" *The American Stage: Writing on the Theatre from Washington Irving to Tony Kushner*. Ed. Laurence Senelick. New York: Library of America, 2010.

Atkinson, Brooks. "At the Theatre." *New York Times* (February 11, 1949): 27.

Banks, Russell. "Foreword." *The Bridge of San Luis Rey*. 1927. New York: Harper Perennial, 1998. xi–xvii.

Ben-Zvi, Linda. *Susan Glaspell: Her Life and Times*. New York: Oxford University Press, 2005.

Bigsby, C.W.E. "Introduction." *Plays by Susan Glaspell*. Ed. C. W. E. Bigsby. Cambridge: Cambridge University Press, 2003. 1–31.

Bryer, Jackson R., ed. *Conversations with Thornton Wilder*. Jackson: University Press of Mississippi, 1992.

Carpentier, Martha C. "Apollonian Form and Dionysian Excess in Susan Glaspell's Drama and Fiction." *Disclosing Intertextualities: The Stories, Plays, and Novels of Susan Glaspell*. Eds. Martha C. Carpentier and Barbara Ozieblo. Amsterdam: Rodopi, 2006. 35–50.

Clark, Barrett H. *European Theories of the Drama, With a Supplement of the American Drama*. Rev. ed. New York: Crown, 1947.

Clum, John M. "Something Cloudy, Something Clear": Homophobic Discourse in Tennessee Williams." *Critical Insights: Tennessee Williams*. Ed. Brenda Murphy. Hackensack, NJ: Salem, 2010. 226–45.

Esslin, Martin. *Theatre of the Absurd*. Garden City, NY: Anchor Books, 1969.

Felski, Rita, ed. *Rethinking Tragedy*. Baltimore: Johns Hopkins University Press, 2008.

Gainor, J. Ellen. *Susan Glaspell in Context*. Ann Arbor: University of Michigan Press, 2001.

Glaspell, Susan. *Complete Plays*. Eds. Linda Ben-Zvi and J. Ellen Gainor. Jefferson, NC: McFarland, 2010.

Goldhill, Simon. "Generalizing About Tragedy." *Rethinking Tragedy*. Ed. Rita Felski. Baltimore: Johns Hopkins University Press, 2008. 45–65.

Green, William Chase. *Moira: Fate, Good, and Evil in Greek Thought*. Cambridge: Harvard University Press, 1944.

Heilman, Robert B. "Tennessee Williams: Approaches to Tragedy." *Tennessee Williams*. Ed. Stephen S. Stanton. Englewood Cliffs: Prentice Hall, 1977.

Kane, Leslie, ed. *David Mamet in Conversation*. Ann Arbor: University of Michigan Press, 2001.

Lahr, John. "Betrayals," *New Yorker* (August 1, 1994): 73.

Leverich, Lyle. *Tom: The Unknown Tennessee Williams*. New York: Norton, 1995.

Lewis, Sinclair. "Text of Sinclair Lewis's Nobel Prize Address at Stockholm." *New York Times* (December 13, 1930): 12.

Makowsky, Veronica. "Susan Glaspell and Modernism." *The Cambridge Companion to*

American Women Playwrights. Ed. Brenda Murphy. Cambridge: Cambridge University Press, 1999. 49–65.

Mamet, David. *Boston Marriage.* New York: Vintage, 2002.

_____. *Three Uses of the Knife: On the Nature and Purpose of Drama.* New York: Columbia University Press, 1998.

Martin, Robert A., and Steven R. Centola, eds. *The Theatre Essays of Arthur Miller*, Rev. ed. New York: DaCapo, 1996.

Matthiessen, F. O. "Figures in a Dream." *New Freeman* (May 10, 1930): 212–13.

McKay, Claude. "If We Must Die." http://www.poets.org/poetsorg/poem/if-we-must-die.

Miller, Arthur. "The Nature of Tragedy." *New York Herald Tribune* (March 27, 1949): sec. 5: 1–2.

_____. "Tragedy and the Common Man." *New York Times* (February 27, 1949): sec. 2: 1, 3.

National Urban League. "State of Black America: Save Our Cities: Education, Jobs + Justice." iamempoweredwww. Web. Accessed March 19, 2015.

Niven, Penelope. *Thornton Wilder: A Life.* New York: HarperCollins, 2012.

O'Neill, Eugene. Letter to Saxe Commins, August 4, 1929. Qtd. in Doris Alexander, "Mourning Becomes Electra," *Eugene O'Neill.* Ed. Harold Bloom. New York: Infobase, 2007. 31.

_____. *Long Day's Journey Into Night.* New Haven: Yale University Press, 1956.

_____. "Memoranda on Masks." *American Spectator Yearbook.* New York: Frederick A. Stokes, 1934.

O'Neill, Joseph P. "The Tragic Theory of Eugene O'Neill." *Texas Studies in Literature and Language* 4.4 (1963): 481–98.

Ozieblo, Barbara. *Susan Glaspell: A Critical Biography.* Chapel Hill: University of North Carolina Press, 2000.

Quinn, Arthur Hobson. *A History of American Drama from the Civil War to the Present.* Vol. 2. New York: Irvington, 1946.

Rosslyn, Felicity. *Tragic Plots.* Aldershot: Ashgate, 2000.

Schvey, Henry I. "The Tragic Poetics of Tennessee Williams." *Études Anglaises* 64.1 (2011): 74–85.

Soyinka, Wole. "The Fourth Stage: Through the Mysteries of Ogun to the Origin of Yoruba Tragedy." *Myth, Literature and the African World.* Cambridge: Cambridge University Press, 1990.

Wallace, Jennifer. *The Cambridge Introduction to Tragedy.* Cambridge: Cambridge University Press, 2007.

Wilder, Tappan. Email to Jackson R. Bryer. March 24, 2015.

Wilder, Thornton. *The Bridge of San Luis Rey.* 1927. New York: Harper Perennial, 2003.

_____. *Collected Plays & Writings on Theater.* New York: Library of America, 1997.

_____. *The Ides of March.* 1948. New York: Harper Perennial, 2003.

Wilson, August. *The Ground on Which I Stand.* Dramatic Context Series. New York: Theatre Communications Group, 2000.

Winther, Sophus Keith. *Eugene O'Neill: A Criticial Study.* Enlarged ed. New York: Random House, 1961. www.eoneill.com/library/winther/XII.htm. Web.

"Woman Satirizes Woman's Honor." *The Herald* (May 22, 1918): n.p.

Politic Silence: Female Choruses in Lochhead's *Medea* and Wertenbaker's *The Love of the Nightingale*

Lydia Craig

Abstract

This essay explores reinventions of the Euripidean chorus in Liz Lochhead's Medea *and Timberlake Wertenbaker's* The Love of the Nightingale, *an adaptation of the Philomele myth, which highlight gender issues still relevant to modern audiences by referencing the unchanging nature of female struggles for agency throughout history. These plays reference the universal female experience with male abuse and resultant powerlessness whenever Lochhead's chorus deviates from their lines in Euripides' original play, or Wertenbaker's chorus rebels against the cohesive, unified structure typical of the Greek female chorus in favor of individuality and resistance. Lochhead's exclusion of Medea's semi-divine nature from her adaptation introduces a new theme—that of instinctive maternity—which her chorus prioritizes over sexual love and betrayal. In contrast, Wertenbaker's chorus recognizes motherhood itself as perpetuating the cycle of violence against women. Male injustice provokes female violence in both plays, a social problem each chorus, biologically trapped and lacking social rights, vainly attempts to resolve.*

The Scottish dramaturge Liz Lochhead's *Medea* (2000) and British-based playwright Timberlake Wertenbaker's *The Love of the Nightingale* (1989) uti-

---

2015 Winner of the Anthony Ellis Prize for Best Paper by a Graduate Student

lize and reinvent the Euripidean chorus to contrast "badly behaved" heroines with a "socially normative" female voice. Prioritizing maternal duty over sexual jealousy, these choruses urge the heroines as women to forget their grievances and sorrow despite demonstrable male wrongs, and instead conform to the roles of wife and mother. In Lochhead's *Medea* an initially supportive female chorus serves a suppressive, didactic function in relation to the titular heroine as her fury against male mistreatment intensifies. The reverse is true for Wertenbaker's female chorus in *The Love of the Nightingale*, an adaptation loosely based on the Philomele myth, which finally responds to masculine tyranny by silently assenting to violence, parodying passive femininity. But neither Lochhead's nor Wertenbaker's chorus directly challenges the structure creating the heroines' problems, recommending silence and restraint instead of voiced, active rebellion. Lochhead's chorus advocates bearing spousal injustice for the sake of children, while Wertenbaker's more radical chorus only becomes complicit in infanticide during the temporary chaos of the Bacchanalian rites. Thus motherhood alternatively represents refuge for Lochhead's chorus, and constraint for Wertenbaker's, both plays portraying the female chorus as unwilling to participate in outright rebellion against patriarchal oppression and powerless to achieve female individual and social rights.

Since both Lochhead and Wertenbaker's choruses are patterned after the Euripidean female chorus in Greek tragedy, consulting the original source texts of Euripides' *Medea*, Ovid's version of the Philomele myth, and various academic studies of the tragic chorus help to clarify each adaptation's ideological point of departure from the classic narrative and "typical" choral behavior. Significantly less common than male choruses in Greek drama, female choruses most often appeared in tragedies involving a female heroine, and were frequently present in ritual theatre. An archetypal female chorus in Greek drama not only interpreted and predicted the action but also provided a wider social context for the given situation (Swift 130). By her own admission, Lochhead has loosely translated Euripides' *Medea* word by word into English and Scots, and then modified or added to each line in accordance with the gendered themes of her adaptation, changing Medea and her chorus's words and perspective in the process (Lochhead v–vi). Since no extant play concerning the Philomele myth exists, Wertenbaker exercises greater freedom than Lochhead in choosing her chorus's composition and situation. She explains "When I wrote *The Love of the Nightingale*, which is inspired by ten lines of Sophocles and looks at the Philomele myth as reported by Ovid and Robert Graves, people kept calling it an adaptation. But there was no 'original' work to adapt, although the work did 'arise from something'" ("First Thoughts" 38).[1] As recounted in Book Six of Ovid's *Metamorphoses*, the story of "Procne and Philomela" describes the rape and mutilation of Philomela by her sister Procne's husband Tereus.[2] After discovering the crime, Procne joins Philomela in killing her son Itys and gruesomely feeding his cooked body to her oblivious husband (Ovid 161–169). Arguably, the original myth already makes a convincing point about oppressed, silenced women fighting back, so why choose to use the Greek chorus at all in this theatrical adaptation? Simply put, Wertenbaker's use of a separated male and female chorus essentially gives a voice to female suffering without disturbing the heroine Philomele's famous muteness and thematically connects the adaptation with Euripides' *Hippolytus*, a play likewise concerned with incestuous desires between men and women, gendered spaces, and the power of language and communication.

Lochhead's *Medea*: The Maternal Chorus

In her transcultural modern retelling of Euripides' *Medea*, Lochhead maintains the original chorus's sex and speaking role in relation to the heroine, but destabilizes their uniform demographic to question whether women of all times and places could understand the reasons for Medea's grief and anger. Furious at her husband Jason's sexual betrayal and upcoming marriage to another woman, King Kreon's daughter Glauke, Medea describes her grief to an initially sympathetic female chorus. However, as she murders Glauke, Kreon, and finally her own children by Jason, the increasingly horrified chorus futilely pleads with Medea to abandon her revenge. Instead of the "singing Chorus of Corinthian women" speaking to Medea as a social equal (Euripides 8), or the Scottish chorus the audience might expect in an adaptation contrasting an English-speaking Medea with Scots-speaking nobility, Lochhead's chorus encompasses women of "all times, all ages, classes, and professions" (Lochhead 7), representing a significant diegetical transposition. As defined by Miriam Chirico in "Hellenic Women Revisited," "a diegetical transposition reveals specific analogies between the earlier depiction of the myth and the latter-day revision; even as anachronisms appear, they underscore both the dissonance *and* similarity between classical antiquity and the contemporary moment and ignite a spark of recognition that is the hallmark of this genre" (18–19). Though the chorus mentions concepts foreign to Euripides' heroine, such as "policemen" and "hospital corridors" (Lochhead 8), as women they still can identify with Medea. Lochhead's chorus and Medea possibly have nothing else in common besides their shared gender, yet this alone prompts them to immediately claim and advise her as their "sister" (7), initially prioritizing womanhood alone, distinct from class or nationality, as sufficient to comprehend her grief. With her diverse female chorus representing women throughout history, Lochhead forces a twenty-first century audience to consider whether Medea's grief and anger at male abandonment resonate the same way now, regardless of time and place.

Because Lochhead's chorus considers frustrated desire and loss to be inevitable components of a woman's lot, they vacillate between angrily recalling male mistreatment and urging Medea to avoid sexual feelings altogether. Cynthia Gardiner claims that the Greek chorus "always plays essentially the same character and role in every drama, such as that of ordinary persons whose limited and often mistaken perceptions contrast with and thus magnify the greatness of the heroic individuals in the play" (3). Lochhead continues this tradition by casting her chorus as women familiar with various kinds of female grief who, instead of confronting the greater social problems lurking behind loss and rejection, opt instead for the safety of repression and self-imposed constraint. Describing Medea's cry at Jason's sexual betrayal as innately part of the feminine experience, uttered by "the woman / opening the door to the telegraph boy in wartime" or "the mother in the hospital corridor / when she sees the doctor's face" heard "from our sisters mothers from ourselves" (Lochhead 8–9), the diverse chorus relates how they themselves have endured similar experiences in their own lives. The chorus claims to hate men like Kreon and Jason, chanting "we promise you we are women Medea / We know men we know who's in the right / punish him for us Medea" (10).

But do they truly comprehend the complicated rationale behind Medea's specific hatred? Besides Jason's adultery, Medea's self-proclaimed grievances against him include committing fratricide for his sake, enduring childbirth after being "gendered" into womanhood by his love, and being "the last to know" about his new affair (10). She is furious at being "transformed" into a gender that can be exploited by men without consequences, a helpless woman who can be tossed aside after bearing the next royal generation for a man she passionately loved. In response, the chorus asks, "what desire is not excessive? gets us into such trouble does us in / drives us wild makes us gluttons for punishment" (22). Medea's inner turmoil, they suggest, is largely self-inflicted and self-indulgent, caused more by her lack of emotional restraint than Jason's supposed mistreatment. Refusing to accept the chorus's advice to accept "celibacy" or "the cosy old / comfy married bed" (22), Medea realizes she cannot "play the part" or "wear the mask" (23) of the moderate chorus. These women from various backgrounds throughout history have survived situations like Medea's by effectively subduing their anger and accepting patriarchy's problematization of female desire. Even at the beginning of Lochhead's *Medea*, the chorus cannot truly relate to this particular woman's understanding of gender or personal "rights."

Furthermore, the female chorus believes a woman's vocal protest against male exploitation and sexual abandonment conflicts with her more instinctive role as mother. Anger at sexual abandonment must be sacrificed to maternal duty—protecting one's young. According to Linda Hutcheon, "Almost always, there is an accompanying shift in the political valence from the adapted text to the 'transculturated' adaptation. Context conditions meaning, in short" (145). As a transculturated adaptation utilizing British accents, with a chorus representing women throughout history, Lochhead's *Medea* intends to provoke comparisons between how women have been regarded and treated at different points in time. The female chorus's prioritization of maternity over sexuality raises strikingly relevant and urgent questions: Who and what is a woman, regardless of social and cultural boundaries? Does her maternal instinct make her a submissive tool of the patriarchy? Despite their hatred of men, Lochhead's chorus differs from Euripides' chorus in believing that maternal duties should be superior to any other feminine instinct in a woman, even frustrated love. A mother should put aside her anger and vengeance for the good of her young. Significantly, the chorus's allegiance to Medea first wavers after her angry dialogue with the "other woman"—pregnant Glauke, who promises to love and care for the children. Glauke passes over the "man and wife" relationship of Jason and Medea to emphasize their primary relationship as "father and mother" to their children (Lochhead 24), a transition the chorus quickly accepts and advocates as a more practical way to defuse the situation. Though they dislike her, the chorus even calls Glauke's naïve cruelty to Medea "understandable," and adds,

> we were shocked at first the mothers among us
> when you said you'd leave them here with Jason
> then we had to see it made good sense
> you said yourself so much so much
> you love your children/you must leave them? [27].

This coaxing assessment of what the chorus hopes Medea's intentions to be perfectly exemplifies Gardiner's observation that Greek "choruses often seem to summarize a character's speech as harsh words needing modification" (39). By speaking for the protagonist using her past words in the manner of a traditional Greek chorus, Lochhead's "modern" chorus preempts Medea's own response to the interaction with Glauke, and outlines the appropriate course of conduct for her to follow. As a rejected sexual partner Medea could vent her wrath without fear of consequence, but as a mother her appropriate course of action dictates that she abandon justified anger for her children's sake, along with her parental rights. Motherhood, by choral definition, is more innately feminine and natural than sexual desire or jealousy. Women must abjure both in order to ensure that the rights and welfare of the next generation are not endangered by their own imprudence and rebellion.

While Euripides' character sees herself as the gods' agent avenging Jason's broken oath, Lochhead removes the divine aspect, allowing the chorus to attack Medea solely on the grounds of being an unnatural mother.[3] However impractically, Medea wants her children to escape the inevitable gendered fate of their parents, which would mean growing up to be either victim (woman) or persecutor (man). She asks, "Can I get philosophy? Sigh and say / 'it happens' 'I am not the first and I won't be the last' / 'in one hundred years it will be all the same'?" (23). Not only do the children represent Jason's dynastic future, they also represent the early stages of the next generation of gender conflict. Charles Segal perceives Euripides' Medea's "sinister magic" to be working "primarily in female domestic space, [moving] from the women's chambers outward to affect the future of kingdoms. Medea not only destroys her own children—her husband's successors—but also ends a dynasty and obliterates her husband's political ambitions" (10). Lochhead's Medea remains conscious of this dynastic aspect of her revenge, but she is primarily motivated by concern for her children. Consequently, when Medea reveals her intention to murder her children to save her sons from becoming "cruel men like their father" and her daughter from experiencing the reality of "womanhood / and this world's mercy" (Lochhead 28), the chorus regards this as an act of murder specifically unnatural. According to "Nature's way," mothers instinctively give their lives for their children (29). This line of argument, employing nature imagery to recall Medea to her maternal "animal" instincts, does not appear in the original and is Lochhead's invention. In the analogy the chorus uses, a "mother sheep offers her own white throat / to the wolf and saves her lambs" (29). If males like Jason represent the "wolf" and menace to the domestic home's stability, then females like Medea must sacrifice themselves to protect their children's future.

Since the female chorus does not share in Medea's guilt, its members feel free to condemn her on the basis of failed femininity until the infanticide itself, emphasizing their particular understanding of motherhood's restrictive, all-encompassing nature. *Transmotivation* is another device Lochhead employs to distance the woman Medea from her divine origins in the original Greek myth. Chirico defines this device as the playwright's revision of a character's intentions (20), which in this instance changes not only how the chorus responds to Medea, but also how the audience rationalizes her heinous act. Because Lochhead's heroine lacks the original Medea's avowed desire for "a glorious reputation" (Euripides 833), concerned instead for her children's future and Jason's punishment, the chorus ultimately blames her for choosing murderous revenge over her identity as nurturing mother. Alternating between calling Medea a "mother" and a "murderer," the chorus again denigrates her suffering as a "domestic commonplace" that she has inflated beyond proportion

(Lochhead 35). They are unable to accept her maternal fear of raising children to perpetuate similar male-female gender roles. Segal addresses Greek tragedy's exploration of a character's hidden motivations as presenting "anxieties that perhaps could not easily be verbalized or otherwise represented with its very one-sided view of male and female relations" (8). Medea's motivation represents a deeply developed understanding of gender dynamics that the chorus, despite its wealth of feminine experiences ranging across history, cannot process. Like them, Medea does understand how maternal sacrifice should be enacted, but refuses to perform her role, knowing that it will lead to future female suffering for her daughters and enable her sons to become tyrants. Instead, the children become the innocent casualties of the matrimonial fracas, dispatched in a pre-emptive act. From the chorus's viewpoint, Medea, not Jason, has doomed the dynasty through succumbing to excessive emotion and unhinged fantasies. The tragedies expose "the dangers of the social system; permit the repressed fears, resentments, desires, and fantasies on both sides to find expression; and then illustrate how ruinous it is to allow full rein to these passions, especially the erotic passions which women are supposedly less able to resist" (Segal 8–9). Medea, instead of man, becomes the unidentifiable Other to Lochhead's chorus, which sees the death of one's children to be the ultimate grief, claiming, "death disease or war / can decimate our hopes / deaths of our children / this is the one pain the Gods should not ask us to survive" (Lochhead 39). However, Medea does survive and glories in her revenge, cementing the chorus' perception of her as an unnatural monster.

Constructing Procne's Suppressed Chorus

Whereas Lochhead deviates from Euripides' original play to "update" *Medea's* themes for a modern audience, Wertenbaker adapts Ovid's "Procne and Philomela" myth in *The Love of the Nightingale* by deriving inspiration from another Euripidean chorus—that of *Hippolytus*. Wertenbaker directly connects the two plays by including an Athenian performance of *Hippolytus* during the crucial scene in which King Tereus of Thrace first desires his sister-in-law Philomele, paralleling Phaedra's passion for her chaste stepson Hippolytus. Though Phaedra "breathes not a word" (*Hippolytus* 40) of her incestuous love, believing her "honor lies in silence" (329), her nurse divulges the secret. After Hippolytus rejects her, Phaedra kills herself and falsely incriminates him as her "rapist" in a posthumous "confession." The tables are turned as Hippolytus finds himself unable to clear his name and destined to die: "So, I'm condemned, and there is no release. / I know the truth and dare not tell the truth" (1090–1). Divided by gender, Hippolytus's fellow huntsmen and

Phaedra's palace women can only witness firsthand what has befallen each representative of their sex, just as neither of Wertenbaker's male and female choruses can predict nor prevent the horrible tragedies that destroy Tereus's family. A male chorus, musing on the nature of man and war, accompanies Tereus during his voyage to convey Philomele to her homesick sister and his wife, Procne. In his absence a female chorus (Hero, Iris, June, Echo, and Helen) reluctantly attends mournful Procne in her husband's absence, unable to verbally or ideologically connect with their mistress. Overcome with lust, Tereus eventually rapes his unwilling sister-in-law, cuts out her tongue to enforce silence, and confines her out of sight. Eventually, Philomele escapes during the feast of Bacchus and tells Procne everything through a dumb show, killing Procne and Tereus's son Itys during the revels while the chorus watches. The two sisters flee from vengeful Tereus, pursued and pursuer inexplicably turning into birds. The choruses of *The Love of the Nightingale* double as Euripides' choruses during the fateful performance, further emphasizing the ideological likeness between the two plays. At its conclusion, they speak their one unified line: "These sorrows have fallen on us unforeseen" (Wertenbaker 24), which represents the only statement both genders can agree on in the aftermath of tragedy. Separated, the male and female choruses will never reach consensus, or even be able to enter into a dialogue about the differences existing between them. Wertenbaker thus emphasizes the spatial and verbal disconnect between genders, both halves of the full chorus unaware even of the full scope of the tragedy until it occurs.

By using Euripides' divided chorus in her adaptation, Wertenbaker can explore how the patriarchal system troubles both male and female choruses, imposing greater restraints and demands on the latter of the two. If and when male abuse occurs, women are expected to hide their shame and stay out of the public eye. Though Tereus identifies with Phaedra in his lustful, illegal pursuit of his sister-in-law, he projects the need for silence onto his victim, Philomele, instead of himself. Exploring Wertenbaker's use of *Hippolytus*'s themes in *The Love of the Nightingale*, Joe Winston reads Phaedra's desire for silence in *Hippolytus* as "resulting from her unquestioning acceptance of a patriarchal moral order which uses shame as a means to oppress her [...] indicative of a political tendency throughout much of history for the voices of women to be silenced" (515). As Procne's chorus knows, there is comparative safety in silence, though not justice. Though the female chorus's constraint occupies the main focus in Wertenbaker's adaptation, the men supporting Tereus are also seen to suffer confusion from the system's demands, though they collude in the very crimes provoking violent female retribution. While women are expected to be voiceless in Thrace, males must remain blind. Instead of responding to flagrant abuses of power, the male chorus "sees nothing" (Wertenbaker 41). Desiring to maintain the status quo, the chorus wrestles with their culpability in aiding and abetting Tereus's crimes, even helping him dispose of the murdered captain's body. "For the sake of order, peace," says one; "But at what price?" answers another (34). Initially, Procne's female chorus also clings to its familiar practices and behavior, seeking safety by conforming to its socially prescribed role within the domestic pace. Philomele's rape can occur because men and women are expected to inhabit these different spheres; as an unprotected, adventurous female she leaves the safety of her parents' house and enters the male realm of action where Procne's influence does not extend, and Tereus wields authority not only over her person, but also commands his men's undying allegiance. In a world where powerful men are not questioned by other men, or held accountable by women, both male and female choruses have come to accept their subservience for the greater good and their own protection, enduring abuse silently instead of challenging the men in authority.

At first conforming to their acceptable gender roles, Procne's chorus gradually comes to recognize their own desire for an independent voice after observing their mistress's grief and misery within the female domestic space. Segal claims, "in the background of the gender divisions of tragedy lies some form of the antithesis of war, male, public realm, action, and glory versus domestic life, private realm, passivity, grief, and weeping" (74). In such a private realm, Procne's chorus originally demonstrates ignorance of their own repression, urging her to join in their customary mindless amusements and abandon her strange moods. Struggling to interpret her melancholy, they label the foreigner's mood "grief," "boredom," and "homesickness," deciding at last that Athenian Procne represents a cultural outsider. June declares, "she is not one of us," which Hero supplements with the observation "a shared childhood makes friends between women" (Wertenbaker 15). Since this chorus has been raised together under the same cultural system, not reared in the comparative freedom of Athenian females, they resent the difference between themselves and their mistress. Procne's listlessness introduces a dangerous element into the domestic space that cannot be ignored, demanding the truth from them, and thus introducing the inconceivable idea of female expression. Claude Calame describes the female choral dynamic as depending "on the friendship of each of them with a girl who is in another position and has a function different from that of the chorus-members" (33). As their leader, Procne introduces previously unvoiced ideas of female agency and expression to her chorus that defy their preconceived social roles and slowly transform their group mentality. Laura Swift elaborates on the fluidity of the tragic chorus's identity as aiding the tragedian's exploration of belonging to a group:

Firstly, the chorus lacks any individual identity on the part of its members: they speak with a single voice, and are defined entirely by the grouping which the poet has chosen to give them. As such, the chorus can easily be used to investigate the phenomenon of group identity and how identities are formed through belonging to particular groupings. Secondly, the choral grouping is never fixed by the myth, but is the free choice of the poet [131].

Procne's position as the chorus's social superior dictates how they must behave, but they are unable to follow her example in demanding the truth. Iris says "We don't know how to act, we don't know what to say" (Wertenbaker 15), suggesting that Thracian culture discourages these women from verbal displays singling them out from the group as the individuals Hero, Echo, Iris, June, and Helen. Having refused to be "initiated" (16) into their female culture of empty play, Procne remains at an impasse with her chorus, trapped with women afraid of speaking out even to warn against sending for Philomele.

Beginning to find fault with the system that keeps them suppressed and dormant, the chorus craves the freedom and ability to uncover the truth. Struggling between the habit of self-effacing silence, and their new longing for answers, Wertenbaker's female chorus begins to voice their thoughts and questions after realizing they share Procne's discontent:

> HERO. Sometimes I feel I know things but I cannot prove that I know them or that what I know is true and when I doubt my knowledge it disintegrates into a senseless jumble of possibilities, a puzzle that will not be reassembled, the spider's web in which I lie, immobile, and truth paralyzed.
>
> HELEN. Let me put it another way: I have trouble expressing myself. The world I see and the words I have do not match [Wertenbaker 32].

These two chorus members are expressing their realization of having been indoctrinated in the belief that women cannot think, reason, or protest when words "do not match" realities. To question the validity of male vocabularies leaves them with no words of their own, and no authentic way to be heard as individuals. When language fails, all that remains is the alternative of taking action, the "senseless jumble of possibilities" which is nearly unthinkable for Procne as well as her women. Indeed, the first truth the women try to tell Procne, that they worry Tereus might take advantage of Philomele, is met with her command of silence, since she herself refuses to disobey her absent husband's command to "look after his country" (33). Until confronted with the evidence of Tereus's betrayal, Procne becomes absorbed in supporting her husband's rule and proving her devotion, deviating from the behavior which first awakened longings for independence in her women. By showing them as gradually realizing their own social helplessness, Wertenbaker seemingly sets the stage for a radical reinvention of the female chorus within her play, which necessitates deviating from *Hippolytus's* choral structure.

The Choral Response to Female Violence

Whereas the female chorus in Lochhead's *Medea* utterly abhors her infanticide, Wertenbaker's chorus progresses from being utterly alienated from Procne to silently conniving in her child's murder while temporarily freed from their domestic and social constraints by the Bacchanalian rites of the god Dionysus. When Lochhead's Medea leaves to kill her children, the chorus cries,

> Gods stop her if Gods you are!
> Mother Earth open up and swallow her now
> before she forever defiles you
> with the spilt blood of her own children
> [...] but stop her
> pointless the pain of giving birth to them? [43].

Their common understanding of woman as the "circle" between "birth" and "death," a fruitful maternal cycle that redeems female suffering and perpetuates humanity, has been utterly shattered (44). Her act negates their own suffering and sense of self-worth as mothers. Procne's chorus, on the other hand, has a markedly different response to her son's murder because of their newly awakened sense of their own gender's oppression. While they do not advocate the deed, the chorus does not act to prevent it. Since liberation is difficult for Procne's chorus within the set spatial boundaries of *Hippolytus*'s choral structure, Wertenbaker takes inspiration from another of Euripides' famous plays, *The Bacchae,* converting the women into a group of rebels taking advantage of the festival's suspension of social order. In *The Bacchae,* the god Dionysus tricks misogynist, order-obsessed ruler Pentheus into spying on the Bacchae gathered for frenzied worship. Pentheus denounces the women who have left their homes and "looms" (*Bacchae* 597) as lascivious propagators of what he terms "obscene disorder" (232). Preoccupied with hunting the women "out of the mountains like the animals they are" (229), Pentheus ignores divine custom, and pays the ultimate price. The Bacchae, which includes his mother Agave, tear Pentheus into shreds and bear his head proudly back to the city, unaware of the atrocity they have committed.[4] Originally Procne's participation in the Dionysian ritual demonstrates the degree to which she has obediently acclimated to her husband's culture: "I will go out with the women of this country. You see how I become Thracian" (Wertenbaker 54).[5] Failing to recall the childhood justice she once believed in, Procne's response to her sister's plight is to drink and pray for aid to Dionysus, a god whose influence "covers the whole of the female experience, but turns on two opposing concepts—that of temperance, wisdom, and that of frenzy, unreason" (Calame

135). Since one "feminine" behavior, silence, has failed to protect Procne and her chorus from male violence, they now rebelliously indulge in chaotic "madness."

Reeling like their mistress from the horror of the truth about Philomele, Procne's chorus look at the experience of women and other marginalized groups throughout time to find an answer for why needless violence occurs, another example of diegetical transposition. Philomele's tongueless plight in Wertenbaker's violent portrayal "brings the whole issue of the silencing of women literally to the forefront of the action [...] its political significance is stressed by the words of the Female Chorus which overtly link the silencing of Philomele with the silencing of oppressed people both today and throughout history" (Winston 515).

> IRIS. We can ask: why did Medea kill her children?
> JUNE. Why do countries make war?
> HELEN. Why are races exterminated?
> HERO. Why do white people cut off the words of blacks? [...]
> HELEN. Why are little girls raped and murdered in the car parks of dark cities? [Wertenbaker 62].

Wertenbaker's chorus has come to believe that female silence and physical and sexual cooperation guarantee the system will continue unchecked. In their minds and Philomele's, motherhood perpetuates the cycle of violence against women by maintaining the dynastic link between father and son. Excluded from the male political and legal spheres, women strike out at what they can reach—their physical offspring. In echoes of *The Bacchae*, Itys falls a victim to Philomele after spying with some soldiers on her revels with the chorus-turned-Bacchae, and entering to rescue his sword from her hold. He shares Pentheus's fate after trespassing as a male and representative of patriarchal lineage into the female realm. Because the soldiers are unaware of what children now represent to these women, they unwisely let Itys trespass on a sacred rite. Hero observes, "A child is the future," to which Hero replies, "This is what the soldiers did not see" (62). By threatening to "Cut off your heads. Pick out your eyes" (63), Itys uses the same verbal threats of physical violence that Tereus has actually perpetrated against a noncompliant woman, causing Philomele to strike out against the representative of her rapist and future male oppressors. In a significant departure from Ovid's narrative (in which both sisters kill and serve Itys to his father as a gruesome meal), Philomele, not her sister, murders Itys, while the chorus and Procne watch in apparent collusion.

Like Philomele and Medea, the female chorus in *The Love of the Nightingale* find recognition and a voice through the enactment of violence, which they first experience prior to Itys's murder by witnessing Philomele's puppets simulating her rape. Unable to tell, she shows, "in a gross and comic way" (56). Similarly, Lochhead's Medea lets the bodies of her children do the talking for her, refusing Jason's request to bury the children with the significant statement "they are not dead to me" (Lochhead 45). This horrendous act and visual image ensures that Medea, the wronged woman and vicious mother, will be remembered eternally. Significantly, though Jason and Tereus remain deaf to the female voice, the perpetration and image of mute violence against their children commands male notice by decisively obliterating the patriarchy's social and lineal future. Both Lochhead and Wertenbaker depict them reacting to female violence and truth with silence and difficulty articulating, reversing the usual gender positions. Instead of seeing and hearing Jason discover the bodies, "JASON enters the house. *A silence*" (44). Choreographing and controlling Tereus's responses, the female chorus parts once to reveal "PHILOMELE [...] Hands bloodied. There is a silence" (Wertenbaker 63); and again to reveal the body of Itys, at the sight of which Tereus can only stutter in horrified comprehension: "Itys. You." Procne responds, "I did nothing. As usual. Let the violence sweep around me" (64). The voiceless female chorus cannot be punished for their non-action during Itys's murder, mocking their own gender's ineffectiveness under regular social conditions. By closing in front of the decapitated corpse, and remaining silent in a parody of patriarchal compliance, the female chorus joins in Philomele and Procne's resistance without verbally expressing their outrage.

In Lochhead's *Medea* and Wertenbaker's *The Love of the Nightingale* a violent female act committed against maternal nature establishes how deeply the patriarchal system has mistreated Medea and the sisters Procne and Philomele. Neither playwright excuses the heroine's murderous act, but rather seeks to explore the history of abuse and physical exploitation leading to such obvious desperation. Lochhead and Wertenbaker's foreign heroines, (an unnatural mother, and a woman freed by Dionysus only to be transfigured into an animal), remain exceptions to the female norm. Meanwhile, their choruses escape social censure through passivity and self-suppression despite acknowledging their common experience of female suffering. Though they occasionally are carried away by empathy, or take advantage of temporary social chaos, the chorus primarily exists in these adaptations to demonstrate what gender roles are permissible in the foreign society that Medea and Procne inhabit, and how similar these concepts are to those of the present day. While infanticide still shocks and appalls the audience, the chorus in each case has shown what difficulty and pain even apparently compliant women endure without hope of redress or justice. By reinventing the female chorus in their adaptations to portray feminine helplessness, Lochhead and Wertenbaker highlight the violent results of defining and suppressing an entire gender's nature based on their sexual and biological use, while endeavoring to reclaim a female voice for both their defiant heroines and their constricted choruses.

LOYOLA UNIVERSITY CHICAGO

NOTES

1. For Wertenbaker's full discussion on translation and adaptation, see "First Thoughts on Transforming a Text."

2. In her adaptation Wertenbaker uses the variant "Philomele" instead of Ovid's "Philomela."

3. On omitting Medea's missing divinity from her play, Lochhead comments "My Medea is not supernatural, not an immortal, but is all too human. [...] The mixed marriage between Jason and Medea isn't between a man and a demi-goddess, but between a man and a woman" (Lochhead vi).

4. Roger Travis sees Pentheus as misunderstanding Dionysiac religion as "the undoing of the distinctions between male and female, public and private, *polis* and *oikos*—those distinctions that create the order of the city at the head of which he stands" (163). Xavier Riu also disagrees with the "tendency to speak of Dionysus's 'danger,'" seeing the god as a proponent of organized chaos that ultimately reinforces the social hierarchy (83–84). In the absence of male interference, the Bacchae would simply perform a civic ritual and return to their duties as wives and mothers.

5. Until hearing Philomele's story, Procne seems to be conforming to Tereus's patriarchal notions while she safeguards his country as temporary ruler, ordering her chorus to remain silent when they suggest Philomele's long journey is suspect (Wertenbaker 33).

WORKS CITED

Calame, Claude. *Choruses of Young Women in Ancient Greece: Their Morphology, Religious Role, and Social Function*. Trans. Derek Collins and Janice Orion. New York: Rowman & Littlefield, 1997.

Chirico, Miriam. "Hellenic Women Revisited." *Dramatic Revisions of Myths, Fairy Tales, and Legends: Essays on Recent Plays*. Ed. Verna A. Foster. Jefferson, NC: McFarland, 2012. 15–33.

Euripides. *The Bacchae. The Complete Greek Tragedies*. Vol IV. Trans. William Arrowsmith. Eds. David Grene and Richard Lattimore. Chicago: University of Chicago Press, 1992.

_____. *Hippolytus. The Complete Greek Tragedies*. Vol III. Trans. David Grene. Eds. David Grene and Richard Lattimore. Chicago: University of Chicago Press, 1992.

_____. *Medea*. Trans. Diane Arnson Svarlien. Indianapolis, IN: Hackett, 2008.

Gardiner, Cynthia P. *The Sophoclean Chorus: A Study of Character and Function*. Iowa City: University of Iowa Press, 1987.

Hutcheon, Linda. *A Theory of Adaptation*. New York: Routledge, 2006.

Lochhead, Liz. *Medea*. London: Nick Hearn Books, 2000.

Ovid. *Metamorphoses*. Trans. Stanley Lombardo. Indianapolis, IN: Hackett, 2010.

Riu, Xavier. *Dionysism and Comedy*. New York: Rowman & Littlefield, 1999.

Segal, Charles. *Euripides and the Poetics of Sorrow*. London: Duke University Press, 1993.

Travis, Roger. *Allegory and the Tragic Chorus in Sophocles'* Oedipus at Colonus. New York: Rowman & Littlefield, 1999.

Wertenbaker, Timberlake. "First Thoughts on Transforming a Text." *International Dramaturgy: Translation & Transformation in the Theatre of Timberlake Wertenbaker*. Maya E. Roth and Sara Freeman, eds. Brussels: Peter Lang, 2008.

_____. *The Love of the Nightingale*. Woodstock: Dramatic, 1990.

Winston, Joe. "Re-Casting the Phaedra Syndrome: Myth and Morality in Timberlake Wertenbaker's *The Love of the Nightingale*." *Modern Drama* 38.4 (1995): 510–19.

Gender, Democracy, and the Justice of Athena's Vote to Acquit Orestes

JACQUELINE LONG

Abstract

This essay examines closely how Athena by chartering the Areopagus court resolves the succession of violence on which Aeschylus centered his Oresteia. *Neither historical nor dramatic and poetic conventions determine whether Athena calls an odd or even number of human jurors, and does or does not vote with them to create their acquitting tie. The interaction of "Orestes', the Erinyes', and Apollo's arguments," together with Athena's reactions, demonstrates that an even-numbered human jury splits equally over whether a human child owes duty more to father or mother. Athena's birth bars her from testing this question on her own sensibility and her celibacy prevents her from testing Clytaemnestra's guilt. Instead she turns to social values. Since judgment of individuals levels out inconclusively, the democratic jury Athena institutes deflects outrage at its verdicts. Similarly, Athena's rule tied jury-votes acquit maximizes satisfaction for the human community within which a case is judged.*

Violence and justice braid together Aeschylus's *Oresteia*. The first two plays of the trilogy unfold its traditional story[1] in terms of retribution and familial obligation: Clytaemnestra says she killed Agamemnon in reprisal for her child (*Ag.* 1413–25), Aegisthus for his father (*Ag.* 1579–611), and Orestes avenges his father on them in turn (*Cho.* 269–305, 925; *Eum.* 455–67). Each claim links its revenge to prerogative to dwell in a homeland (*Ag.* 1419–20, 1583–90, 1605–9, *Cho.* 286–90, 299–305, *Eum.* 462–64), extending familial connotations to country, yet in mid-action the third play, *Eumenides*, transfers the problem of redressing wrongs from the Atreides' native Argos to Athens. Aeschylus's geographical shift thus rooted a political charter in his own and his audience's city-state.[2] The *Eumenides* opens at Apollo's shrine at Delphi. As the oracle bade Orestes kill, his journey back to it closes a loop in time: Delphi will now see his blood-shedding purified. Yet the ritual does not free Orestes to take possession of his ancestral realm and his own future, despite the Chorus's assurance at the end of the *Choephoroe* (*Cho.* 1059–60). Primordial embodiments of retribution, Erinyes, still pursue him. Apollo is obliged to refer Orestes to Athena (*Eum.* 79–84, 224). When the action moves to Athens, Athena moves to meet it. In coming from the act of possessing land assigned her by the Achaeans as a prize of their victory at Troy (*Eum.* 397–402), she closes a larger loop in time by recapitulating the journeys in *Agamemnon* of Clytaemnestra's beacons and of Agamemnon and his entourage. Athena however goes to Athens. As she dislocates Agamemnon's return from Troy, she makes space to correct Agamemnon's disastrous homecoming: when the Athenian jury resolves Orestes' succession to Agamemnon Athena reintegrates the Greek victors' legacy at home. Athens becomes the place where conquest and retribution find stable resolution. And at Athens the decision that restores Orestes to his father's kingdom inaugurates a novel process of justice.[3]

Justice is reconfigured in stages across the *Oresteia*. Reactive, punitive forces drive action from long before Agamemnon's death; the Chorus characterizes the Trojan War itself as punitive (e.g., *Ag.* 40–62). Only Cassandra's prophetic image of a coping-stone makes any suggestion retribution could ever find an end (*Ag.* 1280–85). The vengeance Cassandra foretells is realized in the *Choephoroe*, then spirits of retribution swiftly beset that avenger (*Cho.* 1048–62). Yet whereas the first conspirators Clytaemnestra and Aegisthus both focus so much on their individual grievances they occlude one another as they each assert a virtually solitary revenge,[4] in the Great Kommos Electra and Orestes cooperate to invoke Agamemnon's spirit. They begin to repair the family Clytaemnestra and Aegisthus sundered[5]: more than punishment is at stake. Renewal is moved to Athens in the *Eumenides* and enlarged when Athena, reconciling the Erinyes to Orestes' acquittal, converts them to nurturers. The procession that installs them near the Areopagus and inaugurates their worship as the Semnai Theai[6] swells the denouement to celebration.

The pivotal action of Orestes' trial, however, is harder to trace in Aeschylus's script than the trajectory of his large themes. The jurors' vote is tied. The fact puts into action Athena's declaration that Orestes wins his case even if the votes split equally: it makes the trial a charter-myth for this judicial rule.[7] Within the play the tie vote is part of the truth to which the Erinyes must be reconciled. They rail that acquitting Orestes dishonors them.[8] Athena's first answer is that they were not defeated, but a tie vote yielded a true verdict and did them no dishonor (*Eum.* 795–96). The nature of the tie colors Athena's assertion and the trilogy's ultimate resolution. Modern scholars disagree whether Athena's declaration of approval for Orestes' case, which she describes as "adding a vote to" him (ψῆφον δ' Ὀρέστηι τήνδ' ἐγὼ προσθήσομαι, *Eum.* 735), means that she is voting as a member of the jury or, as presiding goddess, describing her provision for an evenly divided jury-vote.[9] Obviously the presence in the performance of ten or eleven or twelve or fifteen or some other number of human jurors would show viewers whether Athena's vote was or was not part of the equal tally.[10] But the text does not say. The jurors are silent characters. No other character counts them. Axiomatically, ancient scripts deliver information that their playwrights considered important to interpretation, or else rely on audiences' contextual knowledge. The number of jurors and Athena's role in relationship to them should have been obvious.

Whereas other juries of Classical Athens were constituted with odd numbers of jurors, the Areopagus council that in Aeschylus's day judged cases of homicide *ek pronoias* had membership variably odd or even.[11] At least since Solon's reforms in 594 B.C., the men who held the office of *archon* joined the council after their year in office and served on it for life.[12] Demographic estimates put the Areopagites' total perhaps over two hundred in the fifth century.[13] Practical necessity must have made the jury within *Eumenides* a token number, signifying rather than reproducing such a sum. History does not limit the choice of staging for Athena's jury.[14]

Attested conditions of staging also fail to guarantee a specific number for the jury in *Eumenides*. There is no necessity the jury equaled the number of the chorus, for example.[15] Nor is it assured that the ten couplets exchanged by the Chorus and Apollo plus a final three lines by the Chorus (*Eum.* 711–33), after Athena charges the jurors and before she states her own view, correspond to the number of jurors.[16] The passage must be when the jurors vote. Having assembled "the best of [her] townsmen" in order herself to decide Orestes' and the Erinyes' case, Athena now identifies them as judges when she formally ordains the eternal format of trials for murder. Postponing her ordinance to the point the jurors vote marks their act as the crux of the new institution: Athena transfers authority to the court.[17] By holding back her own judgment while her people vote, whether she votes as the last juror or comments outside the voting, Athena keeps her preeminence as patron goddess from any risk of swaying them. The exemplary citizens' collective judgment determines the verdict. But only arbitrary assumption, not evidence, determines the ratio of jurors to lines. The final triplet changes the pace of any assumption built on couplets, but does not guarantee any more human jurors vote or only Athena: possible stagings can be envisaged for different numbers of jurors, without proving anything. Moreover the demonstrative "this" of

Athena's "add[ed] vote" in Orestes' favor (*Eum.* 735) could as easily refer to her next utterance, the rule for tie votes,[18] as to a voting-pebble she casts, if her "vote" is metaphorical rather than a physical prop. No mechanical formula of the text fixes the number of jurors or Athena's role.

Instead, the process Aeschylus's text leaves open for Athena's jurymen to come to their collectivized decision forms the soundest basis for understanding the number of the jury, the nature of Athena's "vote," and the principles of justice on which Aeschylus turned the *Oresteia*. The trial develops a dispute about kinship and culpability. It elucidates the Erinyes' fixed position, their steady imperative to punish Orestes, as Orestes and Apollo propose and explore bases on which to justify Orestes' action. Orestes never denies he killed Clytaemnestra. His violence, like her own and that of Aegisthus, repays a debt of violence each perpetrator feels to be a familial legacy. Against the Erinyes' prosecution Orestes defends himself by the authority of Apollo's oracle and by Agamemnon (*Eum.* 587–88, 593–94, 609–13). The Erinyes do not regard this oracular authority. They mock Orestes for calling on a corpse (*Eum.* 599), but he means his duty to avenge his father's death was greater than his duty not to cause his mother's. He avoids comparing his filial choices directly in terms of gender.[19] Instead he relies on addition: he contends Clytaemnestra "had the trace of two pollutions" because by killing Agamemnon she violated two relationships, hers with her husband and Orestes' with his father (δυοῖν γὰρ εἶχε προσβολὰς μιασμάτοιν, *Eum.* 600; 602). Only the second aspect of the crime makes it Orestes' business, but the Erinyes understand he is measuring Clytaemnestra's guilt against his own, for they object that he is alive whereas "by murder she is free" (ἡ δ᾿ ἐλευθέρα φόνωι, *Eum.* 603). Implicitly they concede Clytaemnestra was accountable, although not for murder aggravated in the way with which they are concerned. They do not, however, go along with Orestes so far as to do sums. Their answer indicates they care only that a crime remains unanswered. Unlike Orestes or the human community at Athens Athena implicates in her decision, the Erinyes are not upset by a succession of vengeance: when one perpetrator suffers, they move on to the next violator of their rules.

Orestes invokes an abstract concept of fairness when he complains the Erinyes did not pursue Clytaemnestra for killing Agamemnon. They reply Clytaemnestra did not share blood-kinship with her victim (*Eum.* 605). Here the argument enters grounds of parentage where gender operates, although the parties recognize its operation differently. Blood ties define Erinyes' interests throughout the *Oresteia*. Clytaemnestra refers to an Erinys for Iphigeneia (*Ag.* 1432–33). In *Choephoroe* Orestes states that Apollo's oracle threatened him with paternal Erinyes if he failed to pay back Agamemnon's murder (*Cho.* 269–84). This connection guarantees that his decision in that play is a true dilemma: he faces the identical retribution for not vindicating his father's death as he does for punishing his mother. The chorus of Erinyes in *Eumenides* does not deny it. They declare to Apollo they "drive mother-strikers from their homes" and to Athena they "drive killers of mortals from their homes,"[20] the notion of eviction again referring to the perpetrators' violations of family. And the closest bond of blood the Erinyes identify is the embodied relationship of gestation and childbirth (*Eum.* 607–8).[21] Kinship is their ideology, gender concomitant. It is Apollo who cherishes patriarchal values and downgrades the female. Having protested ineffectually that the Erinyes ought to punish crimes against marriage, he rails that death at home, in the bath, at a woman's hands dishonored Agamemnon as a ruler and a warrior (*Eum.* 625–39, cf. 213–23). Since the Erinyes yield nothing Apollo finally is pushed to claim they misunderstand parentage entirely: he affirms the father is the only begetter and the mother is not kindred but container to the child, a stranger (τίκτει δ' ὁ θρῴσκων, ἡ δ' ἅπερ ξένωι ξένη / ἔσωσεν ἔρνος, οἷσι μὴ βλάψηι θεός, *Eum.* 658–66). He adduces Athena as proof. The fact Anaxagoras theorized generation this way proves the idea could be taken seriously outside of myth,[22] but the fact the jury splits over it, even with Athena before them, means that Aeschylus was using the theory rather than advocating for it.

For purposes of understanding the jury, the count is crucial. Either Aeschylus grafted the Athenian judicial rule about equal votes onto Orestes' trial with patent arbitrariness or the tie should result from the circumstances and arguments. Apollo clearly expects that by adducing Athena he would carry his point with an Athenian jury voting in her presence. If her citizens were to vote against Orestes in fear of the Erinyes, they would be revealing a lack of confidence in her. Yet if the jury is odd in number and only Athena's own vote creates the tie, a one-vote majority of the human jurors do vote against their city's patron. And a one-vote margin, one-half juror more than one half of an odd number of jurors on the one side and one-half juror fewer on the other, is a precariously arbitrary result. It makes far better sense to understand that the jurors split in reaction to the arguments they have heard than to the confrontation of power Apollo sets up. The Erinyes reject Orestes' arithmetical contention Clytaemnestra's guilt was greater than his. Apollo's image of parentage counters the Erinyes' assignment of primacy to the mother. He and they together restate the dilemma Orestes experiences in *Choephoroe*: to which parent of two does a human child owe duty? If the human jury is even in number, each member the son of one mother and one father, they arrive at a tie perfectly naturally by choosing between two contrary theories about the parentage they experience themselves and dividing in their sympathies. It is the dispute with which the trial presents them. They have only the arguments they have heard, their own reasoning, and their own sentiments to weigh their decisions against. The matter is obscure: human childbirth lacks the clarity of gods with axes to assist maiden gods to spring motherless from their fathers' brows.[23] The tie vote accurately measures human ambivalence before an impossible binary. It doubts without disrespect that Athena's unique parentage is a paradigm for Orestes.

Inevitable as the tie vote is from an even-numbered jury, it does not solve Orestes' quandary. Erinyes following their original nature will punish whatever violator of kinship remains hindermost. But although the Erinyes insist that failing to punish criminal actions will license every crime (*Eum.* 490–565), Orestes' family illustrates that retribution replicates, not ends: it is poignantly futile to wish otherwise.[24] Athens and Athena, however, have an interest in stable resolution of disputes. This case starts with Orestes, but it reverberates into the Athenian future. Orestes' coming as a suppliant to Athena at Athens connects her and her city to himself.[25] Athena recognizes the Erinyes will blight Athens if they feel their prerogative over Orestes is slighted. Therefore she institutes the jury: "the problem is too great for mortal judgment and too inflammatory to be right" to judge herself (τὸ πρᾶγμα μεῖζον, εἴ τις οἴεται τόδε / βροτὸς δικάζειν· οὐδὲ μὴν ἐμοὶ θέμις / φόνου διαιρεῖν ὀξυμηνίτου δίκας, *Eum.* 470–484). A one-vote human majority against Athena's birth and Orestes' choice between filial ties would strain probability in the reasons an odd number of human jurors might vote to that total. By both voting with the jury and declaring a tie vote acquits, Athena would intervene doubly in the jury's result: she would usurp the authority she delegated to her body of respected citizens. By thus hijacking the jury, Athena would break the basis of trust on which the Erinyes accept her as arbitrator, defy them, and bring down on her city the outraged wrath she creates the jury in order to avoid.[26]

It is important to recognize that a jury of humans does not simply exercise individual mortal judgment, the kind Athena remarks is insufficient to the magnitude of Orestes' dilemma. By collectivizing judgment, a jury democratizes. It also very significantly changes the question being decided. As Orestes' trial illustrates, mortals cannot know absolutely the truth of parentage and familial duty, or the facts of many other murders a court could be asked to judge. Yet they can say whether they prefer to live with the prosecution's or the defense's answer, which harmonizes better with their experience, values, and reasoning. The side that gets more votes corresponds to the greater portion of the community that will be more satisfied with the collective result. The same logic of dispute-resolution also explains a rule privileging the defendant in the case of a tie vote. No one in the *Oresteia* speaks of mercy or a presumption of innocence.[27] It is much simpler. If a tie vote were to result in punishment, the defendant's unhappiness in being punished would be added to the sum of jury members who prefer acquittal, making a majority of the community dissatisfied. Privileging the defendant in the event of a tie ensures that the party of the satisfied will always be greater. Athena's mechanism, the jury, is no abler at judging rightfulness than the individual jurors who man it. But by collectivizing their opinions democratically, they serve the community better.

It is wrong to associate Athena's explanation of her vote solely with Apollo's claim about parentage: it would reduce her vote to idiosyncrasy.[28] It also subtracts meaning from the reservation Athena adds to her declaration of support for the male:

> ἐμὸν τὸν ἔργον, λοισθίαν κρῖναι δίκην.
> ψῆφον δ' Ὀρέστηι τήνδ' ἐγὼ προσθήσομαι·
> μήτηρ γὰρ οὔτις ἐστὶν ἥ μ' ἐγείνατο,
> τὸ δ' ἄρσεν αἰνῶ πάντα, πλὴν γάμου τυχεῖν,
> ἅπαντι θυμῶι, κάρτα δ' εἰμὶ τοῦ πατρός.
> οὕτω γυναικὸς οὐ προτιμήσω μόρον
> ἄνδρα κτανούσης δωμάτων ἐπίσκοπον.
> νικᾶι δ' Ὀρέστης κἂν ἰσόψηφος κριθῆι.

> It is my job to render the last judgment.
> I shall add this vote to Orestes.
> No mother exists who gave me birth.
> I approve the male in all things, except for getting married,
> with all my heart: I am very much the father's.
> Thus I shall not give priority to a woman's death
> when she has killed her husband, the head of the household.
> Orestes prevails, even if the judging yields equal votes [*Eum.* 734–41].

If Athena favors the male and rejects marriage both simply as consequences of her motherless birth, her "except" suggests the rejection has an opposite tendency from the partisanship: it reduces her birth's explanatory force for her verdict. Her choice of celibacy is not at issue in *Eumenides* except for this remark. It yokes with Athena's birth as two facts pertinent to her opinion about Orestes' act, however, as it marks her testing for herself, against her own experience, the two perspectives Orestes puts in contention at the trial and the Erinyes accept for debate: was his culpability greater, or Clytaemnesta's? The pair of observations shows Athena following the same evaluative practice as the human jurors. Although the fact she lacks a mother fits with Apollo's claims about parentage, that lack more importantly means she can find no traction when she tries to think through for herself Orestes' decision to kill. Without a mother, she cannot know what it means to respect connection to a mother or to decide to repudiate a mother as Orestes did. Her celibacy similarly blocks her from entering imaginatively into Clytaemnestra's decision and guilt in order to assess their weightiness. Without taking a husband, Athena cannot know what it means to respect a husband or repudiate him, as Clytaemnestra did. Accordingly she turns to social organization as she knows it in Athens. (That is to say, as Aeschylus and his audience knew Athens, to create and to interpret this enacted drama.) The man's responsibility for the household, as Athena sees it, means other lives hang on his. She calculates a different factor than Orestes does, but her arithmetical principle operates similarly. Where an individual choice cannot be assessed conclusively, Athena favors the greater good of the household and the community. The orphaned isolation in which Orestes and Electra each begin the *Choephoroe* confirms Athena's expectation matches the trilogy's events: Clytaemnestra killed in vengeance for a child, yet with the killing she cast off relationship with her other children (e.g., *Cho.* 132–41). Nonetheless, Athena minimizes her intervention. Her approval of the male in this matter goes only so far as refusing to privilege the death of a husband-killer: although Athena's "last judgment" sets a coping stone on the trial, it does so negatively, by halting further action in consequence of the jury's equal vote.

The climax Athena pursues in *Eumenides* ascends from Orestes' trial to her own contest with the Erinyes. She denies they lost the verdict, which she could not do if her own vote in the jury lost it for them. Her "last judgment" in the case and "vote" for Orestes are not part of the jury's activity: if they were inserted into the jury's voting they would preempt the very purpose with which Athena creates a jury to hear murder trials, collectivizing for the community decisions in such serious matters of life and death. Her own unique birth puts her outside the relationships whose violations generate the crisis. Yet the process of decision-making Aeschylus depicts Athena taking matches the ideal process Aeschylus's Athenian audience could have recognized for their own experience of jury trials: she tests the case she has heard against her own knowledge and experience, and she finds the best solution for the community as a whole. Both her system of jury decision and her rule resolving split verdicts in the defendant's favor rest decisions democratically on the collective sensitivity of the community and majority rule. They form a charter for the justice of the Athenian state. Athena's culminating achievement is to win the Erinyes' good will to Athens, by giving their concern for justice positive as well as punitive functions for the community.[29] In contrast to the destructive effectiveness of Clytaemnestra in *Agamemnon* and the abortive restoration Orestes achieves momentarily in *Choephoroe*, motherless, male-favoring but female, democratically minded Athena in *Eumenides* secures a living future.

LOYOLA UNIVERSITY CHICAGO

NOTES

1. See generally Timothy Gantz, *Early Greek Myth: a Guide to Literary and Artistic Sources* (Baltimore and London: Johns Hopkins University Press, 1993): 664–86. I thank several friends for feedback that has improved this paper: Greg Dobrov, Joe Janangelo,

Brian Lavelle, David Posner, Ann Shanahan; also *Text & Presentation*'s editor and anonymous readers, the Comparative Drama Conference's Program Committee and the audience they led to valuable discussion, and my fellow speaker Thomas Faulkner for his excellent paper.

2. Alan H. Sommerstein, *Aeschylus: Eumenides* (Cambridge University Press, 1989): 1–6 concluded Athenian tradition before Aeschylus placed Orestes' trial at the Areopagus, and Aeschylus innovated by making a human jury rather than gods serve as judges; cf. Felix Jacoby, *Die Fragmente der Griechichischen Historiker* III.b Suppl. I.22–25 and notes II.19–29 (Leiden: Brill 1954). Oliver Taplin, *The Stagecraft of Aeschylus: the Dramatic Use of Exits and Entrances in Greek Tragedy* (Oxford: Clarendon Press 1977, corr. 1989): 103–7 discussed Aeschylus's breaks from "unity of place" generally.

3. J. Peter Euben, *The Tragedy of Political Theory: the Road not Taken* (Princeton University Press, 1990): 67–95 insightfully connected Aeschylus's handling of gender and justice by democratic myth in the *Oresteia*, but he avoided the question of Athena's vote (80); cf. R. P. Winnington-Ingram, "Clytemnestra and the Vote of Athena," *The Journal of Hellenic Studies* 68 (1948) 130–47, reprised and extended in Winnington-Ingram, *Studies in Aeschylus* (Cambridge University Press, 1983): 73–174; Sommerstein, *Aeschylean Tragedy*, 2d ed. (London: Duckworth, 2010). Sommerstein and Delfim F. Leão each mapped Orestes' trial onto historical Athenian court-systems, respectively "Orestes' Trial and Athenian Homicide Procedure," 25–38, and "The Legal Horizon of the *Oresteia*: the Crime of Homicide and the Founding of the Areopagus," 39–60, in Edward M. Harris, Leão, and P. J. Rhodes, eds., *Law and Drama in Ancient Greece* (London: Duckworth, 2010). Historical readings of the *Oresteia* include Anthony J. Podlecki, *The Political Background of Aeschylean Tragedy* (Ann Arbor: University of Michigan Press, 1966); David Rosenbloom, "Myth, History, and Hegemony in Aeschylus," in Barbara Goff, ed., *History, Tragedy, Theory: Dialogues on Athenian Drama*, 91–130 (Austin: University of Texas Press, 1995). Martin Revermann, "Aeschylus' *Eumenides*, Chronotopes, and the 'Aetiological Mode,'" in Revermann and Peter Wilson, eds., *Performance, Iconography, Reception: Studies in Honour of Oliver Taplin*, 237–61 (Oxford University Press, 2008), discussed other ways the *Eumenides* transcends time.

4. Clytaemnestra claims the act with aggressive first-person verbs, ἄπειρον ἀμφίβληστρον, ὥσπερ ἰχθύων, περιστιχίζω [...] παίω δέ νιν δὶς [...] καὶ πεπτωκότι τρίτην ἐνενδίδωμι, τοῦ κατὰ χθονὸς Διὸς νεκρῶν σωτῆρος εὐκταίαν χάριν, *Ag.* 1382–87; Aegisthus a distanced responsibility, κἀγὼ δίκαιος τοῦδε τοῦ φόνου ῥαφεύς [...] καὶ τοῦδε τἀνδρὸς ἡψάμην θυραῖος ὤν, πᾶσαν ξυνάψας μηχανὴν δυσβουλίας, *Ag.* 1604, 1608–9.

5. So too by emphases on their likeness Electra's and Orestes' recognition-scene restores brother and sister to themselves as well as to one another: *Cho.* 172–78, 205–10, 220–23, 229–32, 252–54.

6. Sommerstein 1989: 6–12 argued that Aeschylus innovated identifying the Semnai with the Erinyes who pursued Orestes; cf. Pat Easterling, "Theatrical Furies: Thoughts on *Eumenides*," in Revermann and Wilson 2008: 219–36; A. L. Brown, "Eumenides in Greek Tragedy," *Classical Quarterly* 34 (1984): 260–81.

7. See Antiph. 5.51 (*Her.*), Aeschin. 3.252 (*Ctes.*), Ar. *Ath.Pol.* 69.1; A. R. W. Harrison, *The Law of Athens: Procedure* (Oxford: Clarendon, 1971): 47 n. 3. Athena charters the Areopagus court at *Eum.* 681–710 and declares, νικᾷ δ' Ὀρέστης κἂν ἰσόψηφος κριθῇι, 741; Sommerstein 1989: 231–32 *ad* 741. Douglas M. MacDowell, *Athenian Homicide Law in the Age of the Orators* (Manchester University Press 1963): 110 cited only *Eum.* 741.

8. *Eum.* 778–79, 780, ἐγὼ δ' ἄτιμος = 808–9, 810: repetition marks their refusal to accept Athena's initial answer.

9. The two positions have been reviewed and restated by Michael Gagarin, "The Vote of Athena," *American Journal of Philology* 96 (1975) 121–27 for Athena's voting as a juror, and by D. A. Hester, "The Casting Vote," *American Journal of Philology* 102 (1981) 265–74 for Athena's adding her vote conditionally, if the human jury split. See too Richard Seaford, "Historicizing Tragic Ambivalence: the Vote of Athena," in Goff 1995: 202–21.

10. Gagarin 1975: 123 n.9 denied the audience could have been expected to count the jurors, but it would be far harder to be sure nobody counted.

11. Athenian courts: see MacDowell 1963: 39–89; Harrison 1971: 36–64; Alan L. Boeghold, *The Lawcourts at Athens: Sites, Buildings, Equipment, Procedure, and Testimonia*, The Athenian Agora XXVIII (Princeton: The American School of Classical Studies at Athens, 1995).

12. Robert W. Wallace, *The Areopagus Council, to 307 B.C.* (Baltimore and London: Johns Hopkins University Press 1985, 1989): 3–47 contended the pre-Solonian Areopagus was a homicide jury, not a council, and numbered 51, but his arguments cannot securely stretch across the intervening century and a half to control Aeschylus's staging; Mogens Herman Hansen, *The Athenian Democracy in the Age of Demosthenes: Structure, Principles, and Ideology*, trans. J. A. Crook (Oxford, UK, and Cambridge, MA: Blackwell, 1991): 28 cautioned the evidence suggests later Athenians did not know the Areopagus's earliest nature with certainty.

13. Wallace 1985, 1989: 96–97. Mogens Herman Hansen and Lars Pederson estimated roughly 150 for "The Size of the Council of the Areopagos and Its Social Composition in the Fourth Century BC," *Classica et Mediaevalia* 41 (1990) 73–77. Plut., *Sol.* 12.2 gives no warrant for supposing the Areopagus numbered 300. Brian Lavelle proposes in correspondence it may imply the Council was supplemented by non-member *aristoi*; I am grateful to him for discussing the passage with me.

14. Harrison 1971: 47 and Boeghold 1995: 39 n. 60 both observed that tie votes could result from odd-numbered juries if not all the jurors deposited ballots in the voting urn; but this eventuality would have been harder to stage effectively than the *Eumenides'* script supports.

15. So, rightly, Taplin 1977 corr. 1989: 392–93 *ad Eum.* 566; cf. 323 and n. 3 *ad Ag.* 1348–71 and 202–3 *ad Hik.* 234 concerning couplet-counting and the number of Aeschylean choruses, for which Taplin preferred fifteen to twelve.

16. Gagarin 1975: 122 called it the view of "most critics," without citation. He followed, although he noted for example a pair of jurors might have moved at each couplet.

17. First-person and feminine verb-forms bespeak Athena's own agency at *Eum.* 487–88, κρίνασα δ' ἀστῶν ἐμῶν τὰ βέλτατα ἥξω διαιρεῖν τοῦτο πρᾶγμ' ἐτητύμως; at *Eum.* 681–84 she says the Athenians are to "judge" and to serve as a "council of jurors" for all time, πρώτας δίκας κρίνοντες αἵματος χυτοῦ […] αἰεὶ δικαστῶν τοῦτο βουλευτήριον. I take this emphasis on Athena's transfer of authority to have been the point of Colin Macleod's gentle words to Taplin. Taplin himself admitted his arguments for massive displacement and corruption in the trial scene do not resolve neatly (Taplin 1977 corr. 1989: 395–401 *ad Eum.* 574, quoting Macleod at 399 n.1; expressing dubitation, 401; cf. Macleod, "Politics and the *Oresteia*," *The Journal of Hellenic Studies* 102 [1982] 124–44).

18. This common use of the demonstrative is exemplified in the play's first line, εὐχῆι τῆιδε, *Eum.* 1.

19. Froma I. Zeitlin, "The Dynamics of Misogyny: Myth and Mythmaking in the *Oresteia* of Aeschylus," *Arethusa* 11 (1978) 149–84; rpt. in Zeitlin, *Playing the Other: Gender and Society in Classical Greek Literature*, 87–119 (Chicago and London: University of Chicago Press, 1996) made an epochal analysis of deep structures of Athenian gendered thinking. Recent contributions include Emily Zakin, "Marrying the City: Intimate Strangers and the Fury of Democracy," in Denise Eileen McCoskey and Zakin, eds., *Bound by the City: Greek Tragedy, Sexual Difference, and the Formation of the* Polis, 177–96 (Albany: State University of New York Press, 2009).

20. τοὺς μητραλοίας ἐκ δόμων ἐλαύνομεν, *Eum.* 210; βροτοκτονοῦντας ἐκ δόμων ἐλαύνομεν, *Eum.* 421.

21. Clytaemnestra similarly calls Iphigeneia φιλτάτην ἐμοὶ ὠδῖν᾽, *Ag.* 1417–18, cf. 1388–92.

22. Arist. *Gen.An.* 763b31–764a2. See David D. Leitao, *The Pregnant Male as Myth and Metaphor in Classical Greek Literature* (Cambridge University Press, 2012: 18–57); Sommerstein 1989: 206–8 *ad loc.*

23. See Gantz 1993: 51–52, 83–84.

24. Clytaemnestra in *Agamemnon* (1567–76) and the Chorus in *Choephoroe* (1065–76) both express such vain wishes.

25. See John Gould, "*Hiketeia*," *The Journal of Hellenic Studies* 93 (1973) 74–103; F. S. Naiden, "Supplication and the Law," in Edward M. Harris and Lene Rubinstein, eds., *The Law and the Courts in Ancient Greece*, 71–91 (London: Duckworth, 2004), detailed how human laws of ancient Greek communities regulated supplication, with particular attention to Aeschylus's *Suppliants*.

26. Hester 1981: 270 and Seaford 1995: 211–12 indicated this connection briefly. Athena secures the Erinyes' agreement to have her settle the case, *Eum.* 434–35; at the trial Apollo and Athena use εἰσάγω of her role, in Athenian legal contexts the verb for the magistrate overseeing the case (or the prosecutor): *Eum.* 580, 582; LSJ *s.v.*

27. Gagarin 1975: 127 rightly disdained importation of modern sentiment into an argument about ancient literature and values. Ar. *Prob.* 29.13 says a false acquittal is a lesser evil than a false accusation; 13 and 15 say defendants are at a disadvantage.

28. Hester 1981: 271–72 explicitly valorized idiosyncrasy for Athena, as if it made prejudice less objectionable in her; less forthrightly Seaford 1995: 215.

29. On the resolution, see Helen Bacon, "The Furies' Homecoming," *Classical Philology* 96 (2001) 48–59.

WORKS CITED

Bacon, Helen. "The Furies' Homecoming." *Classical Philology* 96 (2001): 48–59.

Boeghold, Alan L. *The Lawcourts at Athens: Sites, Buildings, Equipment, Procedure, and Testimonia.* The Athenian Agora XXVIII. Princeton: The American School of Classical Studies at Athens, 1995.

Brown, A. L. "Eumenides in Greek Tragedy." *Classical Quarterly* 34 (1984): 260–81.

Easterling, Pat. "Theatrical Furies: Thoughts on *Eumenides*." *Performance, Iconography, Reception: Studies in Honour of Oliver Taplin.* Eds. Martin Revermann and Peter Wilson. Oxford: Oxford University Press, 2008. 219–36.

Euben, J. Peter. *The Tragedy of Political Theory: the Road not Taken*. Princeton: Princeton University Press, 1990.

Gagarin, Michael. "The Vote of Athena." *American Journal of Philology* 96 (1975): 121–27.

Gantz, Timothy. *Early Greek Myth: A Guide to Literary and Artistic Sources*. Baltimore and London: Johns Hopkins University Press, 1993.

Gould, John. "*Hiketeia*." *The Journal of Hellenic Studies* 93 (1973): 74–103.

Hansen, Mogens Herman. *The Athenian Democracy in the Age of Demosthenes: Structure, Principles, and Ideology*. Trans. J. A. Crook. Oxford, UK, and Cambridge, MA: Blackwell, 1991.

_____ and Lars Pederson. "The Size of the Council of the Areopagos and its Social Composition in the Fourth Century BC." *Classica et Mediaevalia* 41 (1990): 73–78.

Harrison, A. R. W. *The Law of Athens: Procedure*. Oxford: Clarendon, 1971.

Hester, D. A. "The Casting Vote." *American Journal of Philology* 102 (1981): 265–74.

Jacoby, Felix. *Die Fragmente der Griechichischen Historiker*, vol. III.b Suppl. Leiden: Brill, 1954.

Leão, Delfim F. "The Legal Horizon of the *Oresteia*: the Crime of Homicide and the Founding of the Areopagus." *Law and Drama in Ancient Greece*. Eds. Edward M. Harris, Delfim F. Leão, and P. J. Rhodes. London: Duckworth, 2010. 39–60.

Leitao, David D. *The Pregnant Male as Myth and Metaphor in Classical Greek Literature*. Cambridge: Cambridge University Press, 2012.

MacDowell, Douglas M. *Athenian Homicide Law in the Age of the Orators*. Manchester: Manchester University Press, 1963.

Macleod, Colin. "Politics and the *Oresteia*." *The Journal of Hellenic Studies* 102 (1982): 124–44.

Naiden, F. S. "Supplication and the Law." *The Law and the Courts in Ancient Greece*. Eds. Edward M. Harris and Lene Rubinstein. London: Duckworth, 2004. 71–91.

Podlecki, Anthony J. *The Political Background of Aeschylean Tragedy*. Ann Arbor: University of Michigan Press, 1966.

Revermann, Martin. "Aeschylus' *Eumenides*, Chronotopes, and the 'Aetiological Mode.'" *Performance, Iconography, Reception: Studies in Honour of Oliver Taplin*. Eds. Martin Revermann and Peter Wilson. Oxford: Oxford University Press, 2008. 237–61.

Rosenbloom, David. "Myth, History, and Hegemony in Aeschylus." *History, Tragedy, Theory: Dialogues on Athenian Drama*. Ed. Barbara Goff. Austin: University of Texas Press, 1995. 91–130.

Seaford, Richard. "Historicizing Tragic Ambivalence: the Vote of Athena." *History, Tragedy, Theory: Dialogues on Athenian Drama*. Ed. Barbara Goff. Austin: University of Texas Press, 1995. 202–21.

Sommerstein, Alan H. *Aeschylean Tragedy*. 2d ed. London: Duckworth, 2010.

_____. *Aeschylus: Eumenides*. Cambridge: Cambridge University Press, 1989.

_____. "Orestes' Trial and Athenian Homicide Procedure." *Law and Drama in Ancient Greece*. Eds. Edward M. Harris, Delfim F. Leão, and P. J. Rhodes. London: Duckworth 2010. 25–38.

Taplin, Oliver. *The Stagecraft of Aeschylus: the Dramatic Use of Exits and Entrances in Greek Tragedy*. Oxford: Clarendon Press, 1977, corrected 1989.

Wallace, Robert W. *The Areopagus Council, to 307 B.C.* Baltimore and London: Johns Hopkins University Press, 1985, 1989.

Winnington-Ingram, R. P. "Clytemnestra and the Vote of Athena." *The Journal of Hellenic Studies* 68 (1948): 130–47.

_____. *Studies in Aeschylus*. Cambridge: Cambridge University Press, 1983.

Zakin, Emily. "Marrying the City: Intimate Strangers and the Fury of Democracy." *Bound by the City: Greek Tragedy, Sexual Difference, and the Formation of the* Polis. Eds. Denise Eileen McCoskey and Emily Zakin. Albany: State University of New York Press, 2009. 177–96.

Zeitlin, Froma I. "The Dynamics of Misogyny: Myth and Mythmaking in the *Oresteia* of Aeschylus." *Arethusa* 11 (1978): 149–84. Rpt. Zeitlin, *Playing the Other: Gender and Society in Classical Greek Literature*. Chicago and London: University of Chicago Press, 1996. 87–119.

"Kill the Pity in Us": The Communal Crisis as Crisis of Individualism in David Greig's *Oedipus the Visionary*

PHILLIP ZAPKIN

Abstract

This essay argues that David Greig's Oedipus the Visionary *critiques the socially corrosive effects of neoliberal free market ideology and the society of enjoyment, which erode communal unities in South Africa by positioning every individual as a consumer. Individual isolation threatens traditions of collective action among South Africans which helped undermine and eventually destroy legal apartheid. Greig begins with but ultimately rejects the sacrificial crisis of the Oedipus plot in favor of collective action. This possible solution to contemporary South African problems strengthens communities as an alternative to neoliberalism. Unlike in the Sophokles hypotext, Greig's South African villagers renounce the enjoyment promised by sacrificial violence and Oedipus is brought back into the community, suggesting the possibility of undermining global exploitation under neoliberalism through a common. Form reinforces this thematic purpose as adaptation and theatre become communal methods of re-thinking shared cultural material, creating an intellectual and performative common.*

In the published introduction to his 2000 play *Oedipus the Visionary*, Scottish dramatist David Greig writes that he composed the adaptation as an exploration of power and economics (4). During a trip to the Republic of South Africa (RSA), Greig was affected by the ubiquitous presence of townships segregating the wealthy from the poor, and reflected that, "Perhaps, if our township existed as blatantly as it does in South Africa we would find it intolerable. But, like so much else in Scotland, the architecture of power is rather elegantly executed and so the ugly realities are kept out of sight" (5). One of his great talents as a playwright is utilizing location to explore the pervasive cultural impact of late capitalism across national boundaries. As Marilena Zaroulia writes, "by using these small, unknown locations as the stage of the characters' stories, he indicates how the flow of global capital and its consequences can penetrate people's everyday lives in locations across the world" (178). Pursuing this thematic concern, when Greig wrote *Oedipus the Visionary* he transculturally adapted Sophokles' *Oedipus the King* to a rural community in the mountains of South Africa.[1] Greig has a complicated subject position *vis-à-vis* African drama because he is Scottish but was raised in Nigeria and has spent an extensive amount of time in the RSA. While not an African dramatist per se, he can utilize a hybrid voice influenced heavily by both western and southern African traditions and Scottish/UK traditions.

This *Oedipus* adaptation reimagines the Theban plague as the AIDS crisis currently facing southern Africa, and it critiques global capitalism and continuing structures of economic apartheid for ignoring the plight of many poor Africans. For much of the adaptation, Greig remains quite true to the earlier Sophokles hypotext, despite the transhistorical shift from the Hellenic Heroic Age to the contemporary RSA. Greig's Oedipus is a landowner (possibly white, though Greig neither specifies nor precludes this possibility) who rules a small rural community—an analogue for Thebes—effectively maintaining apartheid-style economic relations without the legal apparatus of a racist state. As in Sophokles, Oedipus pursues the truth about his and the community's history in an attempt to lift the curse of a plague. However, Greig ends his play quite differently than Sophokles, with the community breaking out of the cycle of the sacrificial crisis rather than expelling Oedipus.

This paper focuses specifically on how Greig presents the socially corrosive effects of neoliberal free market ideology and the society of enjoyment, which erode communal unities by positioning every individual as a consumer in a competitive market place. This isolation of the individual threatens traditions of collective action among South Africans which helped undermine and eventually destroy legal apartheid. Following thinkers like Slavoj Žižek and Todd McGowan, I combine psychoanalytic discourses of desire, drive, and identity with Marxist inspired political economics to critique the cultural/ideological reshaping of the human subject under neoliberalism. Greig, I argue, uses the sacrificial crisis of the *Oedipus* plot to promote collective action as a possible solution to contemporary South African problems, thereby strengthening communities as an alternative to neoliberal atomization.

Greig's play, originally just titled *Oedipus*, debuted as part of the Glasgow-based Theatre Babel's Greeks trilogy, which included Liz Lochhead's *Medea* and Tom McGrath's *Electra*. The Greeks production was the brainchild of Graham McLaren, Theatre Babel's artistic director, who sought to bring the timeless Greek tragedies to a turn of the millennium Scottish audience. The project was conceived because McLaren believed "that the plays' sexual, familial and political cataclysms still speak very much to our times, and feels it is crucial that the language of new productions reflect their modern significance" (Brown). Both the playwriting and the performances sought to blend contemporary Scotland (and in Greig's case, contemporary South Africa) with classical Greece, straddling cultural and theatrical lines. This was a difficult performance balance. As one reviewer put it, "Greig has produced a strikingly clean, modern text; Babel's production succeeds in making it look old-fashioned" (McMillan). However much the production may have suffered in its attempts to update/represent Greek performance practices, Greig's play successfully blends the ancient with the modern in ways that shed new light on contemporary late capitalist globalization.

Late capitalist ideology intensifies the individualism already present in Sophokles' Oedipus, combining with the ethics of ownership to shape Greig's *Oedipus*. Benefiting from a racist legacy of land appropriation and economic inequality, Oedipus claims individual ownership of the land: "I came here, I live and farm this land. / *It's mine* as if it were the land that bore me" (28, my emphasis). Similarly, Jocasta tells him, "*This is your land* now. / Rule it. / Make it like it was before" (13, my emphasis). As in Sophokles, Greig's Oedipus is strongly individualistic and justifies his rule based on his own deeds—saving the people from tribulations in the past and his promise to do so again. He establishes his arke—his right to rule—by claiming,

> God didn't build the dam, or road or drive away your
> persecutors it was a man, men. A person. Me.
> If there's a reason for this plague.
> I will find and cure it [16].

In identifying his right to rule based on his deeds, Oedipus conveniently ignores the history of apartheid inequality which dispossessed the lands of indigenous Africans. He ignores as well the continuing economic inequalities that maintain a functional apartheid in neoliberal South Africa. As Geoffrey Schneider writes, "Although apartheid-era laws limiting black mobility and black voting rights have been removed, 'economic' apartheid is being perpetuated in part by neoliberal policies. The ideology of apartheid, which kept the races separate and unequal, is being replaced by the ideology of the market, which is helping to preserve that inequality" (24).

Neoliberalism fundamentally attempts to impose a free market ideology, in which all interaction comes to be viewed in economic terms by atomized consumers. David Harvey puts it clearly: neoliberalism "holds that the social good will be maximized by maximizing the reach and frequency of market transactions, and it seeks to bring all human action into the domain of the market" (3). Neo*liberals* are, in fact, liberal primarily in the sense that they believe in individual freedom as the prime goal of an ethical society (picking up from classical Liberal philosophers like John Locke). Milton Friedman, one of the founding fathers of neoliberal political economics, identified this heritage directly in *Capitalism and Freedom*: "the intellectual movement that went under the name of liberalism emphasized freedom as the ultimate goal and the individual as the ultimate entity in society" (5). Despite contested meanings of the term in the writings of classical Liberal philosophers, what Friedman means by "freedom" is the freedom from coercion by government or economic partners, and the freedom to dispose of one's goods, labor, etc., as one sees fit. He envisions a society with a minimal role for government, guided by the fair hand of a market system in which equally well informed and empowered rational individuals—"a collection of Robinson Crusoes" (13)—trade goods or services *"provided the transaction is bi-laterally voluntary and informed"* (13). In other words, Friedman's philosophical understanding of a free market system ignores the realities of coercion and exploitation that mark the actual functioning of economic systems, particularly for workers, ethnic minorities, and women.

Another practical limitation of neoliberal theory is that it begins from the supposition that all consumers have or can gain access to capital. In areas with histories of inequality, replacing legally enforced segregation with free markets often perpetuates the divisions and inequalities between those with access to capital and those without it. Hand in hand with this belief is the neoliberal assertion that a free market system will break down racism. Milton Friedman made this assertion about the United States (21,108–18), and according to Schneider, the English neoliberal economist and apartheid opponent William H. Hutt's "faith in the redistributive powers of the free market led him to conclude that no redistribution of any kind was necessary in South Africa: all that was necessary was the elimination of apartheid restrictions and the free market would tend to equalize incomes" (26). Friedman based his argument for a racially just capitalism on the premise that "the purchaser of bread does not know whether it was made from wheat grown by a white man or a Negro, by a Christian or a Jew" (109). The basis of the neoliberal argument that free markets create equality is the assumption that all economic players operate rationally and on entirely economic principles, but the theory fails to acknowledge the centrality of prejudice and the roles played by ideology and irrationality in decision making. Again, neoliberalism takes its principles from an ideal vision of the economy—in which rationally based economic decisions outweigh all other concerns—rather than dealing with the vicissitudes of the real world, in which factors such as racism, sexism, sectarian prejudice, homophobia, xenophobia, etc., play a very real role in economic decision making and shaping unequal access to power and capital. Because of the role of prejudice, the reality has been—both in the USA and RSA—that eliminating legal racism without economic redistribution preserves structures of economic, political, and cultural capital that favor white people. Rather than seeing free markets create social justice and economic opportunity, we have seen them maintain exploitation and inequality.

Markets have played a complex role in South African history and culture, a role that tends generally toward social instability rather than the equality and stability that neoliberals promise. My argument here relies on linking local African markets with "The Market" of global capitalism, though I recognize that these two types of markets are nowhere near the same economic entity, and I try to distinguish them as much as possible. However, I make this conflation because, as we shall see, Greig himself collapses the distinction and stages a local market to stand in for the infrastructure of global late capitalism.

Historically, precolonial southern Africa did not have any major markets like those found throughout West Africa. Instead markets were introduced by European colonialists. B. W. Hodder writes, "In many parts of Subsaharan Africa, then, markets post-date European control; are frequently strictly European-introduced phenomena; and in some cases are operated by largely non-indigenous peoples" (101). Working off the model of West African culture and faith in market economics, European colonialists created a network of local markets through southern Africa, thinking that they would fulfill the same social role the markets did in West Africa. Terrence Ranger identifies the imposition of "traditional" markets in southern Africa as part of colonial attempts to "preserve" indigenous cultures. Ranger claims markets are part of "the necessary and unplanned consequences of colonial economic and political change—of the breakup of internal patterns of trade and communication, the defining of territorial boundaries, the alienation of land, the establishment of Reserves" (455). The irony is that imposing a market "tradition" disrupted indigenous economies and power structures in southern Africa, thereby compromising local cultures rather than preserving them.

The contemporary dominance of a global capitalist free market has also had a detrimental effect on South Africa, eroding communal ties that might otherwise have helped create a more economically just Rainbow Nation. The problem is that neoliberal free market ideology—which the ANC made central to South African economics under pressure from the IMF and World Bank

(Narsiah 30)—atomizes individual consumers, focusing principally on individual rights and enjoyment rather than social justice or economic equality. Neoliberals like Milton Friedman identify individual freedom as the primary social good. Friedman writes, "As liberals, we take freedom of the individual, or perhaps the family, as our ultimate goal in judging social arrangements" (12). This focus on the individual as the most important socio-economic unit underpins neoliberalism's suspicion of any sort of collectivist culture. David Harvey notes that this *freedom* bore a paradox: "While individuals are supposedly free to choose, they are not supposed to choose to construct strong collective institutions (such as trade unions) [...]. They most certainly should not choose to associate to create political parties with the aim of forcing the state to intervene in or eliminate the free market" (69). This suspicion of collective culture has been extremely effective in eroding social links—especially in the Global North—leaving contemporary subjects increasingly isolated through lifestyles focused on consumption and the paranoid suspicion that everyone poses a threat to our property/enjoyment. This paranoia is Hobbes's little-acknowledged contribution to the neoliberal worldview. Robert Putnam, in his thoroughly researched book *Bowling Alone*, has traced the decline of social capital and civic engagement in the United States since the 1970s. He argues that Americans are now less engaged with our communities, friends, and governments than our predecessors of the Great Depression and World War II generation. And while Putnam attributes this decline in social capital to the rise of television as an isolating experience, Randy Martin suggests that the financialization of everyday life has created a culture of paranoid suspicion. Martin argues that daily life is increasingly conceptualized through the medium of finance—economic transactions based in assumptions of scarcity, which normalize competition and risk. Martin identifies something schizophrenic about this mode of late capitalist existence: "A hypercompetitive world such as this requires constant attention to opportunity and vigilance as to potential threats. There is nowhere to hide, and no moment of respite from the exertions of financial activity" (36). Martin argues that this unremitting activity has become the norm for subjects of late capitalism.

Of course, Putnam's book is focused on US culture and Martin's book implicitly explores Global North (especially US) cultural trends. While Greig is a Scottish dramatist writing for a Scottish audience, his play attempts to explore economic issues facing both the UK *and* South Africa. But how much do the changes Putnam and Martin identify hold true for the RSA? This is a challenging question, but I think the simple answer is that late capitalist cultural trends affecting the United States and the Global North are increasingly influencing African cultures. James Ferguson argues that theorists of neoliberal globalization—both proponents and opponents—rarely deal thoroughly with

Africa's role in a globalized economy, often preferring to discuss the continent minimally or not at all (25). However, as Ferguson's book *Global Shadows* makes evident, just because no one is talking about African neoliberalism doesn't mean that late capitalism is not reshaping national economies and the continent's position in a global economy. Under neoliberal policies imposed by the IMF and World Bank, there have been few African success stories to mirror the Asian Tigers or the Celtic Tiger, partly because capitalists generally avoid Africa fearing national instability, or because "When capital *has* come into Africa in recent years, it has been overwhelmingly in the area of mineral-resource extraction" (Ferguson 35). While much capital investment has been socially thin—isolated enclaves of Western technicians remaining in insular resource extraction facilities rather than engaging with and spending money in local economies—on the national level neoliberal policies guide much reformation in contemporary African countries. As David Harvey points out, "The IMF and the World Bank [...] became centres for the propagation and enforcement of 'free market fundamentalism' and neoliberal orthodoxy. In return for debt rescheduling, indebted countries were required to implement institutional reforms, such as cuts in welfare expenditures, more flexible labour market laws, and privatization" (29). According to Sagie Narsiah, pressure on South Africa and the ANC from the IMF and World Bank played a large role in shifting the ANC's policies from a socialist focus on economic justice to a neoliberal faith in free markets, particularly through the GEAR program. Responding to pressure from the IMF and World Bank, "South Africa was formally subsumed into a neoliberal, free-market paradigm in 1996—with the adoption of the Growth Employment and Redistribution (GEAR) program. Particular policy positions were adopted as a consequence, promoting fiscal austerity, export oriented development and privatisation" (Narsiah 31). The economic policies Narsiah identifies in South Africa since 1996 largely conform to neoliberal orthodoxy, using free markets and private property to preserve the social order.

In *Oedipus the Visionary* we see the individualizing psychological action of the market staged. Scene Five is set in the town market, where individual members of the chorus imagine what they'll do with the money if they can manage to sell their few personal possessions. Of course, in traditional Greek tragedy (as well as most of Greig's play) the chorus represents a communal voice, or a voice with which the audience is collectively supposed to identify. For Greig to split these chorus members up as individuals within this market sphere is significant. Greig himself points this out, writing in the "Note on the Chorus" that "At certain points they [the chorus] are individuated as 'Man 1' or 'Woman 1.' This individuation should be respected" (8). The market itself is a dismal place, a space of sad dreams, sickness, and despair. Each chorus member—as Greig said, identified only by gender and a number—has his or her own reason for wanting money. Man 1 wants to go to Harvard business school so he can get a good job, Man 2 wants a happy meal, and Woman 2 wants to hear music and see movies (22–24). The specific goals that these chorus members discuss mask the real object of their desire, which is expressed unconsciously through the form of the desire. Their stated goals are the *objet petit a* in Lacanian psychoanalysis. As Lacan explains, the *objet petit a* is "a privileged object, which has emerged from some primal separation, from the self-mutilation induced by the very approach of the real" (83). Or as Todd McGowan puts it, "It is the object that holds out the promise of the ultimate jouissance for the subject. And yet, at the same time, it is an impossible object: it remains always just out of reach" (77). In other words, the *objet petit a* substitutes for the actual desire, which is the castrated phallus, or the experience of the subject's wholeness which has been lost upon entry into the symbolic order. The problem of course is that no object obtainable within the symbolic order can actually replace the phallus, so the search is always in vain.

The guiding force of desire in Scene Five is what Freud called the death drive or death instinct, which is a primordial desire to return to an inorganic state. Freud says of the death drive, "*an instinct is an urge inherent in organic life to restore an earlier state of things* which the living entity has been obliged to abandon under the pressure of external disturbing forces" (30). Trauma can bring the death drive most obviously to the surface by disrupting the balance between the pleasure principle—the desire to seek happiness and avoid unhappiness—and the reality principle—which acknowledges the need for delayed gratification. Amidst the trauma of the AIDS crisis/Theban plague, the characters in the market seek escape, release, sleep, and even death—on a fundamental level they seek a return to the inorganic state. Take, as an example, Man 2. Man 2 wants to consume a McDonald's Happy Meal, which is, of course, a perfect representative of *objet petit a* because the very name "Happy Meal" declares the food to have a privileged connection to enjoyment. And this connection to enjoyment is exactly what Man 2 ostensibly seeks, claiming he wants to "know that I have done what I wanted, only once" (23). However, the *objet petit a* simultaneously obscures and reveals the real object of desire, which is the death drive. Man 2 speaks three times in scene five, and the interaction with the Happy Meal moves from a refined consumer experience to excrement. In his opening line, Man 2 says specifically that he wants to *buy* a Happy Meal; he does not initially say he wants to *eat* a Happy Meal, meaning that this interaction is centered in the space of the commercial, the space of the commodity (22). The next time Man 2 speaks the interaction is more visceral. He claims he wants to "feel the warm burger meat fill my stomach," moving from the realm of the impersonal commodity to the mechanics of digestion

(23). Finally, in his last bit of dialogue in this scene, Man 2 wants to know "what it's like to shit burger meat onto the dry earth by the roadside" (24). This final change is revelatory. In shifting the focus of desire from the consumer purchase of the commodity/*objet petit a* to leaving excrement by the roadside we see the truth of Man 2's desire, which is to escape the consumer cycle so reliant on an economy of enjoyment and return to an inorganic, or perhaps pre-symbolic, condition.

The culmination and most direct representative of the despairing voices in this market is Man 6, the presentation of whom is an almost heavy-handed evocation of the death drive. Man 6 intends to buy alcohol and drink himself into oblivion, then "when I'm no longer conscious of anything. / I'll smash one of the bottles on a rock. / And cut my throat with the glass" (24). More explicitly than any of the other chorus members, Man 6 seeks death in both the figurative and literal senses. The Freudian death drive is not simply or directly about wanting to die, but about achieving "an initial state from which the living entity has at one time or other departed and to which it is striving to return by the circuitous paths along which its development leads" (Freud 32). So both in a simple sense of seeking death directly, and in the more properly Freudian sense of seeking an inorganic oblivion through extreme drunkenness, the object of Man 6's desire correlates with the instinctual dictates of the death drive.

This scene embodies the action of the neoliberal market, and the paradoxical destructiveness of desire within the society of enjoyment. Todd McGowan identifies a contemporary shift from the society of prohibition to the society of enjoyment, that is, to a society in which the fundamental commandment of the Other is to enjoy. This shift is tied to neoliberal political economics because "Global capitalism functions by submitting all cultural life to the process of commodification, and this process can only be sustained if everyone is engaged in the endless pursuit of enjoyment" (McGowan 50). What this means is that global capitalism constructs a new mode of subjectivity for the individual, namely pathological narcissism (34). The pathological narcissist has no interest in or responsibility to a community, but is entirely geared toward seeking his or her own enjoyment in compliance with the Law of the Other. Within the psychological structure of neoliberal capitalism, each individual is pitted against one another, with nothing of value to sell in a market where no one is buying. Greig's presentation of the market condemns neoliberal capitalism for atomizing individuals, each of whom is ostensibly responsible only for his or her own desires, with no space for civic or social unity in the face of the AIDS crisis.

This erosion of community as a valued organizing principle precipitates what René Girard calls the sacrificial crisis, which he argues underpins the movement of tragedy. In a society in crisis, forces like anxiety, tension, dissent, and violence build to potentially explosive or revolutionary levels if not vented. Girard theorizes that a crisis becomes "sacrificial" when the community selects a surrogate victim who can become a kind of lightning rod attracting all the violence that would otherwise destroy the community itself. As he puts it, "The sacrifice serves to protect the entire community from *its own* violence. [...] The elements of dissention scattered throughout the community are drawn to the person of the sacrificial victim and eliminated, at least temporarily, by its sacrifice" (8). In *Violence and the Sacred*, Girard traces this as the fundamental narrative structure of Greek tragedies, and Greig maintains the sacrificial crisis structure into *Oedipus the Visionary* by transplanting almost exactly the plot structure from the Sophokles hypotext. We see the cultural erosion and self-destructive violence building in South Africa in scene five, culminating in the suicidal dream of Man 6. The longing for oblivion and death signifies a larger cycle of violence as the community breaks down, replacing the harmonious dream of the Rainbow Nation with individuals competing in an indifferent free market sphere. We also see this violence and social collapse in Scene One, in which the chorus prays not to feel pity for a dying man. As Friedman says, everyone becomes a kind of Robinson Crusoe, occupying his or her own isolated island and left to the mercies of the market without communal support or unity.

However, African markets also offer the potential for rebuilding unified communities. Although they are not indigenous to southern Africa, in West Africa traditional markets functioned somewhat like the bourgeois public sphere described by Jürgen Habermas. Although in practice the public sphere always fell short, Habermas identifies three ideal characteristics of the bourgeois public: (1) status is disregarded in favor of rational debates between equals, (2) discussions focus on areas of common concern, and (3) anyone can enter the public sphere by meeting certain criteria (36–37). The openness and equality that were the ideals of the European bourgeois public sphere also characterizes West African markets. These markets are community centers in which to meet people, hear and discuss the latest news, and so on. Paul Bohannan and Philip Curtain write that markets "could be used for many purposes other than buying and selling—to meet your girlfriend, settle a legal dispute, get the latest news, or pay your respects to important elders or chiefs. Market places in Africa are almost as important politically and socially as they are economically" (103). Kevin Wetmore, Jr., links African markets to the Athenian *agora*, writing, "the marketplace of Athens was in many ways the cultural, social, economic, political, and geographic center of the city. Similarly, the marketplace in any African village is the center of everyday life" (41). Although markets were traditionally controlled by a local chief or king, their daily functioning was fairly democratic. In this sense, the market made up a kind of commonwealth, or a space of common ownership inhabited by the multitude.

I use the terms *commonwealth* and *multitude* in the sense theorized by Michael Hardt and Antonio Negri. For them the commonwealth encompasses both an environmental commons—air, water, space, etc.—but also the shared products of culture that allow for the continuation and reproduction of culture—language, affect, gesture, style, information, etc. (viii). And they theorize the multitude as a collective group of singularities, or individuals formed by and inextricable from social contexts (111). The multitude allows the coordination of various liberatory struggles in contrast to the organized and powerful forces of oppression because multitude brings together singularities and finds common ground between them. It is through the existence of the multitude itself that the common comes into being; or, as Hardt and Negri put it, "the common is composed of interactions among singularities" (124). Hardt and Negri propose the common as an alternative basis for social organization, contesting late capitalist neoliberalism's emphasis on the individual as isolated consumer in ostensibly beneficial free markets. The openness and communality of traditional markets may offer one model for envisioning an African commons out of which collective action could arise to improve the conditions of the African poor and eliminate the systems of inequality sustained by neoliberal economic apartheid and global inequality.

Indeed *Oedipus the Visionary* envisions collective action in the culmination of the sacrificial crisis. Girard emphasizes the communal nature of selecting a sacrificial victim: "Each member's hostility, caused by clashing against others, becomes converted from an individual feeling to a communal force unanimously directed against a single individual" (79). In *Oedipus the Visionary*, Oedipus comes to stand in for all the evils of colonialism, apartheid, continuing economic apartheid, and the Global North's indifference to the AIDS crisis (in other words Oedipus becomes a new shared *objet petit a*, the object standing in for desire). He must therefore be expelled from the community in an attempt to make it symbolically whole again. As in Sophokles, Greig's Oedipus largely drives his own self-sacrifice, telling the people, "Inside my skin is all the agony the world can make. / I hold it in me. / My skin protects you. / Outside my skin the world is good" (83). In his pain and shame Oedipus tries to retain his individuality—the atomized selfhood which neoliberalism envisions as the human condition. Rather than seeing himself in a context, Oedipus retains his earlier attitude of total ownership, both of his ill-gotten possessions and of his deeds.

This is where Greig really diverges from the Sophokles hypotext. In Sophokles' *Oedipus the King* the titular character is expelled from the community, thereby fulfilling the cyclical movement of the sacrificial crisis. It is also clear in Sophokles that, while the chorus may find an object lesson in his tragedy, they do not identify themselves with Oedipus. At the end of *Oedipus the King* the chorus reflects,

> Look on this Oedipus, the mighty and once masterful:
> Elucidator of the riddle,
> Envied on his pedestal of fame.
> You saw him fall. You saw him swept away [263].

In these final lines of the play the chorus continues to discuss Oedipus as an individual, as an isolated person who can be disconnected from the Theban *polis* and exiled to his fate. And indeed, Oedipus continues to figure as lone individual in *Oedipus at Kolonus*.

By contrast, in Greig's *Oedipus the Visionary*, even in his self-sacrifice Oedipus can never truly be expelled from the community—he remains an integral part of the larger identity of the multitude. In the face of Oedipus' individual suffering, the community experiences a melting of identities into a commonwealth of universal experience. During the play's climax in Scene Sixteen, the priest tells the people,

> His mind and body dissolved.
> He became nothing.
> He became all time.
> Nature shatters all humanity.
> *We* are Oedipus.
> *We* are nothing [76, my emphasis].

Oedipus is brought back into the fold, back into a shared experience of the world through suffering, and therefore back into the commonwealth of humanity. This prayer that incorporates Oedipus back into the commonwealth of humanity stands in stark contrast to the first scene of the play, which serves as a foil for the renunciation of sacrificial violence. In Scene One the chorus watches a man dying of thirst drag himself along seeking water. Instead of helping this man, the chorus prays—establishing a parallel ritual of prayer in scene one and in Scene Sixteen—that God will "kill the pity in us" as they helplessly watch the man die (10). The prayer envisions a god of opulence and enjoyment: this is the god/ Other imagined as having total access to enjoyment in ways denied to subjects within the society of enjoyment. The chorus' prayer addresses,

> Dear fat god.
> Dear drunken god.
> God on your throne of battered gold leaf.
> In your rooms of red velvet.
> With your naked, laughing whores sat on your lap.
> Your mouth stained red with wine.
> Make us like you.
> Give us the power of your hate.
> The power of a God to see pain and feel nothing [10–11].

In this vision of hedonistic enjoyment—of food, wine, sex, texture, color, and indifference—the chorus addresses the Big Other of neoliberal capitalism, which commands enjoyment and simultaneously punishes the subject for never being able to enjoy enough. To this god, the god of enjoyment, the chorus prays for the power of hate, which could eliminate the unpleasure of seeing disease and suffering destroying the community. But this prayer from Scene One is replaced in Scene Sixteen with the prayer to bring Oedipus back into a renewed community, which renounces the enjoyment promised by violence in the cycle of the sacrificial crisis.

This mode of connection characterizes African ritual and drama, as well as Greek theatre, which serve to strengthen communities. Kevin Wetmore identifies the communal effect of sacrifice in African ritual, noting that "sacrifice is a form of reciprocation that unites the realm of the mortals with the realm of the immortals"; and further that "in a group context sacrifice forms a communal bond that joins the participants into a community" (61). While Greig is not an African dramatist, *Oedipus the Visionary* reflects a similar kind of communal experience, a communal connection that allows intersubjectivity to replace isolation. Clare Wallace traces this connectivity in many of Greig's plays as a counterpoint to the erosive force of global capitalism: "If postmodern globalization is often seen to offer a plethora of potentially detrimental or disorienting effects, Greig turns to the ethical resources of human communication and contingent communities as a means of suggesting, however partially, utopian possibilities of transcending those negative conditions" (107).

In Athenian democracy theatre also had political implications, in the sense of opening new possibilities for thinking about the world. In contrast to the relatively limited scope of Athenian democracy in practice, on stage Athenians could imagine vastly expanded political possibilities and democratic openness. In "The Sociology of Athenian Tragedy," Edith Hall argues, "Greek tragedy does its thinking in a form which is vastly more politically advanced than the society which produced Greek tragedy. The human imagination has always been capable of creating egalitarian modes of society even when they are inconceivable in practice" (125). Graham McLaren's original production for Theatre Babel tried to evoke the Greek roots of *Oedipus the King*, though not entirely successfully. In her review for *The Scotsman*, Joyce McMillan wrote that, "Graham McLaren's staging—all oatmeal-coloured robes, stilted body-language, cold-eyed cockney chorus and a single barren tree—somehow looks like nothing more than a string of cliches drawn from some textbook of classic productions." While the *mise-en-scène* may not have been the most aesthetically pleasing choice, the decision to visually evoke the story's Greek roots built connections between the modern audience and the ancient Athenians, including links shared by theatre-goers the world over: the collective experience of theatre as a public art form. The experience of theatre is deeply human, which has the potential to connect audiences across time, space, and culture, producing a commonwealth of spectators. In Greig's play, Oedipus' pain and shame become part of a shared human experience, and it is through the collective recognition and embrace of this common that it becomes possible to break the cycle of violence constituting the sacrificial crisis.

This recognition of the common and renunciation of sacrificial violence gestures toward an end to global capitalism and the society of enjoyment. Obviously Greig is not presenting a simple or transcendental strategy for moving beyond the current political economic mode, but through recognition of our place within the organizing structures of neoliberal capitalism it is possible to affect a resistance by working against the forces of social isolation. The problem created by global capitalism is that "The society of enjoyment works to convince subjects that they exist outside this society, in independent isolation. It thus becomes increasingly difficult to grasp oneself within the universal" (McGowan 193). However, by recognizing ourselves as singularities already existing in the multitude, and therefore already imbedded in the common, we work against the forces of neoliberalism that seek to destroy communities. In the choice not to expel Oedipus from the community—contra Sophokles—Greig's South African community renounces the enjoyment promised by violence, the enjoyment promised by the structure of the sacrificial crisis. Instead of pursuing the *objet petit a* by killing or expelling Oedipus, the community elects to accept its own partial enjoyment, thereby leaving the cycle of consumer-compelled desire. Similarly by coming together in the shared space of the theatre to enjoy and reflect collectively (like Greek and African theatre audiences), we can resist the cultural imperative to enjoy individually and rebuild ties of communal experience.

Ultimately, I propose that adaptation as a form promotes a commonwealth, so when Greig chooses to adapt the *Oedipus* story to protest the cultural and economic violence of neoliberalism, the mode of protest performs a common. In reworking Sophokles' *Oedipus the King*, Greig chooses a well-known piece of Western cultural heritage (which has extensive colonial and postcolonial implications in Africa, as books like Kevin Wetmore's *Athenian Sun in an African Sky* or Astrid Van Weyenberg's *Politics of Adaptation*, among many others, trace in far more detail than I can here). Particularly among African dramatists, adaptation is often a vehicle for multi-faceted political protest, and I think Greig works in this same tradition. Van Weyenberg's central argument in *The Politics of Adaptation* is that postcolonial African dramatists adapt Greek plays to speak politically to (1) the place of Greek drama in a culturally constructed hierarchy of literature, (2) the Global North and (former) imperial nations which continue to assume the superiority of an ostensibly Greek-derived Western culture; and (3) against contemporary African political and economic problems. She locates African adapters like Soyinka, Osofisan, Fugard, and Farber in the struggle against notions of cultural ownership, thereby suggesting innate ties between adaptation and the common. Van Weyenberg writes that "by offering Greek tragedies as theirs, the playwrights indirectly yet effectively undermine eurocentric claims of ownership and authority. They counter these claims by performing, through adaptation, a cultural politics directed at the Europe or West that has traditionally considered Greece as its property" (xii). But she also notes the risk involved in reading African adaptations as merely responses to the Global North, as merely responses to colonialism: "To see these texts mainly in terms of resistance makes the history of colonialism their defining force and the 'West' their sole term of comparison, a perspective that ultimately threatens to reduce African literatures to mere addenda to European culture" (xlix).

In adapting Sophokles' plot to a South African setting, Greig locates himself on the periphery of these trends in postcolonial African adaptation. Obviously Greig does not speak from an originary African perspective and his primary audience is European, but I would argue that his choice to relocate *Oedipus the King* in the Rainbow Nation contests European ownership of the myth and of Greek culture in ways comparable to those Van Weyenberg identifies. It is also significant that in Greig's adaptation it is the African community that transcends the sacrificial and political economic structures of violence that shape the neoliberal Global North. This suggests a reciprocal relationship in which both Europeans and Africans contribute to a common understanding of the *Oedipus* myth and the lessons it can teach us today. Rather than stressing primacy or cultural ownership, Greig envisions an open dialogue between cultures and peoples working toward producing a more just, equal, and welcoming global society. In other words, by addressing a Scottish/UK audience from a hybrid African position, Greig provides a template for social justice and collective action that can be applied to fight the oppressive forces of neoliberalism in both the RSA and the UK. This play combines both Brechtian critical distance—by addressing a UK audience with a South African setting—and simultaneously a cultural hybridity via Homi Bhabha—because Greig draws on both European and African performance traditions to create a new and shared dramaturgy. It is both a critique of Scotland's place in a neoliberal world order (as a member of the UK, one of the major pillars of global capitalism) and a call to Scottish/British people to recognize and resist their own exploitation under a neoliberal world order.

Greig's reworking of this source material becomes a collaborative process between himself and Sophokles, and then with the directors, actors, tech people, audiences, and communities in which the play is performed. Linda

Hutcheon notes that stage performances, like cinema, are extremely complex collaborative experiences with any number of people at various stages of the performance process acting as potential adapters (83). This multiplicity of adapters working together toward a performative project would probably appeal to Michael Hardt and Antonio Negri as a prime example of the common. As they say, multiple people can productively use a single idea and develop it in new and different forms to add to the collective stock of knowledge and culture (Hardt and Negri 381). Hutcheon notes that adaptation is a popular form in the neoliberal era because well-loved source texts bring their own "franchise," or built-in audience predisposed to see the movie, play the game, buy the merchandise, etc. (87). But adaptation also poses a threat to the very notion of ownership, which is fundamental to neoliberalism's ideological investment in property. Hutcheon writes, "Adaptations are not only *spawned by* the capitalist desire for gain; they are also *controlled by* the same in law, for they constitute a threat to the ownership of cultural and intellectual property" (89). Therefore, by adapting we can enact a commonwealth, breaking down neoliberal notions of ownership in favor of intellectual and performative communities of writers, actors, theatre practitioners, audiences, and communities. As with recognizing our own position as subjects whose desire for enjoyment is shaped by neoliberal capitalism, enacting communities offers a means to resist the society of enjoyment and the consumer-isolation that results from it. We create the commonwealth by performing it.

WEST VIRGINIA UNIVERSITY

NOTE

1. I use the term *transcultural adaptation* in the same sense Linda Hutcheon uses it in *A Theory of Adaptation*, broadly meaning a shift from one cultural context to another. She notes, "Almost always, there is an accompanying shift in the political valence from the adapted text to the 'transculturated' adaptation" (145). Within this shift, I see the potential for cultural interconnection, not only between modern and ancient theatre, but within increasingly globalized performance contexts. Diana Taylor writes that transculturation has the potential to produce a commons because "Rather than being oppositional or strictly dialectical, it *circulates*" between dominant and marginalized cultures, thereby potentially decentering hegemonic power structures (71).

WORKS CITED

Bohannan, Paul, and Philip Curtain. *Africa & Africans*. 4th ed. Prospect Heights, IL: Waveland, 1995.
Brown, Mark. "The Man Behind the Mask." *Scotland on Sunday* (March 5, 2000): 9.
Ferguson, James. *Global Shadows: Africa in the Neoliberal World Order*. Durham: Duke University Press, 2006.

Freud, Sigmund. *Beyond the Pleasure Principle*. Trans. James Strachey. New York: Norton, 1961.

Friedman, Milton. *Capitalism and Freedom*. Chicago: University of Chicago Press, 2002.

Girard, René. *Violence and the Sacred*. Trans. Patrick Gregory. Baltimore: Johns Hopkins University Press, 1992.

Greig, David. *Oedipus the Visionary*. Edinburgh: Capercaillie, 2005.

Habermas, Jürgen. *The Structural Transformation of the Public Sphere: An Inquiry into a Category of Bourgeois Society*. Trans. Thomas Burger. Cambridge, MA: MIT Press, 1991.

Hall, Edith. "The Sociology of Athenian Tragedy." *A Cambridge Companion to Greek Tragedy*. Ed. P. E. Easterling. Cambridge: Cambridge University Press, 2001. 93–126.

Hardt, Michael, and Antonion Negri. *Commonwealth*. Cambridge, MA: Harvard University Press, 2009.

Harvey, David. *A Brief History of Neoliberalism*. Oxford: Oxford University Press, 2007.

Hodder, B. W. "Some Comments on the Origins of Traditional Markets in Africa South of the Sahara." *Transactions of the Institute of British Geographers* 36 (1965): 97–105.

Hutcheon, Linda. *A Theory of Adaptation*. 2d ed. London: Routledge, 2013.

Lacan, Jacques. *The Four Fundamental Concepts of Psycho-Analysis*. Trans. Alan Sheridan. New York: Norton, 1981.

Martin, Randy. *Financialization of Daily Life*. Philadelphia: Temple University Press, 2002.

McGowan, Todd. *The End of Dissatisfaction: Jacques Lacan and the Emerging Society of Enjoyment*. Albany: State University of New York Press, 2004.

McMillan, Joyce. "Greek Drama Passes the Test of Time in a Scottish Makeover: Ancient Tragedies with a Modern Malaise." *The Scotsman* (March 20, 2000): 14.

Narsiah, Sagie. "Neoliberalism and Privitisation in South Africa." *GeoJournal* 57.1/2 (2002): 29–38.

Putnam, Robert D. *Bowling Alone: The Collapse and Revival of American Community*. New York: Simon & Schuster, 2000.

Ranger, Terence. "The Invention of Tradition in Colonial Africa." *Perspectives on Africa: A Reader in Culture, History, and Representation*. 2d ed. Ed. Roy Richard Grinker, Stephen C. Lubkemann, and Christopher B Steiner. West Sussex, UK: Wiley-Blackwell, 2010. 450–61.

Schneider, Geoffrey E. "Neoliberalism and Economic Justice in South Africa: Revisiting the Debate on Economic Apartheid." *Review of Social Economy* 61.1 (2003): 23–50.

Sophocles. *Oedipus the King. Sophocles: The Complete Plays*. Trans. Paul Roche. New York: Signet Classics, 2001. 209–63.

Taylor, Diana. "Transculturating Transculturation." *Interculturalism and Performance: Writings from PAJ*. Ed. Bonnie Marranca and Gautam Dasgupta. New York: PAJ, 1991. 60–74.

Van Weyenberg, Astrid. *The Politics of Adaptation: Contemporary African Drama and Greek Tragedy*. Amsterdam: Rodopi, 2013.

Wallace, Clare. *The Theatre of David Greig*. London: Bloomsbury, 2013.

Wetmore, Kevin J., Jr. *The Athenian Sun in an African Sky: Modern African Adaptations of Classical Greek Tragedy*. Jefferson, NC: McFarland, 2002.

Zaroulia, Marilena. "'Geographies of the Imagination' in David Greig's Theatre: Mobility, Globalization and European Identities." *The Theatre of David Greig*. Clare Wallace. London: Bloomsbury, 2013. 178–94.

With Rhyme and Reason:
Hip Hop Hamlet in Prison

Elizabeth Charlebois

Abstract

This essay explores the implications of teaching and producing Shakespeare's plays in prisons. After outlining the pitfalls and problems of traditional approaches that tend to romanticize both the prisoner and Shakespeare, an alternative paradigm is explored through an analysis of a hip-hop adaptation of Hamlet produced in 2015 by St. Louis-based Prison Performing Arts. Hip Hop Hamlet *gave prisoners a fundamentally different way of engaging with and performing Shakespeare that ultimately created a meaningful if provisional site of cultural, artistic, and political resistance, in part because of hip hop's historical alignment with such resistance and the inmates' vital role in composing the script. Furthermore, the ideological significance of the adaptation as both a text and a performance was heightened and even contingent upon the fact that it was developed and produced within the context and confines of the Northeastern Correctional Center in Bowling Green, Missouri, a medium-security state prison.*

This essay asks what it means not only to teach but also to produce Shakespeare's plays in prison. I critically examine approaches to and justifications for teaching and producing Shakespeare in prison—very pointedly including my own attitudes and experiences—while arguing how a collaborative hiphop adaptation of *Hamlet* written and produced with prisoners in 2014 and 2015 provides a provisional, if nonetheless still problematic, model for addressing some of the troublesome implications of employing Shakespeare in a correctional setting.

The proliferation of programs devoted to Shakespeare in prison began in the 1980s and continues to the present. The best known of these is "Shake-speare Behind Bars," Curt Tofteland's program at a men's prison in Kentucky that was turned into a 2003 documentary of the same name. The popular appeal of inmate actors performing Shakespeare seems to stem, at least in part, from the presumed incongruity between the marginalized subject position of the inmate actor and the cultural refinement associated with Shakespeare. Pro-ducing Shakespeare in prison challenges the popular conception of the uned-ucated prisoner who is edified by his articulation and mastery of a sophisticated and heightened language that is ostensibly the antithesis of the slang spoken on the prison yard. Meanwhile, Shakespeare is made culturally relevant again, his well-worn reputation for universality reinvigorated. This complex ideo-logical transaction confers cultural capital on not only the inmate actor, but also the whole field of Shakespearean studies. Rather than being relegated to the esoteric realm of the academy, the study of Shakespeare becomes the most humanizing of the humanities and, in the prison context, quite literally embod-ies the original meaning of the liberal arts as being truly *liberating*.

This perspective is extraordinarily compelling as evidenced by several academics who have written about their experiences teaching Shakespeare in prison, myself included. The language of conversion and redemption domi-nates our accounts, and while there is an emphasis on what studying or per-forming Shakespeare does for the inmate, there is also an implied or explicit conversion in the professor who is given fresh perspectives and insight by inmates who respond to the text without the stultifying accretion of four hun-dred years of scholarship. Shakespeare's texts in essence become the portholes through which the prison inmate and the college professor regard each other.[1]

Despite the tacit or overt critique of traditional scholarship articulated in these accounts, the academy has taken note of these prison programs and their relevance to the discipline of literary study. At the annual meeting of the Shakespeare Association of America (SAA) in 2006 there was a panel devoted to "Big House Shakespeare" and a later issue of *PMLA* featured ten articles by college and university faculty who teach literature in prison, including two by artistic directors of Shakespeare in prison programs.[2] It was at that 2006 SAA meeting that I met Agnes Wilcox, Artistic Director of St. Louis-based Prison Performing Arts (PPA), whose prison production of *Hamlet* is featured in an episode of National Public Radio's *This American Life* with Ira Glass.[3] Seeking to see Shakespeare and my discipline from outside the academy, I spent my first sabbatical working with Agnes Wilcox and PPA as the "Scholar in Residence" on their 2007–08 productions of *Richard III* and *A Midsummer Night's Dream*, at a Missouri men's and women's prison, respectively. I helped inmates learn their lines and better understand their characters, while also witnessing the brutalities and banalities of prison life of which I had previously only the most abstract idea. I found the experience of working with PPA profoundly rewarding, but with time and some distance on what was a very intense and challenging year, I began to question the broader political implications of my work.

While serving as a Shakespeare teacher and dramaturge for PPA, I did learn a good deal about the lives of my prison students as a result of our informal conversations. However, I generally tended to view them through the lens of Shakespeare; the plays' characters and themes remained primary in my imagination, more legible to me—and perhaps less overwhelming—than the real-life suffering and losses of the lives of the inmates I worked with. I saw the inmates and their prison context as compelling contemporary analogues of the plays. Rather than Shakespeare providing me with a means to better understand these men and women, they gave me a renewed understanding and appreciation of Shakespeare. My intimate familiarity with the language of the plays enabled me to "translate" the vastly different lives and experiences of my prison students into an idiom that I already knew. Unwittingly, I had created a romanticized fiction that reinforced the self-absorption of the academy in precisely the ways that I had sought to avoid. My habits of mind protected my own privilege and authority in ways that now nearly make me cringe with embarrassment.

The chapter I wrote for *Performing New Lives: Prison Theatre* about my experience working with PPA on *Midsummer* at the Women's Eastern Reception and Diagnostic Correctional Center in Vandalia, Missouri, is a testimony of my point of view at the time. I concluded with an elaborate analogy between my own experience and the themes and language of *Midsummer*: "I came to prison for my 'sabbatical' and, despite or perhaps because of the ubiquitous ironies of the play and this place, found myself transformed. I didn't enter the magic world of the forest like the mortals in Shakespeare's play, but the strange world on the other side of the prison airlock where I witnessed two dozen women commit to and create another reality, a shared reality, the world of the play. I saw a group of actors turn a set made of raw wood and milk crates under florescent lights into a lush forest on a beautiful moonlit, midsummer night. For a magic moment, our minds were truly 'transfigured so together,' despite all that divides us" (Charlebois 269). The extent to which I had subordinated the inmates and their experiences to my own reading of a particular passage of *Midsummer* is right there—in *my own words.*

While I didn't want to further indulge this self-serving narrative, I had found my teaching in prisons nonetheless very fulfilling and thought about returning to PPA for my next sabbatical. That vague notion took specific shape after I saw a brilliant hip-hop adaptation of *Othello* called *Othello, the Remix* at the Chicago Shakespeare Theater in May 2013. The show, written and performed by the Chicago-based Q Brothers, had been originally commissioned by the Shakespeare's Globe in London for their Globe-to Globe-Festival in the Olympic Year of 2012.[4] As a Shakespearean, I knew *Othello* particularly well, perhaps better than any other play in the canon, but knew comparatively little about hip-hop. Nonetheless, I emerged a complete convert, bowled over by the energy and insight of the production where four male actors performed all of the roles. *The Remix* comically updated and transformed Shakespeare's original while still conveying the play's central themes. What it did for me, as an academic, was legitimate hip hop. It was performed at Chicago Shakespeare and even on the stage of Shakespeare's Globe in London. As Linda Hutcheon points out in *A Theory of Adaptation*, "one way to gain respectability or increase cultural capital is for the adaptation to be upwardly mobile" (91). By taking on Shakespeare the Q Brothers' adaptation had elevated hip hop.

Almost instantaneously, I came up with the idea: For my next sabbatical I would return to Prison Performing Arts and write and produce a hip-hop adaptation of *Hamlet* with the inmates at the Northeast Correctional Center in Bowling Green, Missouri. I thought of *Hamlet* because PPA's Artistic Director Agnes Wilcox had begun her career directing inmates in a production of of *Hamlet*, the one featured on *This American Life*. I also thought she would be enticed by the prospect of returning to the play for her last semester with the company before her retirement. But this would be different and more democratic. We would be developing an original script with a class of inmates who would not only be actors but also the authors of the script. Agnes Wilcox and I returned to Chicago where we met with the Q Brothers who, having just performed *Othello, the Remix* for inmates at Cook County Jail, very enthusiastically agreed to come to the prison to help us launch our project. But that was over a year away.

Meanwhile, my recognition of the problems and tensions of traditional approaches to producing Shakespeare in prison was sharpened when I moderated a panel devoted to the work of Brazilian director and political activist Augusto Boal at the "Shakespeare in Prisons Conference" at the University of Notre Dame in November 2013. Boal was a teacher and an inspiration for several theater practitioners who now produce Shakespeare in prison. Most famous for his book *Theatre of the Oppressed*, which takes its name from Paulo Freire's 1968 educational manifesto *Pedagogy of the Oppressed*, Boal's approach is Brechtian in its aesthetic and political engagement and seeks to "stimulate the spectator to transform his society" (Boal, *Theatre* 47). In a provocative talk, entitled "Banishing Romeo," University of Southern California Professor of Theatre Brent Blair challenged the compatibility of producing Shakespeare in prison with Boal's *Theatre of the Oppressed*, arguing that doing so encourages behavioral compliance and adherence to conventional authority and social norms rather than giving inmates the tools to challenge such norms. Blair, a committed Boal practitioner, no longer teaches Shakespeare in prison after going through what he terms an "ethical crisis" where he came to see such work as not engaging what he believes is the central purpose of art—"to assist in liberation." Rather than being consistent with Boal's radical philosophy and dramatic practice, producing Shakespeare in prison remains "expert and text centered," where inmates are "colonized" by a process whereby "we bring them into a house that we've already built" (Blair).

Blair's critique of Shakespeare in prison both infuriated and challenged me to further consider some of the implications of my previous work with prisoners. I had to admit that programs like Prison Performing Arts are allowed in correctional settings because in Boal's words they "bridle the individual" (47).[5] Programs commonly boast that prison actors have fewer behavioral infractions and comply with authority much more readily when participating. As Amy Scott-Douglass points out in her book *Shakespeare Inside*, programs like this "while they might be liberating or freeing to a certain extent, also serve a very practical function for the prison in that they help to keep the inmates complacent and under control" (96). While much recent Shakespearean scholarship sees in many of the plays a skeptical critique of the gender, racial, and religious orthodoxies of the playwright's own day, mainstream public opinion still largely regards Shakespeare as an icon of elite Western culture and studying his work as the epitome of traditional learning, implicitly if not explicitly aligned with conservative values, broadly construed. With such cachet, producing Shakespeare in prison makes the culturally marginalized prisoner-actor acceptable and even impressive to conventional audiences.

And maybe even to me. Rather than speaking in their own diverse and dissonant voices, they spoke to me in the powerful reputedly universal idiom of Shakespeare. Perhaps like prison uniforms that conceal or disguise what are, in fact, vast differences among the prison population, having inmates perform the beloved works of the playwright who was at the center of my professional life, having them articulate the famous lines that have echoed in theaters for centuries, rendered virtually invisible the economic, racial, cultural, and educational disparities that divide prison inmates not only from one another, but also, perhaps especially, from me. I had to face the possibility that Shakespeare's reputation for universality takes on a darker meaning if deployed in the service of creating an illusory homogeneity that obscures the diversity of the inmate actors and masks their profound alienation from the culture that keeps them behind bars.

Not all scholars or theater-in-prison practitioners share this critical view. Another speaker on the Boal panel at Notre Dame's Shakespeare in Prisons Conference in 2013 countered this highly skeptical perspective. Rob Pensalfini,

Senior Lecturer in Drama and Linguistics at the University of Queensland and the Artistic Director of the Queensland Shakespeare Ensemble, produces plays at the Borallon Correctional Centre through the Australian Shakespeare in Prison initiative. Like more recent scholars who approach Shakespeare from a left-leaning perspective, Pensalfini sees Shakespeare as a "vehicle for political theater" that is consistent with Boal's philosophy and ideology, contending "that the things it takes to perform Shakespeare are antithetical to the context of prison." Pensalfini uses "Theatre of the Oppressed" (TO) games and strategies in his rehearsals and workshops with prisoners and points out that Boal himself used "TO" techniques when he worked on *Hamlet* with the Royal Shakespeare Company in 1997 (234). According to Pensalfini, Shakespeare's text enables inmates to explore their own lives "at a more heightened level," allowing them "to express some aspect of their own experience that they had not been able to articulate with such a degree of passion and precision" (235).

Shawn Whitsett as Hamlet in *Hip Hop Hamlet* (courtesy blueShadow Photography).

PPA's Agnes Wilcox, taught by Augusto Boal himself and inspired by his politics, is an NYU-trained director and only uses Boal's games for actors as warm-up exercises, focusing on producing the play in performance rather than foregrounding the actors' experiences and their relevance to the text. However, she also sees performing Shakespeare as liberating the prisoner rather than confining him or her to social expectations and authority. In contrast to my characterization of Shakespeare's language as a kind of prison uniform, Wilcox observes, "Inmate actors in costume look like a group of actors or a group of characters in a play. They do not look like 'inmates'; they do not look like the 'mug shots' on their prison ID cards. [...] When the audience believes, the character emerges and the inmate is erased. The character is free to behave according to different rules. [...] She may even behave in a way that violates prison regulations, like touching another inmate, wearing a silk peignoir, or using language to seduce another person" (Wilcox 248, 250). Rather than seeing the language and characters of Shakespeare as a mask behind which to hide or a uniform that conceals their individuality, Agnes Wilcox sees it as a vehicle for personal change and growth, an opportunity to "slough off her identity and previous images of herself, which are often images of failure and victimhood" (250).

It is with these questions and tensions in mind that I returned to the *Hip Hop Hamlet* project on my second sabbatical with Agnes Wilcox and Prison Performing Arts. While not without a host of problems of its own, I will show how *Hip Hop Hamlet* gave prisoners a fundamentally different way of engaging with and performing Shakespeare that ultimately created a meaningful if provisional site of cultural, artistic, and political resistance, in part because of hip hop's historical alignment with such resistance and the inmates' vital role in composing the script. Furthermore, the ideological significance of the adaptation as both a text and a performance was heightened and even contingent upon the fact that it was developed and produced within the very specific context of the Northeastern Correctional Center (NECC) in Bowling Green, Missouri, a medium-security state prison.

From one perspective, the hip-hop medium is ideal for an adaptation produced in a correctional institution due to what Jeffrey Ogbar characterizes as its historical association with "biting criticism of prisons, white supremacy, political corruption, and police brutality" (105). One of the first break-through hip-hop albums, Public Enemy's *It Takes a Nation of Millions to Hold Us Back* (1988), features members of the group behind the bars of a prison standing on the American flag. Ogbar claims that the influential album was hip hop's "first major reference to prisons as an extension of racist social control" (147). Since then, he argues, "no issue [...] has been as central to the discourse of hip-hop radicalism and its collective self-expression as the prison industrial complex. From conscious rappers to nihilistic thugs, from commercial to underground, and from every region in the United States, prisons would be a prominent trope in hip-hop" (146).[6]

However, the radical roots of hip hop, which traces its origins back to the 1970s in the Black Power and Puerto Rican nationalist movements, were diluted by 1996 when it had "outsold every other genre of music" and had fully penetrated the American music scene (Ogbar 3). Indeed, now more than 70 percent of hip hop in the United States is consumed by whites (Hurt 2006), and its mainstream global popularity has made it a commercialized and corporate phenomenon that undermines its association with marginalized populations and radical politics. As prominent scholar of hip hop Tricia Rose argues, "Corporate record companies, while claiming to be mere middlemen distributors of authentic black ghetto tales, are product makers. [...] They want to sell records and thus they promote, tailor, encourage, discourage, sign, and release artists based on two crucial factors: what they think will sell as many copies as possible and what they think won't cause too much negative attention, friction, or resistance from society and government" (143). Of course, the fact that the Q Brothers' hip-hop adaptation of *Othello* was commissioned by Shakespeare's Globe Theatre in London for a major international festival is itself evidence of the degree to which the genre has been assimilated into, if not entirely coopted by, mainstream culture. In the context of a prison production in 2015, hip hop equivocally signaled both dangerous subversion and benign affirmation of social norms.

While the adoption of hip hop as a medium could be variously understood, the act and process of adaptation itself has radical potential and implications. I would argue that those implications are heightened when the adapters are prison inmates reimagining a paradigmatic literary text and doing this work in a correctional setting. As Linda Hutcheon points out, the process of adaptation "can destabilize both formal and cultural identity and thereby shift power relations" (174). The script of our hip-hop adaptation of *Hamlet* was roughly based on the plot of Shakespeare's play and contained occasional words, phrases and entire lines from the original, while largely consisting of rhymed couplets written in contemporary, urban-inflected English slang, and a few quotations from well-known hip-hop lyrics. Adaptation is, by definition, "a form of intertextuality," an extended intertextual engagement with the adapted work" (Hutcheon 8). Further, the richly intertextual nature of *Hip Hop Hamlet* has an affinity with "sampling," a prominent characteristic of hip hop where artists incorporate beats and other musical features of previous works into new creations that bridge past and present as well as the citationality so common in early modern literature and drama. Shakespeare himself was a master of the common Renaissance practice of "imitatio," a sort of early modern "sampling," whereby artists demonstrated artistic flair and talent by citing and transforming their existing source materials. As an example of one of the most popular dramatic forms of its time, Shakespeare's *Hamlet* is a revenge tragedy that cites its contemporaries, while self-consciously resisting and parodying the expectations of its genre.

One of the prisoners in the cast of *Hip Hop Hamlet* perceived the natural affinity between hip hop and Shakespeare and the way they illuminate one another. In a post-show discussion he said, "I didn't know nothing about Shakespeare, but I do like hip hop. I'm a fan of hip hop, and this was a way for me to sit down and dissect the Old English to Modern English and put it with something that I love, which is hip hop. And I think they complement each other: the literary piece of Shakespeare and the culture of hip hop. Together they bring awareness to each other."

However, many members of the cast weren't as enthusiastic about doing a hip-hop production. In particular, some of the white actors who had worked with Agnes Wilcox on other productions clearly felt that the choice to do a hip-hop adaptation was an accommodation to black inmates. Their black counterparts didn't seem that enthused about it either, some resenting the expectation that they would or should be knowledgeable or competent in the genre in ways they weren't. Aside from three or four students of an initial class of forty, no one else identified himself as a fan. I had assumed, wrongly, that prisoners would be more familiar with hip hop than Agnes and I, but it turns out that for most of the actors it proved to be another alien poetic language that had to be learned, nearly as unfamiliar as Shakespeare's iambic pentameter. I also wondered whether the extent to which hip hop is often maligned for replicating and even glamorizing the worst stereotypes of African American men as violent, homophobic, and misogynistic might have negatively influenced the receptiveness of both white and black actors to the idea, perhaps especially in the context of a prison theater class where participants hope that their work with PPA will challenge rather than reinforce popular perceptions of prisoners as "thugs" and "ganstas."

From the onset my idea was fraught with problems. Despite fairly widespread reluctance, if not downright resistance to the hip hop medium, the project had been launched. The Q Brothers were all lined up to come to prison, and we would move ahead. We had only six months to teach Shakespeare's play, write the adaptation, and stage it. In retrospect it is obvious that a more deliberate effort to familiarize the class with the origins and history of hip hop would have been helpful, but I shied away from it, not feeling comfortable teaching something that I was hardly an expert in and fearful that an open discussion might provoke the latent racial tensions that I perceived in the group. Instead I took comfort in the Q Brothers assurance that if Shakespeare had been alive today he would have been a rapper.

It is unclear whether the prison administration was more provoked by the hip-hop nature of the production or not. PPA had dealt with countless obstacles in previous productions, so it was hard to tell. When the Q Brothers came to lead workshops, prison staff required GQ to remove his camouflage vest and JQ to take out his nose ring before entering the institution. While consistent with prison regulations, the fact that the Qs' appearance, even after the rest of their jewelry, hats, and other accessories had been left in the car, needed to be additionally censored, seemed to signal that there was something illicit about the semiotics of hip hop.

Certainly, there was a problem with the acoustics of hip hop. The one thing that seemed pointed was the administration's denial of our request to provide the inmate actors with access to the musical beats we selected to accompany the script so the actors could practice saying their lines in rhythm outside of rehearsal time. We tried every conceivable option, including suggesting that we only make them available to listen to on headphones in the prison library, but we were ultimately denied, in January, six weeks before our first performance. While the security risks of having inmates listen to CDs, tapes, or digital audio files were generally cited as reasons for the decision, I wondered if the adamant refusal of the prison officials on this crucial point was fueled by a tacit assumption that there was something inherently subversive about those hip hop beats. While Shakespeare can go with the inmate back to his cell, the musical beats were out of bounds. Not surprisingly, the decision had the very practical and devastating consequence of making it clear that we were going to have to produce what was essentially a musical with only a few opportunities to rehearse with the music! Not surprisingly, this obstacle exacerbated the already-present anxieties and doubts among the actors who were no more hip-hop artists and rappers than Agnes and I were.

These tensions remained throughout a good deal of the script development and rehearsal process. Even on the night of the final performance, the white stage manager surprised me by playing heavy metal rock as preshow music for the audience. When I asked him why he wasn't playing hip hop as he had done for all other performances, he responded, "This is for me," which I interpreted to be a very clear assertion of not only his musical preference but his racial identity as well. Nonetheless, others were able to laugh and joke about it by the end of the process. During a post-show discussion with a public audience, the white actor who played Hamlet reflected on the difference between the more traditional adaptation PPA had produced the previous semester and *Hip Hop Hamlet*: "I don't know nothing about hip hop. Not a clue. I'm white. I didn't want to do it, but I stuck with it, and I'm glad I did." The Assistant Stage Manager, a black man in his mid–40s, followed up by saying that after being in several plays with Agnes Wilcox over the course of fifteen years, he thought he wanted the part of Hamlet in this production, but when he found out that it was a hop-hop adaptation he changed his mind: "I said 'No way.' It ain't only white guys that can't rap." This public exchange demonstrated that even if hip hop is enormously popular among white mainstream audiences, the white prisoners in the company still associated it with African American culture, even at the end of the project, as if whiteness itself precludes even basic knowledge of the genre. Interestingly, the response by the black stage manager humorously dispels what is the tacitly racist assumption that blackness involves a natural affinity with hip hop by denying any aptitude or even taste for it.

However, these sentiments were countered by other members of the cast. A young black inmate originally from Senegal saw hip hop as a way to understand the language of Shakespeare better: "English is my fifth language, and the original Shakespeare was so difficult for me to understand. The hip-hop version [...] I enjoyed it a lot more than last semester. I understand it. Everybody understands it." A white inmate talked about how the hip-hop medium made perfect sense: "Shakespeare was writing for his contemporaries. He wrote 400 years ago on issues that people understood at that time. With *Hip Hop Hamlet,* the story was essentially the same [...] but by putting it [...] in hip-hop we adopted a language that works for our contemporaries."

Despite the ideological and practical tensions attendant on choosing the hip-hop medium, one result was a significant reduction of my power and authority as an academic specialist. It put me on more equal footing with the inmates as we all struggled to write the script. In that respect the process was significantly more democratic than a traditional adaptation where I would have been the expert on the author and text. However, during the first phase of the project, we read and studied the play together in a fairly traditional class setting, where I was very much the teacher and the expert.

We met once a week on Wednesdays from 1:00 to 3:00 and 6:00 to 9:00 p.m. Forty inmates with vastly disparate educational backgrounds and levels of familiarity with Shakespeare and *Hamlet* undertook the task of deeply comprehending this extraordinarily complex play. There were students with college degrees in English, writing a prequel to *Hamlet* in iambic pentameter, who were sitting next to students who hadn't graduated from high school and struggled to understand plot summaries of the play, let alone Shakespeare's verse. We read the text aloud in class, pausing to break down the language and vocabulary and to discuss plot, character, language, and theme. It was slow going, but despite their various backgrounds, the men were astonishingly patient with each other as we made our way through Shakespeare's *Hamlet.*

Between class meetings, the men met in ten small groups organized by their housing units since inmates aren't allowed to congregate with anyone else outside of class. They worked on a series of "adaptation exercises" I devised that asked them to paraphrase portions of the text and condense and adapt the dialogue of the play into the rhymed couplets of hip hop. Some of the groups excelled at this work, while others struggled, but all managed to contribute. An inmate describes how the adaptation process allowed the members of the company to have ownership of the work: "In doing the traditional Shakespeare we all learned our parts and did our parts, but [*Hip Hop Hamlet*] was like no other because we never had to write [the script.] Since we broke it down into such small sections, we learned the original language page by page by page. [...] We would paraphrase first and then take three paragraphs of paraphrase and turn it into twelve lines. So in writing those twelve lines you've got to understand what the text is saying, which is a challenge, and also you've got to make it rhyme!"

We are immeasurably indebted to the Chicago-based Q Brothers whose internationally acclaimed hip-hop version of *Othello* had inspired the project. JQ and GQ flew in from Chicago and met us at the prison on three occasions during the script-development process. In late August they performed a scene from their show, *Othello, the Remix,* and conducted a workshop on a scene from the original text of *Othello* as a warm-up exercise to prepare us for work on our own adaptation of *Hamlet.* They returned to lead writing workshops, the first in October 2014, which resulted in the drafting of the first verse of Hamlet's "to be or not to be" soliloquy, and the second in January 2015, when we worked on portions of the play's final scene. During these workshops JQ and GQ stood at a white board, fielding ideas and suggestions from the class, using their expertise to facilitate and occasionally adjudicate between competing ideas. They provided us with a model for hip-hop Shakespeare and the process of composing the adaptation, as well as the confidence and inspiration to continue, despite so many obstacles and setbacks.

From the material generated during our weekly workshops as well as the vast amount of work the inmates produced in their small groups, Agnes Wilcox and I stitched together a rough draft of the script, which we edited and supplemented with material we wrote together. The Q Brothers gave us sixteen of their original musical beats for the project, a collection from which we selected the accompaniment for each of the play's ten scenes.

The text of the script itself served as a powerful antidote to the more conservative implications of staging traditional Shakespeare. The inmates decided to set their adaptation in contemporary corporate America. Rather than the royal family of Denmark, our script featured the business leadership of "Elsinore Enterprises."[7] Claudius is the new CEO who pushed his brother off the thirteenth floor of the office building while they were enjoying drinks by the rooftop pool, the same pool in which Ophelia later drowns. Hamlet is an art student; Laertes is in law school at Yale and, perhaps predictably, on the fencing team. Ophelia is a spoiled teen who reads *Seventeen* magazine and writes love songs to Hamlet, much to her brother's annoyance. The contemporary setting, allusions, and comedic touches cumulatively served to turn the adaptation not only into a parody of Shakespeare's original but also a critique of corporate America and pop culture.

In our production all of the dramatic roles were played by men, as was the case in Shakespeare's England, although such a choice in the context of a twenty-first-century prison production is subversive of conventional expectations of male prisoners who are expected to maintain a hyper-masculine guise at all times.[8] "Playing the woman's part" in such a context might make an actor especially vulnerable, but in this production it proved to be a surprising source of power. Two weeks before our first performance, the inmate who was originally cast as Gertrude was sent to "the hole" (the colloquial term for solitary confinement). Even after he was released back into general population he was not allowed to return to the company, despite our urgent appeals to the warden. While we had lost two other actors for similar reasons, we simply recast or eliminated their roles, but recasting Gertrude so close to our first performance was a more complicated matter, and the administration was well aware of that fact. In the end, Gertrude was played by a bald, sleek-headed, fifty-five-year-old African American man with a very obvious mustache. His willingness to take on the substantial and potentially problematic part at the eleventh hour was largely due to his remarkable dedication to the company but perhaps also aided by the fact that Wilcox provided him with the option of wearing an African dashiki, a more gender-neutral costume than the more feminine or professional attire that would have been expected of the self-described "stockholder and socialite" *Hip Hop Hamlet's* Gertude purports to be. The actor challenged expectations of the prison by embracing and playing his role without embarrassment, fear, or apology.

One of the most compellingly subversive choices the inmates made in adapting the script of *Hamlet* was turning the play-within-the play into a full-blown parody of an episode of *The Jerry Springer Show*. It turns out that despite his high status, Claudius is a huge fan of the raunchy series, and Hamlet presents tickets to Gertrude and Claudius as a "late wedding present." As Hamlet, Laertes, Polonius, Ophelia, Gertrude, and Claudius sit among members of the theater audience, Jerry introduces "The Mousetrappers," a dance company hired by Hamlet to do a routine to the 1972 R & B classic "Backstabbers" by the O'Jays.[9] While the song's lyrics and pointed choreography noticeably unnerve Claudius, it is Jerry's guests who make him storm out of the studio audience. We meet "Gracie Mae" who married her deceased husband's brother, "Cleedus," a month after his untimely demise [see Figure 2]. "Hank" is the surprise guest who confronts Cleedus and accuses him of murdering his father. A fight predictably breaks out, requiring security to remove the guests from the stage, after which Jerry announces, "Join us tomorrow when we hear from two star-crossed lovers contemplating suicide because their families simply can't get along." The collision between the exaggerated pop-culture ethos of *Jerry Springer* and the presumably high-brow world of *Hamlet* heightens the comic impact of the scene, while simultaneously emphasizing the tawdry nature of the Shakespearean plots, which suits the *Jerry Springer* format surprisingly well.

The metadramatic implications of the scene are further enhanced by the dubious status of the *Jerry Springer Show* as a "reality" television show given its outrageous guests and implausible scenarios. Consistent with the rest of the show, the female part of Gracie Mae was played by a male inmate, but unlike the play's Gertrude who spoke in his natural speaking voice, Gracie adopted an exaggerated Southern accent and spoke at a much higher pitch. The African American actor who played Gracie is 6'2" tall and weighs 245 pounds. Gracie's fawning over the oblivious and nearly mute Cleedus was rendered more comical not only by the actor's size but by the juvenile dress embroidered with flowers he wore that barely contained his muscled physique. Unlike the other instances of cross-dressing in the play, in the context of *The Jerry Springer Show* it was treated ironically, a strategy which seemed to serve as a kind of safety valve where the anxieties about the other men playing female roles could be released.[10]

Another way in which the script of *Hip Hop Hamlet* constituted a political critique rather than a capitulation to conventional authority was in its creation of several narrators, all of whom are employees of Elsinore Enterprises, including a janitor, an administrative assistant, a door man, mail room

Figure 2: Delmar Drummond, left, as Gracie Mae and Joe Cowles as Cleedus in *Hip Hop Hamlet* (courtesy blueShadow Photography).

clerk, and courier. While serving a practical and dramatic function, the narrators thematically represent the invisible labor that keeps the corporate engine of "Elsinore Enterprises" running smoothly. These characters, both literally and figuratively on the margins, not only summarize the action but often comment on it and critique the characters by directly addressing the audience. This dramatic device called attention to the fact that these inmate actors were profoundly removed from the privileges enjoyed by Shakespeare's characters, contributing to adaptation's critique and parody of corporate America.

Furthermore, by mediating between actors and audience and offering their opinions on characters and the action, our narrators also call attention to the distance between Shakespeare's *Hamlet* and their own. They foreground the interpretive act that is at the core of the adaptation process (Hutcheon 18). One of the narrators functions as the only other actor on stage during Ophelia's mad scene. The fact that Ophelia can see and hear a narrator, unlike any of the other characters, is a sure sign that she "must be crazy." While the scene is comedic for the most part, the narrator also remarks to the audience after Ophelia has left the stage to go for swim: "To see the loss of her mind is terrible. / There are things in life that are simply unbearable."

As if the challenges of teaching the play, writing the script, and staging the show in six months while only meeting one day a week weren't enough on their own, working in a prison context presented additional obstacles. Every single thing associated with the class and the production had to be approved in writing—every pencil, pad of paper, prop, costume, and even those subversive hip-hop beats. The administration also censored the script, oddly in places where it was faithful to Shakespeare's original, while allowing the social and political critique to remain. For example, in the first draft of the script submitted to the prison administration for review, Claudius introduces himself as a character who "lies, cheats, breaks the law, and even kills." The administration demanded that the text be "toned down," even though that character is true to the Claudius that Shakespeare created. All references to drugs, and words that are commonplace on primetime television such as "ass" and "bitch" were cut. Ironically, however, the most overtly political content, the company's version of Hamlet's famous "to be or not to be" soliloquy, was not censored, even while the recent events of close-by Ferguson, Missouri, seemed to resonate with every word it.[11]

> *Chorus*:
> To be or not to be, somethin' that I wonder:
> Should I live this life or let the world take me under?
> —There's got to be more than this monotony.
> The ultimate question, to be or not to be.

Verse One:

> It's the question we ask when things get narrow:
> Why should I suffer these slings and arrows?
> To die, to sleep, to dream forever—
> What do we dream at the end of this endeavor?
> Do any of us know what will happen—
> Lyin' in the ground with our hearts not tappin'?
> We take it, we fake it, to get through life.
> Somehow we make it, we avoid the knife.

Verse Two:

> For who would bear the whips and scorns of time
> When even our leaders are guilty of crimes?
> The cops get paid to look away
> While the 1% control the U.S.A.
> Scandal and heartbreak go hand in hand.
> The common man can't make a stand.
> The rich get richer, the poor without a dime,
> Greed and oppression at the same damn time.

Rather than a soulful articulation of the privileged prince's dilemma, the soliloquy became a collective complaint about the crushing boredom of prison life and the existential anxieties exacerbated by it, as well as the political and economic injustices that at least frame if not explain their incarceration. "The oppressor's wrong," "the law's delay" and the "insolence of office" that Hamlet complains of (3.1.71–73) became, "The cops get paid to look away / While the 1% controls the U.S.A." Agnes Wilcox commented on the implications of the process that resulted in this speech: "The freedom to insert topical references gave actors political agency—especially in 'to be or not to be,' in which they discussed corruption in American institutions. In their writing, inmates critiqued 'the system.' Without explicitly identifying corrections as a part of that system, they took license in acknowledging the dishonesty, meanness, and suppression that 'the system' encourages" (Interview).

The decision to turn this most famous soliloquy into a group speech was partly sparked by a class discussion where one of the inmates, a white college graduate in his mid-twenties from an upper-middle class background, took issue with the group's take on injustice. Pulling me aside after a writing workshop devoted to the second verse of the speech, he asked "Would Hamlet complain about the economy? He's in the 1%." I talked about the fact that Hamlet never uses the first-person pronoun in the entire speech, and despite the acute nature of his own situation, his comments can be read as a more general commentary on the suffering, uncertainty, and injustice that befall all of humankind of any time period. This sparked a later discussion in class that led to the decision to divide the lines of the adapted speech and chorus among all twenty-seven members of the cast. This choice and the content of the speech itself also deepened the democratic ethos of the production. Not only was the script itself the result of a group process, but its most famous speech was spoken by all of the actors. Furthermore, this speech made our *Hamlet* a distinctly contemporary American play by calling attention to the police corruption and the widening income disparity in the country.

One of the most subtle but powerful ways in which the production worked against the status quo was by creating a genuine community of men who would likely have little to do with each other either on the prison yard or back "on the streets." Bringing together old and young, black and white, urban and rural, the PPA company at NECC truly worked collaboratively not only in class and rehearsal, but when they met and worked on their own. Further boundaries were broken when they performed the play for audiences of other prisoners who laughed and cheered enthusiastically, giving the actors an unprecedented standing ovation, entirely unheard of at the men's prison where wariness and reserve are the norm. Several remarked that during the duration of the forty-five minute show, they entirely forgot they were in prison. One audience member said he had been locked up a very long time and few incidents stood out in his mind. He said, "I remember Reagan getting shot and the Space Shuttle blowing up—and now, this performance." (Of course, the fact that he was comparing the show to disasters of one sort or another was, I hope, unintentional....)

The pleasures that the inmates experienced from the performance were fueled largely by the irreverent dimensions of the production, a subversive element that was heightened by its setting in a correctional institution. And context largely determines the impact and implications of an adaptation: "an adaptation, like the work it adapts, is always going to be framed in a context— and time and a place, a society and a culture; it does not exist in a vacuum" (Hutcheon 142). Turning a Shakespearean tragedy into a comedy and adding elements of contemporary political critique became a two-pronged act of resistance; the inmate actor/authors were simultaneously challenging the authority both of Shakespeare and of the dominant political and cultural institutions that presume to control his meaning and message.

The pleasures that the college professors and their students in attendance for the public performances took from *Hip Hop Hamlet* were undoubtedly different, largely because of their greater familiarity with the Shakespearean source. They appreciated the inside jokes and picked up on more of the Shakespearean allusions and subtleties in the script. Linda Hutcheon describes this pleasure as being key to the reception of adaptations, "Part of the pleasure ... comes simply from repetition with variation, from the comfort of ritual combined with the piquancy of surprise" (4). There are many moments when the script veers very close to or even cites its Shakespearean source while creating a different context and meaning for those lines. For example, the show begins with Hamlet entering the stage alone in jeans and a knee- length leather jacket, while his cell phone rings. He answers the phone with the famous first words of Shakespeare's script, "Who's there?" a line which initiates a prologue where each of the play's characters subsequently enters and introduces himself. Audiences very familiar with Shakespeare's play would immediately recognize the line, while appreciating its radically new cultural and dramatic context, experiencing what "the palimpsestic doubleness that comes with knowing" (Hutcheon 127). The different responses of inside and outside audiences emphasizes how contingent and variable the meaning of any adaptation is and the extent to which context is dependent not just upon physical setting but also the various frames of reference that exists for individual adapters and audience members alike.

During a reception after the public performances the cast, still dressed in their costumes that looked very much like regular street clothes, mingled with members of the audience, and for a while the boundaries between them and even the presence of the prison guards and security cameras around us all receded. While not especially provocative on the surface, I believe this was one of the most compelling elements of the show. PPA's costumes are almost conspicuously ordinary. Blazers, dress shirts, jeans and t-shirts are the mainstays. For the most part inmates on stage look very much like ordinary men, and after the show, when they are seamlessly mingling with the audience, the distinction between them and the public is blurred even further. However brief, this informal post-show socializing is one of the most treasured aspects of being in the company for the actors. They relish the opportunity to get out of their state-issue grey uniforms and into clothes they might have worn on the outside. Both on and off stage they are able to assume an identity other than "offender." While they talk with and enjoy the praise of the audience, it is the silent uniformed guards who now look "other." This is a palpable act of resistance. Agnes Wilcox thought this resistance was heightened in this production because it was an adaptation. Not only were the audience members praising them for their performances but for the play they wrote: "Their adaptation was a pointed display of intellectual competence—a slap in the face to prison staff who have power over inmates, but are painfully like them in race, class, and education. The inmates were exhibiting their new found abilities in front of staff members who are unable to do the same scholarly and creative work (whether from lack of opportunity of lack of aptitude)" (Wilcox, Interview).

As my title implies I think there is both "rhyme and reason" to producing a hip-hop adaptation of Shakespeare in prison, but the project as we both conceived and executed it ended up replicating some of the very problems and tensions I had hoped to avoid. We had imposed hip hop on the inmates rather than letting it emerge organically as it would have if we had operated in a way consistent with the collaborative practice and ethos of devised theatre companies. As much as I am proud of the intellectual and creative work the inmates did and believe that it gave them far more agency and involvement than a traditional adaptation of *Hamlet* would have, Agnes Wilcox and I functioned ultimately as the very kind of experts Brent Blair eschewed in his critique of Shakespeare in prison programs. The college professor and the professional director, while not punitive prison guards, were the ultimate authorities on both the text of the script and the staging of the production itself. While the exercise of such authority is not uncommon in other educational or theatrical contexts—and is, in fact, the basis for much of traditional academic learning—when working in a correctional setting, we cannot forget that coercion is in the air we breathe. As artists and teachers, we like to think of ourselves as liberators in this context and to a significant extent we are. Nonetheless, there is a complex negotiation among various sources of authority, not only the prison's and the State's but mine and even Shakespeare's—or rather the cultural authority that he has come to signify. The inmates themselves assumed authority by becoming "co-authors" with me, with Agnes Wilcox, and with Shakespeare, and the production became a source of artistic and political power, power that we hope will continue to find expression when we publish the script with all twenty-seven inmates listed individually as contributing authors.

Boal himself, whose memoir is entitled *Hamlet and the Baker's Son,* had a life-long relationship with Shakespeare's play and uses it to frame what he hopes for the possibilities of theater: "Shakespeare used to say—not used to say, but he said in *Hamlet* that the theater should be and is like a mirror in which we look at the mirror and then we see our vices and our virtues. I think that's very nice, but I would like to have a mirror with some magic properties in which we could—if we don't like the image that we have in front of us to allow us to penetrate into that mirror and then transform our image and then come back with our image transformed. The act of transforming, I always say, transforms she or he who acts. So to use the theater as a rehearsal for transformation of reality" (Boal, Interview).

While lingering questions remain for me about what it means to teach Shakespeare in prison, even a hip-hop Shakespeare, I do hope that the project contributed to the transformation of the actors and the audiences of *Hip Hop Hamlet*—and that the process itself, however flawed, gave us all a glimpse, even a kind of magic mirror to help us imagine a more just and civil society. While the carceral state and the racial and economic inequities that fuel it persist, I believe that *Hip Hop Hamlet* constituted a meaningful act of resistance to the brutalities experienced locally within the confines of a Missouri prison and has the potential to become a liberating model for future Shakespearean educational projects and theatrical productions on both sides of the razor-wire fence.

St. Mary's College of Maryland

Notes

1. See for example, Laura Bates, *Shakespeare Saved My Life: Ten Years in Solitary with the Bard* (2013); Amy Scott-Douglass, *Shakespeare Inside* (2007); Jean Trounstine, *Shakespeare Behind Bars: The Power of Drama in a Women's Prison* (2001).

2. See *PMLA* 123.3 (May 2008), especially Jonathan Shailor's "When Muddy Flowers Bloom: The Shakespeare Project at the Racine Correctional Institution" (632–42) and Jean Trounstine's "Beyond Prison Education" (674–77).

3. The episode, entitled "Act V," originally aired in 2002 and rebroadcast many times since, features journalist and author Jack Hitt's interviews with inmate actors about *Hamlet*, their roles in it, and its relevance to their lives and their crimes.

4. The Globe-to-Globe festival featured adaptations of all of Shakespeare's plays from all over the world with the promotional tagline "37 different plays, 37 different languages." The Q Brothers' *Othello, the Remix* represented North America in the "language" of hip hop.

5. Boal's critique of Aristotle's *Poetics* resonates with Blair's skepticism about the more conservative implications of Shakespeare-in-prison programs: "Let there be no doubt: Aristotle formulated a very powerful purgative system, the object of which is to eliminate all that is not commonly accepted. [...] It appears in many and varied shapes and media. But its essence does not change. It is designed to bridle the individual, to adjust him to what pre-exists" (*Theatre* 47).

6. For Ogbar's detailed account of the prison trope in hip hop, see his Chapter 5, "The Prison Industrial Complex and Social Control."

7. While I chose to show only scenes from Kenneth Branagh's and Franco Zeffirelli's film adaptations of *Hamlet* in class because they were set in the historical past and wouldn't influence what the inmate adapters created for their own contemporary context, Michael Almereyda's film of *Hamlet* staring Ethan Hawke is similar to *Hip Hop Hamlet* in its overall conceit. Rather than being the new CEO of Elsinore Enterprises, Almereyda's Claudius is the head of "Denmark Corporation."

8. With only one exception, previous PPA productions had employed professional actors from St. Louis to play the female roles to avoid what Agnes Wilcox saw as a potential risk for inmates who took on the roles. In this respect Wilcox is somewhat atypical. Her peers, Jonathan Shailor and Curt Tofteland have always cast male inmates in the female roles.

9. This song was chosen because of the affinity between the lyrics and Hamlet's famous aphorism that "one may smile, and smile, and be a villain" (1.5.106). St. Louis-based choreographer and renown hip-hop dancer Anthony "Redd" Williams came to the prison on two occasions to teach the men a routine that he had created for the show.

10. The particular function of the *Springer* scene was especially evident in the per-

formances done for other inmates who laughed uproariously, many to the point of tears, as Gracie Mae camped it up on stage.

11. On August 9, 2014, an unarmed African American, eighteen-year-old Michael Brown, was shot and killed in Ferguson, Missouri, by a white police officer, Darren Wilson. Local protests, some peaceful and some violent, spread across the country in response to what many saw as a pattern of excessive force on the part of police officers against unarmed African American men. While never explicitly discussed in class, the events of Ferguson provided an important context for the writing of *Hip Hop Hamlet* at NECC, located eighty miles north of Ferguson.

WORKS CITED

"Act V." *This American Life*. NPR. WBEZ, Chicago. August 9, 2002. Radio.

Bates, Laura. *Shakespeare Saved My Life: Ten Years in Solitary with the Bard*. Naperville, IL: Sourcebooks, 2013.

Blair, Brent. "Banishing Romeo." Shakespeare in Prisons Conference. University of Notre Dame, South Bend, IN. November 16, 2013. Conference Presentation.

Boal, Augusto. Interview. *Democracy Now*. June 3, 2005. Web. Accessed May 3, 2014.

_____. *Theatre of the Oppressed*. Trans. Charles A. and Maria-Odilia Leal McBride. New York: Theatre Communications Group, 1985.

Charlebois, Elizabeth. "'Their Minds Transfigured So Together': Imaginative Transformation and Transcendence *in A Midsummer Night's Dream*." *Performing New Lives: Prison Theatre*. Ed. Jonathan Shailor. London and Philadelphia: Jessica Kingsley, 2011. 256–69.

Hip Hop: Beyond Beats and Rhymes. Dir. Byron Hurt, 2006.

Hutcheon, Linda. *A Theory of Adaptation*. New York: Routledge, 2006.

Ogar, Jeffrey O. *Hip-Hop Revolution: The Culture and Politics of Rap*. Lawrence: University Press of Kansas, 2007.

Pensalfini, Rob. Shakespeare in Prisons Conference. University of Notre Dame. South Bend, IN. November 16, 2013. Conference Presentation.

_____. "Shakespeare of the Oppressed." *Teaching Shakespeare Beyond the Centre*. Ed. Kate Flaherty, Penny Gay, and L.E. Semler. London: Palgrave Macmillan, 2013. 225–236.

Rose, Tricia. *The Hip Hop Wars: What We Talk About When We talk About Hip Hip Hop—And Why It Matters*. New York: Basic, 2008.

Scott-Douglass, Amy. *Shakespeare Inside: The Bard Behind Bars*. New York: Continuum, 2007.

Trounstine, Jean. *Shakespeare Behind Bars: The Power of Drama in a Women's Prison*. New York: St. Martin's Press, 2001.

Shakespeare, William. *The Tragedy of Hamlet, Prince of Denmark*. Ed. Sylvan Barnet. New York: New American Library, 1998.

Wilcox, Agnes. "Inmates, Actors, Characters, the Audience, and the Poet." *Performing New Lives: Prison Theatre*. Ed. Jonathan Shailor. London and Philadelphia: Jessica Kingsley, 2011. 247–253.

_____. Personal Interview. August 21, 2015.

Strange Interludes: Wallace Stevens and the Theatrical *Event*

D OUG P HILLIPS

Abstract

If, as the philosopher Simon Critchley argues, philosophy is born out of two kinds of disappointment—religious and political—then I would like to add a third: theatrical disappointment. *What follows is a philosophical reflection, in thirteen parts, on what I believe theatre must do in order to be an* Event *rather than a disappointment. To help make my case I draw upon the work and life of the poet and playwright Wallace Stevens—as well as upon a range of theorists and philosophers—to offer, in Shelley's words, "a prismatic and many-sided mirror" of the theatrical* Event, *defined here as that which has the capacity to* turn lives around. *To experience such an* Event—*a rupture in the fabric of the everyday, of business as usual—would be to experience a subjective transformation, and therefore be anything but a* disappointment.

1—Theatre of Trope

A blackbird was for Wallace Stevens the object of thirteen ways of looking and so too it happens was *theatre*, a word which appears in precisely thirteen different lines—and thirteen lines *only*—throughout his 400-plus published poems.[1] In one such line, from "Notes Toward a Supreme Fiction," Stevens refers to the "Theatre of trope" (1997: 343), an apt if radically condensed description of what was, for him, poetry's chief *raison*: to dramatize in often exuberant language the myriad ways we metaphorize our world. Through a play of words, thought Stevens, we fashion and refashion reality into whatever fictions best suit our lives. As he explains in his 1941 lecture "The Noble Rider and the Sound of Words," "what makes the poet the potent figure that he is, or was, or ought to be, is that he *creates the world to which we turn incessantly* and without knowing it and that he gives to life the supreme fictions without which we are unable to conceive of it" (1951: 31, italics mine). If poetry is a *theatre of trope*—a staging of "supreme fictions"—then what might theatre itself be? At root, a trope, from the Greek *tropos*, refers to a *turning* (as in a *turn* of phrase or speech). So we might think of theatre, at its very best, as a *theatre of turning*. That is, what happens in the theatre—the theatrical *Event*— is what *turns* us around: it turns around not only the lives on stage, but possibly as well the lives of those who happen to be looking. The playwright, like the poet, *creates the world to which we turn incessantly*.

Interlude

That Wallace Stevens (1879–1955) wrote plays—all *three* of them between the years 1916 and 1917—is a fact hardly remembered, and may have been forgotten altogether were it not for their publication in the posthumous volume *Opus Posthumous* (1957). Stevens himself seems to have put his plays quickly out of mind after writing them, forgoing even the opportunity to attend the first production of his first play, *Three Travelers Watch a Sunrise*,[2] at the Provincetown Playhouse in 1920. A few weeks after the performance he wrote to Harriet Monroe: "I was in New York while they were doing the play but did not have the opportunity to see it or even to see anyone to make inquiries. So much water has gone under the bridge since the thing was written that I have not the curiosity even to read it to see how it looks at this late day" (1996: 216).

To be sure, Stevens's plays are few (one of the three was published posthumously), brief (two are roughly a dozen pages in length; the other is half that), and *weird* in a way that points toward the theatre of the absurd.[3] Sounding every bit like Beckett, Stevens characterized his second play, *Carlos Among the Candles*,[4] as a "theatre without action or characters" (1996: 203). His stint as a playwright was short-lived. In a 1951 letter, he explains: "I gave up writing plays because I had much less interest in dramatic poetry than in elegiac poetry" (1996: 729).

Stevens was no doubt turned around by his brief experimentation with theatre, which is to say he was *turned* away from it,[5] but the plays themselves— in particular *Three Travelers Watch a Sunrise*—give example to what I'm calling the *theatre of turning*. In *Three Travelers,* three Chinese characters gather atop a wooded hill where they philosophize on the way reality shifts when affected by light and time (a theme Stevens will revisit in *Carlos Among the Candles*):

But when the sun shines on the earth,
In reality
It does not shine on a thing that remains
What is was yesterday.
The sun rises
On whatever the earth happens to be [1997: 603–04].

Meanwhile, a young gentleman has hanged himself in the forest in front of his young lover, "his neighbor's daughter" (608), an event the three characters (whose collective role seems to be that of a chorus) anticipate and comment upon. Not only are we confronted by a continuous *turning* of perspectives[6]—including one speech toward the end that Stevens referred to as the "point of the play"[7]—but by a suicide: a *turning*, as it were, *in extremis*. For Slavoj Žižek, suicide is "the act *par excellence*" (1992: 44),[8] the ultimate transformative *Event* whereby one is obviously not "the same as before" (44).

What Kafka has to say about the reading of certain kinds of books—that they should affect us "like a suicide"—applies equally to what I'm calling (and *calling for*) the *theatre of turning*, the theatrical *Event*. As you read Kafka's 1904 letter below, addressed to his schoolmate Oskar Pollak, try substituting the word "play(s)" for "book(s)," and "see(ing)" for "read(ing)," and you'll see what I mean:

I think we ought to read only the kind of books that wound and stab us. If the book we're reading doesn't wake us up with a blow on the head, what are we reading it for? So that it will make us happy [?] [...] Good Lord, we would be happy precisely if we had no books, and the kind of books that make us happy are the kind we could write ourselves if we had to. But we need the books that affect us like a disaster, that grieve us deeply, like the death of someone we loved more than ourselves, like being banished into forests far from everyone, like a *suicide*. A book must be the axe for the frozen sea inside us. That is my belief" [16, italics mine].

Once more, with "plays" inserted: "But we need the *plays* that affect us like a disaster, that grieve us deeply, like the death of someone we loved more than ourselves, like being banished into forests far from everyone, like a suicide."

Such a disaster would be a *turning*; such a suicide, the *Event*.

2—Scenes of the Theatre

Rooted in the Greek *theatron* or *thea*, the word *theatre* refers to a place of *looking*—or rather, a place of *seeing*. To look at it another way, Stevens's poem "Thirteen Ways of Looking at a Blackbird" is—as a *theatre of trope*—a panoramic *looking* at a blackbird's *turnings*. In the third section, for example, we get:

> The blackbird whirled in the autumn winds,
> It was a small part of the pantomime [1997: 75].

And in the eleventh section, this:

> The river is moving.
> The blackbird must be flying [1997: 76].

We might call these turnings, to borrow a line from Stevens's poem "The Auroras of Autumn," the "scenes of the theatre" (1997: 358). And what we see in such scenes—in such *turnings*—isn't what's static but what's *possible*.[9] To experience the theatrical *Event*, then, is like looking at Stevens's blackbird: it's a *looking* at what's *possible*.

Interlude

The predominant, recurring theme of Stevens's poetry is the relation between *Reality* and the *Imagination*. That is, Stevens is interested in the way our poetic *Imagination* gives rise to what we call *Reality*,[10] which for him is another word for "supreme fiction." At its best, theatre does much the same thing. As a place of imagination, it turns us toward new ways of looking, of envisioning new realities. And as a place of looking, it turns us toward new ways of *imagining*. In short, the theatre is a place of supreme fictions (i.e., a *theatre of trope*) where we are compelled to *look* and taught to *imagine* and turned toward the *possible*.

Hugh Kenner tells us that "in Stevens's world there are no actions and no speeches, merely ways of *looking* at things" (78, italics mine). Likewise, writes Irving Howe, "in Stevens's poetry the eye is the central organ of consciousness [...]. Stevens is a revolutionist of the *imagination*, neither exhorting nor needing to exhort but demonstrating through poetry the *possibilities* of consciousness" (58, italics mine). For Howe, Stevens's recurring use of the subjunctive "as if"

> charts a characteristic *turning* or soaring of his mind, which is then followed by another opening of perception. And these, in *turn*, are openings to the *drama* of the mind as it reaches out toward new modes of awareness [...]. There may be thirteen or three hundred and thirteen ways of *looking* at a blackbird, but what matters is that the eye, and the mind behind the eye, should encompass the life of these *possible* ways and the excitement of their variety [58, italics mine].

Oscar Wilde draws upon a similar notion of looking[11] in his dramatic dialogue *The Decay of Lying*, with an emphasis on the aesthetic: "Things are because we see them, and what we see, and how we see it, depends on the Arts that have influenced us. To look at a thing is very different from seeing a thing. One does not see anything until one sees its beauty. Then, and then only, does it come into existence" (312). Stevens's own take on art and *looking* and the "drama of the mind" (as Howe puts it) can be found in his notebooks:

> The relation of art to life is of the first importance especially in a skeptical age since, in the absence of a belief in God, the mind *turns* to its own creations and examines them, not alone from the aesthetic point of view, but for what they *reveal*, for what they validate and invalidate, for the support they give [1997: 916, italics mine].

With all of this emphasis on *looking*, one could easily get the impression that Stevens's work—as well as my conception of the theatrical *Event*, of the *theatre of turning*—is something (*à la* Wilde) purely aesthetic rather than, in Stevens's words above, *supportive* or even *political*. To take this position, however, would be to dismiss or ignore altogether the implications of the *possible*, which is precisely what *looking*—and the *imagination*—opens us to. A political act, after all, begins with an imagined future; it is born out of a belief in what is *possible*—and belief, for Stevens anyway, is another word for *imagination*, for ways of *looking*. Such is the case with Stevens's late, long poem "The Auroras of Autumn," a ten-part *look* at the way possibility opens to other possibilities; the way myth succeeds to other myths; the way "scenes of the theatre" lead to other scenes. In the words of Marie Borroff, there is in the poem a "theatrical celebration of the world," as well as a "theatre motif" running throughout. This motif includes various nods to *Hamlet*,[12] and to its eponymous hero whom we know of course to be a consummate looker.

3—And If It Be Theatre for Theatre

The first sentence of the last section of Stevens's poem "Repetitions of a Young Captain" opens with the words "And if it be theatre for theatre" and closes with "the choice is made" (1997: 274). With his usual ambiguity, Stevens opens himself to multiple interpretations; however, I would like to consider this statement—in isolation from the poem in which it appears—as a proposition generally reflective of what many people understand to be the purpose of theatre. That is, "if it be theatre for theatre"—if it be theatre for the sake of theatrical entertainment—then "the choice is made," which is to say everything is carefully orchestrated in advance for the enjoyment of theatregoers. Nothing, in other words, is left to chance, though the chance *Event*, as every seasoned director knows, can't be so easily corralled or kept at bay. But no matter. It's the chance *Event* that often saves an otherwise mediocre and forgettable production from historical obscurity. In this way, the chance *Event* is rather like Stevens placing a jar in Tennessee,[13] around which everything else—memory especially—adheres.

Interlude

For those of us who frequent the theatre on a semi-regular basis, we have our stories, and here are two of mine:

(1) In NYC in 2008, at the Theatre for the New City, I attended a production of Rebecca Schull's *On Naked Soil: Imagining Anna Akhmatova*. As the title indicates, the play is about the life of the poet Anna Akhmatova, much of it set in war-torn Russia among the displaced and starving. In one such scene Anna is conversing at a kitchen table, on top of which is a bowl containing, among other things, a juicy-looking orange with its little blue produce sticker (Sunkist?) easily visible to those of us in the front row. It's winter. It's Russia. The war is going badly. The people are hungry. Prop-wise the Sunkist orange seems, well, *out of place*.

(2) In the summer of 2012, on the Greek Island of Hydra, I had the pleasure of watching contemporary theatrical spins on the figures of Iphigenia, Elektra, and Ajax. Because this was Greece, and because the theatre was outdoors, cats would sometimes wander un-scripted onto the stage, observe the action for a second or two, then wander back off. While I remember each of the three plays to be quite good—all of them lively and well-performed—the particulars have long since faded. Except for the cats. The cats I'll never forget.

The point of my two tales in relation to the theatrical *Event*—specifically, the chance *Event*—has everything to do with what Roland Barthes calls the *punctum*, a term he applies to photography, but which I find equally useful for theatre.[14] If for Barthes the *studium* of a photograph is what's apparent, obvious, easily recognized, and digestible, then the *punctum* refers to the accidental, the incidental, the charming or disarming detail or chance *Event* that "pricks" the viewer by disrupting, subtly or unsubtly, the photograph's (in our case, the stage's) gloss and composition. The same is true of theatre: to experience the *punctum*—the Greek cats, the Sunkist-stickered orange—is to experience the *pricking* of the theatrical *Event*.

4—A Tempest Cracked on the Theatre

A turn of events, we are prone to say, when things go in a way we're not usually expecting, when what we previously thought impossible opens suddenly to the *possible*. Whether we are open to *living* the *Event* so-turned is another question, however. "A tempest cracked on the theatre," begins

Stevens's poem "Repetitions of a Young Captain," after which we're told, "The people sat in the theatre, in the ruin, / As if nothing had happened"[15] (1997: 306). If something were to happen—an *Event*, after all, is a thing that *happens*—then how would the people know, and in what way might their lives be *turned*?

Interlude

In his letters, Stevens references his poem "Repetitions of a Young Captain" only once, apparently in response to a translator's query. Later, in this same letter from 1945, Stevens confesses: "I read little or no fiction, and really read very much less of everything than most people. It is more interesting to sit round and look out the window" (490). Whether he realized it at the time, Stevens's predilection for looking out the window speaks in important ways, I think, to the content of "Repetitions of a Young Captain," as well as to that poem's recurring metaphor of theatre. Both experiences—the *looking* out of windows and, as I have been describing it, the experience of the theatrical *Event* (the *theatre of turning*)—tap into one of Stevens's most persistent themes: the "making interior of the exterior" (Sharpe 20).

In his explication of "Repetitions of a Young Captain," Alan Perlis describes a captain returned from war who is trying to reconcile the reality of his exterior world—of what he has done and seen—with the interior of who he now imagines himself to be:

> We gather from the poem's beginning that the captain, while overseas and in the midst of war, has experienced an *event*, possibly the one that he narrates, that has been traumatic for him. Having returned to America, he realizes that the *event* has lost its clear edges in the time-warp of memory [69–70, italics mine].

"What he hopes to accomplish in his new environment," explains Perlis, "is a total change of consciousness" (71); eventually, "he has acquired the ability to transform" (72). Perlis then offers the following encapsulation: "The captain's heroic victory signals a pervasive theme in all of Stevens's major poems written after World War II: constant meditation on the world of objects brings with it a self-understanding in the human spirit" (72). Might this "meditation on the world of objects" be the very thing we do when we look out windows? And might the experience of theatre—that place of seeing—be akin to looking out windows, whereby we make interior the exterior of what we are seeing?[16] Whereby, for example, Hamlet's existential ruminations on whether life is worth living become part of our own interior?

A contemporary of Stevens, American artist Edward Hopper (1882–1967)[17] is perhaps the great painter of people looking out windows, all of whom appear to be "making interior of the exterior."[18] A life-long lover of theatre and opera, Hopper makes frequent use of these subjects in his paintings. Like those depicted looking out windows, his theatregoers and ushers are typically figured in reflective isolation as though the "scenes of the theatre" were scenes of their own psyches. In the presence of theatrical *Event*, they often appear "in ruin," as if something has most definitely *happened*.

In his essay "The Importance of Staring Out the Window," Alain de Botton writes,

> The point of staring out of a window is, paradoxically, not to find out what is going on outside. It is, rather, an exercise in discovering the contents of our own minds. It's easy to imagine we know what we think, what we feel and what's going on in our heads. But we rarely do entirely. [...] If we do it right, staring out the window offers a way for us to listen out for the quieter suggestions and perspectives of our deeper selves [Botton].

The theatrical *Event*, like that of staring out the window, affords us—and Hopper's introspective figures—"suggestions and perspectives of our deeper selves." This is what it would mean to be *turned*. This is the moment when the "audience listens," as Stevens writes in his poem "Of Modern Poetry," "not to the play, but to itself" (1997: 218).

5—Then the Theatre Was Changed

In "Of Modern Poetry," Stevens, drawing yet again upon the metaphor of theatre, identifies what he understands to be the condition and task of modern poetry in a new century:

> Then the theatre was changed
> To something else [...]
> And it has to find what will suffice. It has
> To construct a new stage [1997: 218–19].

"As early as 1909," observes Sara Ford, "Stevens considered the modern condition in terms of the theatre" (97). In a letter to his wife that same year, he writes, "We are where we have been, listening to what we have never heard. We are in a dark place listening [...]. And is it all on stage? And can't you possibly close your eyes and, by imagination, feel that it is perfectly real?" (qtd. Ford 97). "Of Modern Poetry," adds Ford, is Stevens's "best known example of the theatrical metaphor" (97), a poem that—like so much of his work—imagines new possibilities, new realities, and therefore "makes any stable, actual world, any world that is not invented, a distanced one, one very much not of ourselves" (97).

Interlude

Not only poetry but theatre *itself* is in need of a new stage, argues the philosopher-playwright Alain Badiou in his short philosophical treatise, *Rhapsody for the Theatre*: "I would like for the theatre not to be a mirror, or a redoubling, of the confused, frenetic and stagnant world to which the somber dictatorship of profit confines us. I would like it to be a lightning strike, an elucidation, and an exhortation" (*Rhapsody* 156). Here, Badiou's wish for a "lightning strike" brings to mind not only Stevens's image of a tempest cracking on the theatre,[19] but also Žižek's concept of the *Event*: "an event par excellence strikes us like lightning and shatters our entire life" (2014: 79–80). For Badiou, such a life-shattering theatrical *Event* would be "something that brings to light a possibility that was invisible or even unthinkable. An event is not by itself the creation of a reality; it is the creation of a possibility, it opens up a possibility. It indicates to us that a possibility exists that has been ignored" (*Philosophy* 9).

If, however, most theatre—with the exception of improvisation, of course—is carefully scripted, blocked, directed, and rehearsed, then what chance is there for a chance *Event* (beyond, that is, an unintentionally ridiculous prop or errant cat), for something momentous to *happen*, for lightning to strike in such a way that it "shatters our entire life"? How in other words might theatre open us to the *possible*—to the *Event*—when the very notion of possibility seems to be foreclosed from the start?

Such a line of questioning presumes of course that theatre is only and ever a *representation* (re-presentation) of sameness, rather than an occasion for what Gilles Deleuze calls *repetition*, a term he uses in connection with the *Event*. As Timothy Murray explains, "It is the philosophical aim of the theatre of representation to leave identity intact, whether character, author, actor or spectator" (203). Deleuze, however, "wished to mess up representation's sameness with the intensities, movements and repetitions of a theatre whose end is to problematize the final object of knowledge, or the final recognition of anything traditionally understood as identity" (Murray 204). Much like Deleuze's "repetitions of a theatre," Stevens's poetry ("Repetitions of a Young Captain," for example) disrupts our notion of a "stable, actual world" (Ford 97). To put it another way, Max Startkiewicz explains that "Repetition, Deleuzian repetition, just like rereading, is always a repetition of the different, displaying the uniqueness of any gesture, of any word" (110). With every repetition, then, comes the experience of *difference*, which disrupts our sense of identity, much in the way Stevens disrupts the identity of a blackbird through his thirteen repeated viewings. This disruption of identity, in turn, makes room for the new, the *possible*. That is, with repetition comes the possibility for invention, for new imaginings.

In "Of Modern Poetry" Stevens suggests that a world unmade by war—the ultimate life-shattering *Event*—requires yet still more poetry (*repetition*), but of a new order (*difference*). That is, in a post-war world (the "theatre," Stevens calls the world), the once stable order of poetic forms and subject matter no longer suffice. We might, however, read these same lines in such a way that they give additional example to Deleuze's theory on performance and repetition, which goes something like this: Each time you experience a performance of, say, *Waiting for Godot*, the scene will indeed be set and the actors will *repeat* what's in the script (in the case of Beckett, they *must* do these things *or else*!); and yet, for Deleuze, the experience of "true literature" is never the *re-presentation* of sameness. Instead, each experience, while a repetition, is also different. Perhaps the easiest way to understand this is to consider the two-act structure of *Godot*, a play in which one critic famously said "nothing happens, twice."[20] We know, though, that the second act of *Godot* is not merely a re-presentation of the "nothing" of the first act; rather, Act Two *repeats* the "nothing" of Act One, but with *difference*. The same can be said of the entire play, were one to see it night after night, for the entire run.

To state the obvious: no two experiences of *Godot* can be same, if only because you (and the players on stage) won't be the same person you are tonight as you were the night before. And you're certainly not the same person you are now, this very moment, that you were two decades ago, when you first saw *Godot*. On the repetition of so-called "true literature," Claire Colebrook, in her study of Deleuze, writes, "The only thing that is repeated or returns is difference; no two moments of life can be the same" (121). To experience the *Event*, then, depends as much on the particulars of each performance as it does on the circumstances of your own life, no matter how scripted or conventional or off-kilter the overall production. In other words, there's much that is contingent in terms of how theatregoers will be affected by what they see and hear. This is another way of conceptualizing the chance *Event* in theatre (apart from a cat and a Sunkist), the *difference* in every repetition.

As for the theatre of Stevens's poetry, time and again we encounter poems composed of variations on a particular theme or idea, from "The Idea of Order at Key West" to "Variations on a Summer Day" to "Thirteen Ways of Looking at a Blackbird." *Repetition* in Stevens's work is *everywhere*—especially the *Reality-Imagination* idea—but always in relation to *difference*. Together repetition and difference destabilize our notions of identity and so open us to the possible *Event*.

6—As at a Theatre

"As at a Theatre" is the only poem of Stevens's in which the word "theatre" appears in the title. In its last stanza a line reads, "The curtains, when pulled, might show another whole" (1997: 456). To put it another way, a pulled curtain occasions the truth of the *Event* just as Toto occasioned the truth of Oz. And if behind the pulled curtain is "another whole"—a whole other man, let's say, who urges us not to pay attention to him—then we know ourselves to be in the presence of the theatrical *Event*.

Interlude

In Stevens's poetry there are only two references to the word "event," one of which appears in the concluding line of his late poem, "A Discovery of Thought," and speaks crucially to every individual's crowning life event, the survival of birth: "Surviving being born, the event of life" (1997: 459). The other instance of "event" appears in his poem "The Comedian as the Letter C"[21]: "he humbly served / Grotesque apprenticeship to chance event" (1997: 32). Of course, in Stevens's day the word "event" as a philosophical concept did not yet have the currency which later theorists such as Badiou, Derrida, and Deleuze would give it. It's worth noting, though, that William James—who was teaching at Harvard at the turn of the century when Stevens was a student there—uses the word "event" in his 1907 study *Pragmatism* to describe a truth-process: "The truth of an idea is not a stagnant property inherent in it. Truth *happens* to an idea. It *becomes* true, is *made* true by events. Its verity *is* in fact a truth, a process" (78). More than a century later Badiou will speak in quite similar terms: "For me, truth is an undertaking: it is a process made *possible* by the *event*" (*Philosophy* 12, italics mine).

In contrast to the scant references to "event" in Stevens's work, the word "possible" appears thirty-one times, dispersed among twenty-one different poems and one play. Stevens's interest in the *possible* is even written into the title of his poem "Prologues to What Is Possible." To experience the *possible* in the theatre is, as I have been suggesting, to experience the theatrical *Event*, a "process of truth" that begins the very moment the curtain is pulled—when, in Stevens's words, "another whole" might be shown. Such a truth-process recalls Heidegger's notion of *Event*, which, explains Žižek, "designates a new epochal disclosure of Being, the emergence of a new 'world'" (2014: 31). With regards to Stevens's own potential disclosure of Being—that of "another whole"—we might also recall Heidegger's notion of *enframing* as it pertains to the *Event*. Here again Žižek is helpful, explaining that "at its most elementary, event is not something that occurs within the world, but is *a change of the very frame through which we perceive the world and engage in it*" (2014: 10).

The "event"—as Stevens implies and as Žižek defines—is another way of understanding the theatrical *Event*. To pull a curtain and disclose "another whole" is to change the frame "through which we perceive the world and engage in it." Thus we are turned by our experience.

7—A Theatre Floating Through the Clouds

For the philosopher Deleuze, writes Claire Colebrook, "Love is the encounter with another person that opens us up to a *possible* world" (17, italics mine); likewise, I have argued, is our encounter with the theatrical *Event*. It too opens us up to a *possible* world. However, what's meant exactly by a *possible world*? "For Badiou," explains Kenneth Reinhard in his introduction to Badiou's play *The Incident at Antioch*, "theater functions as a kind of laboratory for the experimental production and investigation of new subjectivities, new ideas, and new temporalities" (*Incident* XXIV). Imagine then, as Stevens does in "The Auroras of Autumn," "a theatre floating through the clouds" (1997: 359), on whose stage characters and ideas continually shift and *become*, and that, I think, is something like the theatrical *Event*.

Interlude

Could it be that the chief appeal of academic conferences in general, but of the Comparative Drama Conference in particular,[22] is a longed-for encounter with the *Event, as at a theatre*, which *might show another whole*? Not just *any* event, mind you, of which there are many at the CDC, most notably the presenting of some hundred-plus papers, but an *Event* in the Badiousian sense of the term: that is, the capital-E Event after which, suggests Badiou, your thinking is so upturned that *business* cannot go on *as usual*. Along with the presenting of papers, each a possible big-E Event in its own right, there's also something like a quote-unquote *main* Event at the CDC, be it the Keynote address or the live theatrical performance or the end-of-the-conference hors d'oeuvres and boozy blow-out overlooking the moon-blanched bay. Then too there are the looser, less formal, late-night events, those across the way and around the corner at the *James Joyce Pub* or down the road at *The Horse You Came in On*, where conference-goers reportedly dance drunkenly with the spirit of Edgar Allan Poe. Or perhaps the *Event* you have in mind—and which Badiou cites as its most obvious, most universal example—has something more to do with *love*, in this case the much mythologized if seldom realized conference *hook-up*, the upshot of which is you in a U-Haul six-weeks hence, Westward-bound to your new Squeeze's cat and three-story walk-up.[23] But what of your love for the theatre? What must the nature of the theatrical

Event be like *for you* in order to fall in love? To float through clouds? To turn your life around in such a way that business *can't* go on as usual? Or am I asking too much? At the very least, asks Stevens in "Of Modern Poetry," what must *suffice*?

8—In the Theatre's Bricks

In an interview on the subject of love, Badiou was asked to describe his love of theatre "from the inside [...] from the point of view of the actor you once were" (*Praise*: 91), to which he replied, "It is a unique love that requires you to give up your own body in prey to language, in prey to ideas. As you know, *every philosopher is an actor*, however hostile he feels towards games and simulation" (91–92). Badiou adds that, while philosophers "have been much criticized for being magicians, for captivating people by artificial means and leading them to unlikely truths via paths of seduction," there is also in philosophy "always an element of baring oneself" (92). Similarly, in her book *Talk to Me*, Anna Deavere Smith has this to say about acting: "Acting is the furthest thing from lying that I have encountered. It is the furthest thing from make-believe. It is the furthest thing from pretending. It is the most unfake thing there is. Acting is a search for the authentic, it is a search for the authentic by using the fictional as a frame, a house in which the authentic can live. For a moment. Because, yes indeed, real life inhibits the authentic" (8). From the inside—from "in the theatre's bricks" (1997: 367), as Stevens writes in his poem "In a Bad Time"—we might conceive of the theatrical *Event* as "a house in which the authentic can live" (Smith 8).

Interlude

No modern poet—with perhaps the exception of T. S. Eliot—knew as well as Stevens the ways in which "real life inhibits the authentic" (Smith 8). Like his contemporary Eliot, who, for a time, lived a whole other life as a banker in London, Stevens fashioned a career-long double life working in insurance, first in New York, then in Harford, Connecticut, where he would spend the rest of his life. Unlike Eliot, however, Stevens lived the most untheatrical of lives, having married but once, having never travelled abroad, having never gotten into trouble, having never really even fooled around—having in fact virtually no nose for drama except perhaps that one time, in Key West, when he and Ernest Hemingway exchanged punches.[24]

"I certainly do not exist from nine to six, when I am at the office," writes Stevens in a 1909 letter to his wife, Elsie. "There is no every-day Wallace," Stevens adds, "apart from the one at work—and that one is tedious.—At night

I strut my individual state once more" (1996: 121). Walking each day from home to office, then back again, Stevens would work out poems in his head then put them onto paper the first chance he got. While strutting his "individual state once more," he would, in Smith's words, use "the fictional as a frame" and so, like all poets, don the actor's mask and voice in the creation of his supreme fictions. In this sense, his life was indeed infused with the theatrical, along with "the need for an audience, the need to have his talent appreciated" (Sharpe 61).

9—The Immensest Theatre

> And now I am going to say something which, perhaps,
> is going to stupefy many people.
> I am the enemy
> of theatre.
> I have always been.
> As much as I love the theatre,
> I am, for this very reason, equally its enemy [qtd. Derrida 249].

The words are Artaud's, though I confess I share something of his expressed love-hate relationship with the theatre. It's also a sentiment shared by Badiou, who expresses his own mixed-love toward the stage by distinguishing between what he terms small-t and capital-T Theatre, both of which, he says, are the object of a certain kind of love as well as a pronounced kind of scorn. Of capital-T Theatre, which Badiou ultimately champions for its capacity to turn us around:, "there exists a specific hatred [...] which every soul is capable of. Theatre is of all the art forms the most hated, under the cover of the adoration devoted to 'theatre'" (*Rhapsody* 21). As for this small-t kind of theatre, which Badiou further indicates by always putting it into quotation marks and which, he insists, so many theatregoers adore, it entails "the ritual insipidness of a celebration of self, some laughs, culture, recognizable figures, feeling always one foot ahead, answers that 'hit the nail on the head,' sublime décor, communion during intermission" (*Rhapsody* 23). Plus, adds Badiou, small-t theatre is "fulfilling," for it is "a 'theatre' of established meanings, a 'theatre' from which nothing is lacking and which, abolishing chance, induces a convivial satisfaction in those who hate truth" (21). None of this is a good thing for Badiou, by the way. In contrast, the experience of big-T Theatre is akin to a rupture and so by definition an *Event*. And such theatre, writes Badiou, demands that "its spectator [...] feel the hardness of his seat" (24), for it "entails the process of a truth, of an elucidation whose spectacle would be the event. [...] Because under these conditions, theatre makes it known to you that you will not be able innocently to remain *in your place*" (23). To borrow from Stevens's poem "To an Old Philosopher in Rome," Big-T Theatre is, we might say, "the immensest theatre" (1997: 434). It's the kind of theatre that turns us around.

Interlude

Stevens's use of "immensest" to describe a certain kind of theatre—a word, incidentally, much appreciated by Scrabble enthusiasts but unrecognized by Spellcheck—is typical of his verbal art, the stretch and invention of which are *Events* all their own, in the very way that Joyce's or Shakespeare's uses of language are. Regarding the latter, Stevens expresses in a 1909 letter to his soon-to-be wife, Elsie, his admiration for Shakespeare's "glorious" line: "What a piece of work is man! How noble in reason! How infinite in faculty!" (1996: 143). He continues:

> The quotation from Shakespeare is particularly serviceable to me now, for I have lately had a sudden conception of the true nobility of men and women [...] their nobility does not lie in what they look like but in what they endure and in the manner in which they endure it. [...] One might say that their appearances are like curtains, fair and unfair; the stage is behind—the comedy, and tragedy [1996: 143–44].

Stevens's conception of nobility in relation to endurance, to appearances, and to the stage, points, I think, to another way of conceptualizing the *Event*. If, as both Badiou and Žižek remind us, the *Event* is that which ruptures the fabric of our everyday lives (in the form of falling in love, say, or having just witnessed a *really* good production of *Hamlet*), then what matters next is the manner in which we endure the rupture, the manner in which we live the *process of truth* made possible and set in motion by the rupture in question. For Badiou, such endurance is an ethical principle, what he calls "fidelity to the Event."[25] An example of this idea on stage can be seen in Neil Labute's play *The Mercy Seat*: a young man and his boss have been carrying on an affair, and they happen to be having sex at her apartment the morning of 9/11, rather than tending to business in their appointed offices in the World Trade Center, thus surviving the calamity. The rupture in the fabric of their lives opens up a truth process by which the "real" nature of their love for one another is tested. Will he at last answer his persistently ringing phone and assure his wife and children he's well and fine? Or will he keep silent and pretend to have died so he may begin a new life with his lover? Will his lover consent to such a plan? Will the two of them, in other words, endure the *Event*—that is, will they show their fidelity to it?

There is, however, another way to consider Stevens's verbal art in relation to such writers as Joyce and Shakespeare, which is at the level of syntax and diction, and so a kind of linguistic *Event* on the page whereby the fabric of the ordinary is ruptured by the *choice* word, the *arresting* phrase. In her biography of Stevens, Joan Richardson writes, "As he became more of a poet, Stevens became involved with words in the way others might become involved with children. He played with them, he fondled their sounds, he helped them grow into strong, commanding presences" (446). For R. P. Blackmur, "The most striking if not the most important thing about Mr. Stevens' verse is its vocabulary—the collection of words, many of them uncommon in English poetry [...] and such phrases as 'thrum with a proud douceur,' or 'A pool of pink, clippered with lilies scudding the bright chromes'" (183). Shakespeare's uses of language strikes a similar chord in the mind of the rhetorician Richard Lanham, who recounts what was for him a transformative *Event* of reading Shakespeare: "I saw not the customary Shakespeare of profundities, moral and political, but a Shakespeare infatuated with language and playing wild games with it just for fun, creating characters who would never say 'I don't like it' when they could say 'it is most retrograde to my desire'" (3–4). In contrast to his reputation for being philosophical and difficult, a creator of "high art" on the same order as Eliot and Pound, Stevens—like Shakespeare—was "infatuated with language and playing wild games with it just for fun." Such theatrics are a breaking of form, a piercing of the clichéd. Such language, as both Stevens and Shakespeare stage it, is the *Event*.

10—The People Sat in the Theatre

If the people, as Stevens writes in "Repetitions of a Young Captain," continue to sit "in the theatre [...] as if nothing happened" (271) after a tempest has cracked, then what's happened is decidedly *not* the *Event*.

Interlude

Artaud's poem-like notion of theatre, referenced at the start of #8 above, continues thus:

> The theatre is a passionate overflowing
> a frightful transfer of forces
> > from body
> > to body.
> This transfer cannot be reproduced twice [qtd. Derrida 249].

Written in 1946, Artaud's experience of theatre compresses much of what he argued a decade earlier in his manifesto, *The Theatre and Its Double*. The theatrical *Event*—by definition a passionate, frightful, unreproducible overflowing—cannot be conceptually contained or pinned-down, despite our best efforts to interpret what we've seen. In her essay "Against Interpretation," Susan Sontag warned against our tendency to do just that, *interpret*: to reduce, minimize, fix, formulate, or neuter art as a way to manage our anxiety in the face of its "frightful transfer of forces." Let me explain. I've a friend[26] with whom I sometimes go to the theatre, and whom, after the show, I can always count on to come up with an apt, usually three-part encapsulation-interpretation of whatever it is we've just seen. "It was *Godot* crossed by *Streetcar* crossed by *A Doll's House*," he tells me. "It was Shakespeare meets Chekhov meets David Ives," he sighs. Only when he leaves the theatre with nothing to say, he tells me, is there *really* something worth talking about. Only then, he insists, have we experienced something like an *Event*; only then do we feel the *overflowing*. The result of such an overflowing, Badiou reminds us, is that we can't remain in our place. The tempest cracks and we are swept-up or knocked-over or turned-around, our lives opened to possibility, pointed in new directions.

Unfortunately for Stevens, who envisioned himself early on to be a playwright rather than a poet, this was not the case. His plays reportedly left audiences perplexed and irritated and anything but moved (except quickly out the door!). For Stevens, playwriting turned out to be a non–*Event*, though I suppose it can be said that a non–*Event*—what doesn't happen—can be an *Event* all its own, rather like the non–*Event* of the no-show Godot; or John Marcher of Henry James's story "The Beast in the Jungle," whose singular non–*Event* of life is to be the man to whom nothing happens. In 1935, years after his first two plays were performed to the bafflement of critics, Stevens wrote, "I think it quite likely that I should have been more interested in the theatre if those two experiments had not given me the horrors" [1996: 291].

11—In a Theatre, Full of Tragedy

Of theories and prescriptions and manifestos for what is needed in order for theatre to be an *Event* there are many. For Artaud, it's that which can't be reproduced twice. As Derrida explains, "*Artaud wanted to erase repetition in general.* For him, repetition was evil, and one could doubtless organize an entire reading of his texts around this center. Repetition separates force, presence, and life from themselves" (245). As mentioned already, however, Deleuze recuperates the notion of repetition in relation to difference; that is, repetition opens the way to what is possible. To reiterate, Deleuze's concept of repetition is distinct from the *re-presentation* of the same, which is what Artaud railed against. Derrida too writes of the vitality of repetition (as opposed to representation), especially as it pertains to Artaud's Theatre of Cruelty, arguing that the "menace of repetition is nowhere else as well organized as in the theatre" (247). Long before Derrida and Deleuze and Artaud, however, Shelley made a similar case in *A Defense of Poetry* against representation or, as he calls it, "reiteration." As an *Event*, the theatre resuscitates a universe made dormant if not annihilated by familiarity. Specifically, Shelley writes that poetry—of which Athenian drama was for him the finest specimen—"purges from our inward sight the film of familiarity which obscures from us the wonder of our being. It compels us to feel that which we perceive, and to imagine that which we know. It creates anew the universe after it has been annihilated in our minds by the recurrence of impressions by reiteration" (354). For Shelley, this is the *Event* of theatre, its necessary "atmosphere," as Stevens might characterize it in his poem "Lettres D'un Soldat": "In a theatre full of tragedy, / The stage becomes an atmosphere / Of seeping rose—" (1997: 544).

Interlude

Repetition in Stevens's second play *Carlos Among the Candles* (1917) approaches Beckettian proportions as Carlos—"an eccentric pedant of about forty" (1997: 615)—lights a dozen candles before extinguishing them one by one, first reflecting upon the changing nature of self amid the flames and shadows, then upon the transitory condition of all things. In the course of the play's brief six pages, the stage eventually becomes an atmosphere, if not of "seeping rose" then of dimming light—a theatre, we might say, tilting toward tragedy. The situation recalls Shelley's argument in *A Defense of Poetry* for the way in which drama "purges from our inward sight the film of familiarity which obscures from us the wonder of our being" (354). This purging of familiarity and subsequent revealing of the wonder of our being is, in fact, Stevens's entire dramatic and poetic project.

A Defense of Poetry, writes Harold Bloom, was for Stevens the "most inescapable" (134) of Shelley's prose, though one can also find in Stevens's poetry allusions to a number of Shelley's poems, and even a direct reference to Shelley himself in the long poem, "Owl's Clover":

> On pattering leaves and suddenly with lights,
> Astral and Shelleyan, diffuse a new day [1997:155].

In a 1940 letter, written largely to address and explicate the section above, Stevens writes, "What is necessary is to recognize change as a constant. Life is chaos" (1996: 367). Shortly after, in the same letter, Stevens observes the way in which we transform the world—via our poetic imagination—even if the "structure of nature" repeats and remains the same:

The astral and Shelleyan lights are not going to alter the structure of nature. Apples will always be apples, and whoever is the ploughman hereafter will be what the ploughman has always been. For all that, the astral and the Shelleyan will have *transformed the world* [367, italics mine].

The theatrical *Event*, I'm proposing, is for Stevens the very experience Shelley puts forth in *A Defense of Poetry*: "It creates anew the universe after it has been annihilated in our minds by the recurrence of impressions by reiteration" (354).

12—The Theatre Is Spinning Round

"The theatre is spinning round" (311), writes Stevens in his poem "Chaos in Motion and Not in Motion," but what might be the consequence of this chaos—the effect of all this spinning—for both spectator and actor? In other words, what becomes of us in the presence of the theatrical *Event*?

Interlude

If *Event* it indeed be, then the spectator, I submit, undergoes the very transformation which Stevens claims for the blackbird, and which Badiou claims for the actor: "the actor exhibits onstage the evaporation of every stable essence. The decisiveness of the bodily and vocal gestures in which he or she presents himself or herself serves above all to establish, in delight and surprise, that nothing coincides with itself" (*Rhapsody* 63). Given that his own work-life in insurance was a world apart from his poetic life, Stevens knew as well as anyone that nothing coincides with itself.

"I know myself to be incalculable," says Carlos in Stevens's play *Carlos Among the Candles,* "since the causes of what I am are incalculable" (1997: 619).

13—The Theatre Is Filled with Flying Birds

"The drama, so long as it continues to express poetry," argues Shelley in *A Defense of Poetry*, "is as *a prismatic and many-sided mirror*, which collects the brightest rays of human nature and divides and reproduces them from the simplicity of these elementary forms, and touches them with majesty and beauty, and multiplies all that it reflects, and endows it with the power of propagating its like wherever it may fall" (346, italics mine). To think of it another way, as Stevens does in "The Auroras of Autumn," "The theatre is filled with flying birds" (1997: 359). The trope is clear enough: In the theatre what we see taking flight is ourselves. The stage, an impetus toward new turnings; the theatrical *Event*, a transformation of self.

Interlude

In Stevens's play *Carlos Among the Candles*, the lone character Carlos poses a question that sets in motion the fall of the curtain: "What is there in the extinguishing of light?"

His answer: "It is like twelve wild birds flying in autumn" [619].

UNIVERSITY OF ST. THOMAS

NOTES

1. In a late, uncollected poem titled "Lynton Strachey, Also, Enters into Heaven," there does appear the word "theater," though notice its alternative spelling. My source text for all of Stevens's poetry is the Library of America's fine and authoritative volume, *Wallace Stevens: Collected Poetry & Prose*.

2. Published in 1916 in *Poetry*.

3. In *Letters of Wallace Stevens*, the editor (Holly Stevens—daughter of) writes, "Stevens's letter of October 31, 1917, to Harriet Monroe contains a comment on it that is particularly relevant in light of today's theater of the absurd" (189–90).

4. *Carlos Among the Candles* was published in 1917 in *Poetry* and first performed the same year. Scheduled for a two week run, it was basically incomprehensible to both spectators and critics, and so closed after the first night.

5. "In terms of his personality," writes Joan Richardson in her biography of Stevens, "his romance with playwriting showed how fragile he was [...] when a production of another of his plays met with failure, he turned completely away from the theatre" (452).

6. A "turning of perspectives" or "variations on a theme" pretty much describes the whole Stevens oeuvre.

7. "The point of the play, by the way, is [...] in the last sentence of the final speech" (1996: 195), wrote Stevens in a 1916 letter to Harriet Monroe. Those lines read: "Sunrise is multiplied, / Like the earth on which it shines, / By the eyes that open on it, / Even dead eyes, / As red is multiplied by the leaves of trees" (1997: 613).

8. Žižek's use of the word "act" can be, I think, understood as a theatrical metaphor.

9. "The imagination," writes Stevens in his essay "Imagination as Value," "is the power of the mind over the *possibilities* of things [...] it is the source not of a certain single value but of as many values as reside in the *possibilities* of things" (1951: 136, italics mine).

10. See Stevens's 1951 collection of essays, *The Necessary Angel: Essays on Reality and Imagination*. As for his poetry, Stevens's 1936 collection of poems, *Ideas of Order*, is—in title, anyway—most overtly expressive of his interest in the *Reality-Imagination Idea*, as is the most remembered poem from the collection: "The Idea of Order at Key West." The philosopher-playwright Alain Badiou shares Stevens's interest in the *Idea*, and links it to the philosophical concept of the *Event*: "I name the 'idea' that which, regarding a given question, proposes the perspective of a new possibility. [...] An idea is associated with an event because the event is the creation of a possibility and the Idea is the general name of the new possibility" (2013: 14).

11. In her review of Stevens's first book of poems, *Harmonium* (1923), Marianne Moore compares Stevens to Wilde: "so wakeful is he [Stevens] in his appetite for color and in perceiving what is needed to meet the requirements of a new tone key, that Oscar Wilde [among others] seem children asleep in comparison with him" (92).

12. In a lecture on Stevens's poem "The Auroras of Autumn," Marie Borroff explains that there are "a number of allusions in the poem to the play *Hamlet*." Plus, she says, "There's a lot of theater. Theater is one of the motifs of the poem [...] you see it again and again."

13. See Stevens's poem "Anecdote of the Jar."

14. For more on the *punctum*, see Barthes's *Camera Lucida*. Plus, see Wayne Koestenbaum's introduction to Barthes's *A Lover's Discourse*.

15. This "As if" line is an example of Irving Howe's commentary on Stevens's use of the subjunctive (in relation to *turning*) mentioned earlier.

16. Strindberg was especially fascinated with the importance of windows—and window symbolism—in relation to theatre, about which Hans-Goran Ekman offers instructive commentary in his study *Strindberg and the Five Senses*.

17. Stevens and Hopper were born but three years apart and just down the road from one another.

18. In his study *Remaining Light: Ant Meditations on a Painting by Edward Hopper*, John Taggart opens by drawing a link between Hopper and Stevens, suggesting therefore "the possibility of reading Stevens through Hopper" (1).

19. See Stevens's poem "Repetitions of a Young Captain."

20. The quip belongs to Vivian Mercier.

21. Title-wise, Stevens's poems have the same intrigue and curbside appeal as the titles of Raymond Carver's short stories. One can no more resist Stevens's "The Emperor of Ice Cream" or "The Final Soliloquy of the Interior Paramour" than one can Carver's "What We Talk about When We Talk about Love" or "Would You Please Be Quiet, Please?"

22. Also known as the "CDC," the Comparative Drama Conference began in 1977 at the University of Florida and is now hosted by Stevenson University in Baltimore. Yearly it draws scholars from around the world who gather to present their latest findings on all things related to theatre.

23. True story.

24. See Ernest Hemingway's letter to Sara Murphy, dated February 27, 1936.

25. For more on fidelity in relation to the *Event*, see Badiou's *Ethics: An Essay on the Understanding of Evil*.

26. The old codger.

WORKS CITED

Badiou, Alain. *Ahmed the Philosopher: Thirty-Four Short Plays for Children and Everyone Else*. Trans. Joseph Litvak. New York: Columbia University Press, 2014.

_____. *Ethics: An Essay on the Understanding of Evil*. New York: Verso, 2012.

_____. *The Incident at Antioch*. Trans. Susan Spitzer. New York: Columbia University Press, 2013.

_____. *In Praise of Love*. Trans. Peter Bush. New York: New Press, 2012.

_____. *Philosophy and the Event*. Cambridge: Polity, 2013.

_____. *Rhapsody for the Theatre.* Trans. Bruno Bosteels. New York: Verso, 2013.

Baker, Carlos, ed. *Ernest Hemingway: Selected Letters, 1917–1961.* New York: Scribner, 1981.

Barthes, Roland. *Camera Lucida: Reflections on Photography.* Trans. Richard Howard. New York: Hill and Wang, 1979.

Blackmur, R.P. "Examples of Wallace Stevens." *Form and Value in Modern Poetry.* New York: Doubleday, 1957.

Bloom, Harold. *The Anatomy of Influence: Literature as a Way of Life.* New Haven: Yale University Press, 2011.

Boroff, Maria. "Lecture 20—Wallace Stevens." Open Yale Courses. ENGL 310: Modern Poetry. oyc.yale.edu/english/engl-310/lecture-20. Web.

Botton, Alain de. "The Importance of Staring Out Windows." *The Book of Life.* www.thebookoflife.org/the-importance-of-staring-out-the-window/ Web.

Colebrook, Claire. *Gilles Deleuze.* London: Routledge, 2002.

Derrida, Jacque. "The Theatre of Cruelty and the Closure of Representation." *Writing and Difference.* Trans. Alan Bass. Chicago: University of Chicago Press, 1993.

Ekman, Hans-Goran. *Strindberg and the Five Senses.* London: Bloomsbury, 2001.

Ford, Sara J. *Gertrude Stein and Wallace Stevens: The Performance of Modern Consciousness.* New York: Routledge, 2002.

Howe, Irving. "Another Way of Looking at the Blackbird." *Critical Essays on Wallace Stevens.* Eds. Steven Gould Axelrod and Helen Deese. Boston: G.K. Hall, 1988.

James, William. *Pragmatism.* 1907. New York: Dover, 1995.

Kafka, Franz. *Letters to Friends, Family, and Editors.* Trans. Richard and Clara Winston. New York: Schocken, 1977.

Kenner, Hugh. *A Homemade World: The American Modernist Writers.* New York: Knopf, 1975.

Labute, Neil. *The Mercy Seat.* New York: Faber, 2003.

Lanham, Richard A. *Style: An Anti-Textbook.* Philadelphia: Paul Dry, 2007.

Moore, Marianne. "Well Moused, Lion." *The Complete Prose of Marianne Moore.* Ed. Patricia C. Willis. New York: Viking, 1986.

Murray, Timothy. "Like a Prosthesis: Critical Performances á Digital Deleuze." *Deleuze and Performance.* Ed. Laura Cull. *Edinburgh*: Edinburgh University Press, 2009.

Perlis, Alan. *Wallace Stevens: A World of Transforming Shapes.* New Jersey: Associated University Presses, 1976.

Richardson, Joan. *Wallace Stevens: The Early Years 1979–1923.* New York: Beech Tree, 1986.

Sharpe, Tony. *Wallace Stevens: A Literary Life.* New York: St. Martin's, 2000.

Shelley, Percy Bysshe. "A Defense of Poetry." *The Critical Tradition: Classic Texts and Contemporary Trends.* Ed. David H. Richter. New York: Bedford Books, 1997.

Smith, Anna Deavere. *Talk to Me: Travels in Media and Politics.* New York: Anchor, 2001.

Sontag, Susan. "Against Interpretation." *Against Interpretation: And Other Essays.* New York: Picador, 2001.

Startkiewicz, Max. *Rhapsody of Philosophy.* University Park: Pennsylvania State University Press, 2009.

Stevens, Wallace. *Letters of Wallace Stevens.* Ed. Holly Stevens. 1966. Berkeley: University of California Press, 1996.

_____. *The Necessary Angel: Essays on Reality and the Imagination.* New York: Vintage, 1951.

_____. *Opus Posthumous: Poems, Plays, Prose.* New York: Knopf, 1957.

_____. *Wallace Stevens: Collected Poetry and Prose.* New York: Library of America, 1997.

Taggart, John. *Remaining Light: Ant Meditations on a Painting by Edward Hopper.* New York: State University of New York Press, 1993.

Wilde, Oscar. "The Decay of Lying." *The Artist as Critic: Critical Writings of Oscar Wilde.* Ed. Richard Ellmann. Chicago: University of Chicago Press, 1982.

Žižek, Slavoj. *Enjoy Your Symptom! Jacques Lacan in Hollywood and Out.* New York: Routledge, 1992.

_____. *Event: Philosophy in Transit.* London: Penguin, 2014.

Spirits in Black and White: Ethiopia as the Black Columbia in African American Pageantry

Lurana Donnels O'Malley

Abstract

During the Progressive Era, Caucasian pageant performances in the U.S. typically featured a pageant woman as a guide or narrator. She often took the form of Lady Columbia. Pageants written and produced by African Americans metamorphosed Columbia into Ethiopia. Just as the classical connotations of Columbia's iconography asserted a U.S. claim to a civilized past, African Americans reclaimed their Egyptian/African heritage through the figure of Ethiopia. Ethiopia revealed the choices faced by African Americans in the early twentieth century: assimilating into the American nation or celebrating their unique history, talents, and heritage. This essay analyzes a few of these Ethiopias: in W. E. B. Du Bois's Star of Ethiopia *pageants (1913–1925), in four educational pageants of the 1920s, and in a short pageant Du Bois wrote in 1932. Taken together, these female Spirits reject prevalent stereotypes of black women and express the tensions between assimilation and cultural celebration.*

Long before the stern Uncle Sam and the curvaceous Wonder Woman, the United States was allegorized as the Lady Columbia: a regal figure, vaguely Greek or Roman, draped in a flowing flag, and often wielding a mighty sword. That allegorical representation of nationhood was animated by women acting in pageant dramas produced in the Progressive Era in both Caucasian and African American contexts. In a fiercely segregated time, each of these two cultural contexts produced educational pageant performances that again and again featured a central female Spirit character as a guide or narrator. Countless

Columbia figures appeared in mainstream American pageantry. But in pageants written and produced by African Americans, African American writers metamorphosed Columbia into Ethiopia. Just as the classical connotations of Columbia's idealized dignity asserted a U.S. claim to a civilized past, imagery of Egypt and Africa allowed African Americans to reclaim their heritage in multiple ways. Egyptianism and Ethiopianism did for African Americans what the Hellenized image did for America: they provided status and authenticity. For black spectators in the 1910s and 1920s, Ethiopia,[1] while borrowing her proud stance and quasi–Grecian robes from the all-American Columbia, connoted both ancient Egypt and the contemporary African continent. As U.S. historian Julie Des Jardins argues, textbook writers under historian Carter Woodson's mantle were torn between celebrating black uniqueness and advocating assimilation to white standards (121). Writers of pageant dramas for educational settings faced similar challenges. Ethiopia revealed the choices faced by African Americans in the early twentieth century: assimilating into the American nation or celebrating their unique history, talents, and heritage. By her very existence as an alternative to Columbia, Ethiopia usually expresses this cultural celebration, a reveling in the cultural splendor of Africans as equal to the glory that was Greece.

I will analyze a few of these black Columbias, starting with the first: a queen named Ethiopia in W. E. B. Du Bois's historical-allegorical pageant *The Star of Ethiopia* (elaborately staged on several occasions from 1913 to 1925). I will then examine Ethiopia variations in four 1920s pageants, written for school and church audiences. These pageants differ in the degree to which they express assimilationist ideals. *Out of the Dark,* in particular, echoes Du Bois's purpose of celebrating African heritage through its presentation of a sculpture by Meta Warrick Fuller. Finally, I return to Du Bois with a look at his narrator in the much later play *George Washington and Black Folk* (1932). This narrator is not Ethiopia but rather the Witch of Endor, a mysterious and powerful figure who mounts a pointed critique of the titular president.

These female figures—whether called Ethiopia, Spirit of Negro Progress, Chronicler, or the Witch of Endor—were deliberately fashioned, with inspiration from the white Columbia, as rejections of stereotypical black females of the era. When Trudier Harris, scholar of African American folklore and literature, surveyed popular magazines from 1900 to 1930 she discovered that images of black women mandated "size, subservience, and a stylized role as servant" (Harris 4). Ethiopia figures combat these requirements, refuting both the passive, nurturing mammy and the highly sexualized Jezebel, both stereotypes derived from Caucasian representations on stage, in literature, and in film (Banks 68–72). Instead, Ethiopia resembles another type, prominent within both the propagandistic and folk strains of early twentieth-century

African American literature: the "capable matriarch" that Du Bois hoped would lead reform in black communities (Hewett 199).

The allegorical Ethiopia characters of these pageants enact many roles. They are queens, slaves, mothers, and leaders. Cultural critic Michele Wallace wrote in 1979 of the African American superwoman, a figure of "inordinate strength," "the embodiment of Mother Earth, the quintessential mother" (Wallace 107). The Ethiopias exhibit this power. When they are narrators, they control the stage, order events, and retell history. They experience abjection but also rise in triumph. Their visual appearance works against stereotypes and makes a strong statement about women and uplift. Both Columbia and Ethiopia, women standing with arms upraised, are propagandistic images. Du Bois famously claimed in his 1926 essay "Criteria of Negro Art" that "all Art is propaganda [...]. I do not care a damn for any art that is not used for propaganda" (296). With *Star of Ethiopia*, he set the tone for future black pageants, putting art in the service of propagandistic revisions of history and cures for social ills. These pageants and their female Spirits express the tensions between assimilation and cultural celebration.

Columbia and Ethiopia

Lady Columbia was born out of a European practice of portraying women as allegorical personifications of nationhood, a practice that underscored a "cultural message of European superiority" (Wintle 27). Examples include Britannia (who emerged in the seventeenth-century with the formation of Great Britain) and Germania (a potent symbol in the Romantic era). The visual appearance of these female figures was shaped by ancient and Renaissance depictions of the Roman warrior goddess Minerva, who co-mingled wisdom with martial strength. The first printed reference to Columbia as the female symbol of the emerging United States came in the midst of the American Revolutionary War: in the 1775 poem "To his Excellency George Washington" by African American slave Phillis Wheatley. Wheatley portrays Columbia as a divine goddess who can spur Washington to victory as head of the Continental Army. Beginning in the early nineteenth century, visual representations of Columbia were plentiful in art and editorial cartoons (such as those of Thomas Nast), in which she was often linked to a progressive, pro-immigrant agenda ("Chinese Question," "Columbia Welcomes," Nast). Columbia shares many attributes with Liberty (later known as Marianne), the symbol first of the French revolution and then of the first French republic. In her earliest pro-revolutionary depictions, Marianne often assumed a fierce stance and sported the Phrygian cap—first worn by freed slaves in Rome, and sometimes called the "liberty cap," it was associated with both the French and American revolutions (McKinley 123). Like Marianne, Columbia's visual iconography varies considerably from image to image but typically the shape of her robes connotes the classical, and she might wear a Minerva-like helmet or a Phrygian cap. She might carry a sheathed or unsheathed sword or a bayonet with a covered tip, and might also hold a shield or laurel wreath. Frequently, the U.S. flag print fabric of her robes connects her to America. From her first appearance in print in Wheatley's poem, Columbia epitomized dignity, beauty, competence, and strength.

Once pageantry made its mark in the United States in the early twentieth century, Columbia moved from the printed page to embodiment on the stage. The historian David Glassberg uses the term "pageant woman" to refer to the various female Spirit characters of pageantry. He describes the pageant woman as "a woman in classical garb who reappears throughout the pageant [...] the idealized female image represented in public statues, murals, and posters of the period" (136). Variations on the pageant woman character, with names such as the Spirit of Home (Glassberg 85) or the Spirit of Philadelphia (151), appeared in countless U.S. pageants, from the beginnings of American pageant mania in 1905. These pageant women were often depicted through the iconography of Columbia. For example, in *The Vision of Columbus: A Pageant of Democracy*, by F. Ursula Payne of the Brooklyn Training School for Teachers (published 1919), a photograph shows the character United States wearing a pointed crown and a flag-like robe, and wields a sword [see Figure 1]. In Hazel Mackaye's suffrage pageant *The Allegory*, staged in 1913 on the steps of the Treasury building as the

Figure 1: United States, frontispiece in *The Vision of Columbus* (1919) by F. Ursula Payne (courtesy Lurana Donnels O'Malley).

climax to Alice Paul's large-scale suffrage march, the helmeted figure of Columbia, holding a staff topped with an eagle, strikes a pose of triumph ("German Actress") [see Figure 2].[2] Although Columbia was active in promoting both suffrage and World War I war efforts, Uncle Sam soon overtook her in popularity after the passage of the nineteenth amendment, and her popularity faded, as did the popularity of U.S. pageant drama, by 1930.[3]

As African Americans looked to pageantry as a performative assertion of their history and culture, they created their own Spirits, most often in the form of a female character called Ethiopia. She began as an amalgam of two movements in the Progressive Era: Egyptianism and Ethiopianism. These trends forged connections between Africa and Egypt in order to promote a sense of culture and tradition among African Americans. The Egyptian revival was an architectural movement that began in early nineteenth-century Europe as a result of Napoleonic archeological expeditions. In the U.S., it created a strong association between the nascent imagery of America and symbols of Egyptian power such as pyramids and obelisks. Throughout the nineteenth century, the racial makeup of the ancient Egyptians was the subject of much debate, with white phrenologists such as Samuel George Morton denying the

Figure 2: Hedwig Reicher as Columbia in Hazel Mackaye's *The Allegory*, Washington, D.C. (1913) (Library of Congress).

African origins of the creators of this civilization (Giguere 149), and black historians such as George Washington Williams, Joseph Casely Hayford, and Du Bois refuting these claims. Williams, in his *A History of the Negro Race* (1883), asserted that Egypt was the cradle of Greek and Roman civilization as well as the cultural ancestor of the African continent; Casely Hayford, the Ghanaian author of *Ethiopia Unbound* (1911) sought to counteract imperialist ideologies by using Ethiopia as a symbol of African independence (Ugonna). Du Bois's own Egyptianism is apparent in his writing and in his stage productions. In 1913, he wrote that "Egyptian monuments show distinctly Negro and mulatto faces" (*Negro* 17), and Egyptian imagery was manifest in the set and costume designs, in the characters, and in the Egyptian regalia and ceremony in his pageants.

Ethiopianism also pervaded poetry and the arts at the turn of the century; for African Americans, Ethiopia's status as an uncolonized nation made it a symbol of freedom and hope. In Paul Laurence Dunbar's poem "Ode to Ethiopia" (published in his collection *Oak and Ivy* in 1893) he feminizes/allegorizes Ethiopia as "O Mother Race!" (5) and predicts her future glory in classical imagery of the scroll and the lyre: "Be proud, my Race, in mind and soul; Thy name is writ on Glory's scroll / In characters of fire" (6). "Aethiopia" is itself an ancient Greek term, referring to various geographical locations in Africa. Ethiopianism in America can be said to derive from the era of U.S. slavery, when African Americans encountered the name of the African country in the Bible, as a land that would be delivered. News of Ethiopia's successful resistance to Italian invasion in 1896 led to Ethiopia eclipsing Haiti in symbolic power for blacks in America. As the allegorical personification of Africa/ African America, the female Ethiopia character may have first taken the stage in 1915 in Washington, D.C.

Star(s) of Ethiopia

The earliest pageant written by and produced by an African American was likely the massive spectacle authored by Du Bois, first called *The People of Peoples and their Gifts to Men* and later titled *The Star of Ethiopia*. These Du Bois pageants were seen by thousands of spectators, and various contemporary accounts of them were published.[4] Du Bois first produced the pageant in 1913 in New York's Twelfth Regiment Armory as part of the National Emancipation Exposition (a celebration of the fiftieth anniversary of the Emancipation Proclamation). The prelude and six episodes proceed from stormy early Africa to the civilization phase of Egypt through the slave trade to the Haitian revolution; the pageant ends with emancipation in America. Two photographs of the pageant show that its backdrop was a replica of an Egyptian temple constructed within the Armory, with two obelisks in front; one photograph depicts the dance of "forty maidens [...] before the enthroned pharaoh Ra, the Negro" ("National"; "Historical"). This New York pageant had no character named Ethiopia, but its pageant woman, the Veiled Woman, appears in the first episode: "At last, dimly enhaloed in mysterious light, the Veiled Woman appears, commanding in stature and splendid in garment, her dark face faintly visible" (Du Bois, "National Emancipation" 339). Although she is not central to the performance in this script, the pageant's climactic procession ended with her transformation: "the all-Mother, formerly the Veiled Woman, now unveiled in her chariot with her dancing brood, and the bust of Lincoln by her side" (341). Removal of her veil was thus equated with freedom; veil imagery was deeply significant in Du Bois's other writings, as a symbol of an African American duality.

Du Bois adapted his pageants to circumstances. *The People of Peoples* highlighted the theme of Africans' gifts to civilization; its emphasis on emancipation imagery suited its celebratory and commemorative context. Because the description of this pageant was published in *Crisis* in November 1913, it has been anthologized as the definitive version of this performance under the title *The Star of Ethiopia*.[5] But several later pageant versions (known from a 1915 article in *Washington Bee*[6] and from several drafts in Du Bois archives) were each titled *The Star of Ethiopia*, despite significant differences in their characters and events. These scripts, the basis for productions in Washington, D.C., in 1915, in Philadelphia in 1916, and in Los Angeles in 1925, show Du Bois's first use of Ethiopia as a character, making the D.C. production likely the first stage representation of Ethiopia as a representation of Africa.

Woman-centered imagery increased substantially from the 1913 *People of Peoples* performance, as the pageant transformed into the story of Ethiopia and her quest to reclaim a lost Star of Freedom.[7] A 1914 manuscript of *Star of Ethiopia*, developed for a meeting of the National Federation of Colored Women's Clubs,[8] focuses on women in several key ways: its female Herald narrator, its queen Ethiopia, and its closing pageant scene of modern women. In this version, the Herald, dressed "gorgeous and woman-wise" (Du Bois, *Star of Ethiopia, 1914* 1)[9] provides narration throughout, and introduces "Ethiopia the Black, All-Mother, mystic queen of men, bearing on her mighty hands, the Star of Freedom—Freedom divine, long sought for, unattained" (2). After a stately initial scene in which Ethiopia receives a crown, and the Star is placed on her bosom, she is attacked by the figures of "Bigotry, Industry, Passion and Greed," who, according to the Herald, "bound and raped and slew the Queen of Heaven" (2). She is "offered up in burning sacrifice" (3) not only by slave trader figures but by other characters referred to as "Mohammedans," "Yorubans," and "Bantu." But Ethiopia rises again: the African Thunder God, introduced in the first scene, later revives the queen. Upon her resurrection she gains white wings, and the Star is restored to her breast. Soyica Diggs Colbert makes an insightful analysis of this attack on Ethiopia as a counter-ritual to the era's public lynchings of black men (84–86). Although Du Bois made deliberate effort to primarily feature music composed by African Americans in all his pageants, here Ethiopia exits to the march from Verdi's *Aida*, whose titular character is also an Ethiopian princess. In the next sequence, accompanied by "modern Negro music," twenty "women in modern dress" appear: "Doctor, nurse, teacher, musician, actress, hairdresser, book-keeper, stenographer, merchant, reporter, cook, artist, photographer, dressmaker, milliner, and 5 women of fashion" (4). In this final sequence, Ethiopia is initially "veiled as a witch" but is later unveiled (like the 1913 version's Veiled Woman) and revealed.[10] Du Bois's Ethiopia is a figure of dignity and power throughout the pageant. Yet she is also one of abjection. The image of her burned body links her to ancient Greek tragedy, as well as to the slave trade, to plantation abuses, and to contemporary lynching. Her resurrection is Jesus-like. While the characters of "women in modern dress" present examples of achievement in contemporary arenas, this Ethiopia herself, like Columbia, expresses a connection to antiquity.

The first staging of a version called *The Star of Ethiopia* was probably the 1915 production in Washington, D.C. I have yet to find evidence that the 1914 women's club version described above was ever staged. The *Washington Bee* newspaper gives a detailed account of the production, which was performed outdoors at the American League Baseball Park and featured over a thousand participants. This version is quite similar to the 1914 script, although the newspaper description omits the rape of Ethiopia. "At last the Traders discover her and set fire to the rock as she flees. She burns […] and the Rock becomes her tomb" ("Star of Ethiopia" 1). After her resurrection with wings and a flaming sword, Ethiopia calls the three Rivers (Congo, Nile, and Niger) who aid in constructing an allegorized structure (with foundation of Knowledge, stones of Labor, Science, Justice, and Art, and a capstone of Love) (1).

A full-length photograph of Eleanor Curtis in the role of Ethiopia in this production reveals her as a black Columbia (Du Bois, "Star") [see Figure 3]; Curtis was also the costume designer. The image is flanked by photographs of Adella Parks and Gregoria Fraser as the Queen of Sheba and Candace of Meroë, both historical Ethiopian queens. These latter costumes are significantly more decorative, with long necklaces and elaborate beadwork; they are costumed as African historical characters, rather than as allegories. Ethiopia herself is more plainly dressed, and more reminiscent of Columbia. She stands grandly in her long robes, and holds the Star of Freedom aloft. She also wears the white wings she has gained upon resurrection. Two group photographs from the May 1916 Philadelphia pageant ("Philadelphia") each show numerous cast members in front of a four-columned temple. Ethiopia is at center raising the star with her right hand, although her wings are not clearly evident [see Figure 4].

Du Bois's *Star of Ethiopia* pageants are complex texts, difficult to analyze without full information about the music, dance, costume, sets, and staging that are the center of this very visual allegorized narrative. Du Bois did not shy away from the opportunity to create a black Columbia as a symbol of his people's struggle, part African queen, part Egyptian princess. Hewett convincingly argues that this Ethiopia embodies what Du Bois espoused again and again in *Crisis*: that the black woman could be the

Figure 3: Eleanor Curtis as Ethiopia in *The Star of Ethiopia* (1915). From *Crisis* 11.2 (December 1915): 90.

capable matriarch who "presides over and aids in the creation of Du Bois's notion of the 'talented tenth'" (199). Although she can be seen as a model for middle-class uplift, Ethiopia is also a metaphor for the suffering of slavery and Reconstruction. Although the exact actions vary from version to version, Ethiopia is always burned and must be resurrected before her final triumph. In some versions, she is violently assaulted and raped. Her victorious rise as a

Figure 4: *The Star of Ethiopia* **cast in Philadelphia (1916). From** *Crisis* **12.4 (August 1916): 172.**

glorious winged being, seen by large audiences of African American spectators, is both tragic and triumphant as a narrative of cultural celebration.

Pageants of Assimilation vs. Cultural Celebration

Du Bois's first *Star* variations inspired many more African American pageants, although none were done on the immense scale of his productions. In the 1920s, African American educators (many of them women) created numerous pageant scripts for educational and community settings. These pageants, like those of Du Bois, emphasize visual spectacle, and often feature narrators who resemble teachers, guiding a class through historical narratives and facts about black achievement. Ethiopia-type characters appear in these four pageants: *Two Races, Out of the Dark, The Light of the Women, and Ethiopia at the Bar of Justice.* All were published in the 1930 anthology *Plays and Pageants from the Life of the Negro,* compiled by African American playwright Willis Richardson. Carter Woodson's Associated Publishers (the first African American publishing company in the U.S.) intended for the scripts to reach both readers and potential producers in other educational and religious institutions nationwide. Although not much information is available on productions, two of the pageant authors make practical notes about the details of previous performances in a school setting. In contrast to Du Bois's complex and sometimes disturbing spectacle, these didactic pageants simplify history, exude positivity, and generally avoid violence. Their Ethiopias are figures of tranquil inspiration. Like Du Bois, these authors all write propaganda, using drama as a means of persuasion.

Two Races by Inez M. Burke expresses a typical American pageant goal of assimilationist pluralism, in contrast to *Star of Ethiopia*'s message of Africa as a dominant contributor to world civilization. Burke was an elementary teacher at "the primarily African American Charles Young School" in Washington, D.C. (Smith 46). Burke's appearances in and contributions to the *Negro History Bulletin* lead Smith to conclude that she was Carter Woodson's colleague (60).[11] In *The Journal of Negro History*, the reviewer of the anthology (likely Woodson himself) comments, "Inez M. Burke, appearing here for the first time with a pageant for children in the seventh grade, may well take courage to write another" (Anonymous).

Taking place in the present on a Washington, D.C., sidewalk, the play's Columbia stand-in is called Spirit of Negro Progress. There are also two named characters: "Sam, a Negro Boy," and Gilbert, "a white boy." When Gilbert boasts to Sam that his ancestors "built this country"–he mentions Columbus, Washington, Hamilton, and Lincoln–Sam is speechless and dejected, unable to articulate a response. Spirit of Negro Progress enters the scene, and proceeds to introduce the boys to an assortment of female "Talkers" (Adventure, Invention, Bravery, Oratory, Poetry, and Music) who detail various black accomplishments. The author notes that Spirit of Negro Progress appears in "flowing white robe," a crown, and an optional sash bearing her name; the Talkers "may wear white dresses with ribbon sashes bearing their names" (296). The utopian vision of *Two Races,* of whites and blacks jointly building America's future, is expressed both via the pageant genre's emphasis on the visual, and by the Talkers' lecture-like speeches. Gilbert learns from the Talkers: "Why, Sam, I see now that your race, too, has helped to make the United States" (302). At the end of the play, Uncle Sam enters, calling the two boys "the future builders of America" and urging them to unite to make America great. Burke's female Spirit of Negro Progress has assisted both Sam and Uncle Sam in understanding "the glorious achievements of the Negro Race" (302) but the pageant gives Uncle Sam the final word, a message of assimilation.

Dorothy C. Guinn's pageant *Out of the Dark,* on the other hand, emphasizes cultural heritage and celebration, especially through a closing living tableau that visually represents Ethiopia as an Egyptian woman with African features, in imitation of Meta Warrick Fuller's sculpture. Several facts point to a connection between the play and the Young Women's Christian Association.[12] The pageant recalls Du Bois's *People of Peoples* in its episodic approach to African American history: the four episodes (The Rape of a Continent, Slavery, A New Day Breaks, What of To-Day?) take the spectator on a chronological history of oppression and achievement. Guinn's costume descriptions recall Lady Columbia and the Attic mania of the era. The female Chronicler "wears a long flowing robe and carries a scroll which she begins to unwind" (311). She wears "long flowing Grecian costume of soft white silk. Hair bound with narrow ribbon, Grecian effect" (327). Chronicler's scroll connects her to classical knowledge, and endows her with authority to address her historical subject.

In the final episode, What of To-Day?, Chronicler, now in the present, invites commentary by female performers representing Music, Literature, Science, and Art. The script's closing Suggestions state that Music wore a "long flowing robe. We used a large woman, to represent MUSIC as fully grown. She wore a lavender robe" (328). These allegorical figures mention various African American luminaries by name (writers, composers, scientists, etc.). Art, the final figure, names the sculptor Meta Warrick Fuller and says that the audience will see "one of her latest pieces" (322). At this late moment in the pageant, the stage finally presents its Ethiopia: an actor presenting a living tableau of Fuller's sculpture "Ethiopia Awakening" [see Figure 5]. Art speaks these words: "See, Ethiopia is awakening and she is beginning to realize the glories of her past and the possibilities of her future. In this statue of Meta Warrick Fuller, see symbolized the soul of this people today" (322).

Figure 5: *Ethiopia Awakening* by Meta Warrick Fuller (Art & Artifacts Division, Schomburg Center for Research in Black Culture, The New York Public Library, Astor, Lenox and Tilden Foundations).

The living tableau, a performance form popular in America from the 1830s through the early twentieth century, presents a tribute to an artwork through embodiment: live actors posed in stillness in imitation of the original sculpture or painting. Living tableaux had much in common with American pageantry, particularly in their reliance on the power of the visual and their goals of social, educational, and spiritual uplift. Caucasian *tableaux vivants* typically promoted canonical masterpieces, often in imitation of sculptural originals in white marble. Art historian Robin Veder (139) notes the "eugenicist agenda" behind the imitation of these classical white figures. The Fuller sculpture, brought to life via tableau, subverts this agenda with its black, female Ethiopia. In the sculpture, Ethiopia has an Egyptian headdress and her lower body appears to be encased in Egyptian funerary wrappings; her "facial features are clearly modeled on black physiognomy" (Ater, *Remaking* 106).

The aesthetic strategy of presenting a sculpture through a living tableau is particularly complex in the case of the Guinn pageant. The tableau would have featured a live performer embodying Fuller's sculpture through stillness; the sculpture is a frozen representation of a living figure caught in the first moments of unwrapping her mummy bindings. Although the sculpture's title indicates the woman's "awakening," the mummy imagery instead implies a resurrection, one that recalls Du Bois's Ethiopia.

In fact, "Ethiopia Awakening" was likely directly inspired by Du Bois's theatrical vision of Ethiopia as a female symbol of Africa. Fuller (using her unmarried name Warrick at the time) had met Du Bois in 1900 in Paris (he was there for the Paris Exposition as the head of the African American pavilion there; she was there to study at the Académie Colarossi and the École des Beaux Arts). In 1913, as part of the upcoming fiftieth anniversary of the Emancipation Proclamation, Du Bois (as a member of the New York State Emancipation Proclamation Commission) commissioned Fuller to create a sculptural tribute to the occasion, to be featured at the Emancipation Exhibition. Her sculpture, *Emancipation Proclamation*, is an eight-foot-high plaster sculpture that features a male and two females. Of the women, one is sorrowful, but the other is proud, stepping out into the world to meet the challenges of her newly won freedom. This female has a nude torso, and carries none of the adornment typical of female allegorical figures; she is human, not supernatural. Since Fuller would almost certainly have seen Du Bois's pageant *People of Peoples*, performed at the same occasion, this exhibition marked the first instance of the sculptor's work and writer's pageant sharing a joint space.[13]

In 1921, again at Du Bois's suggestion, James Weldon Johnson (NAACP leader and Chairman of the Exposition's Americans of Negro Lineage Executive Committee) invited Fuller to create "Ethiopia Awakening" as part of the "Americans of Negro Lineage" pavilion of the America's Making exhibition. The exhibition aimed to present a varied demonstration of the contributions of various immigrant groups to the United States as part of its ambitious assimilationist project. In the words of John H. Finley, the president of the America's Making committee: "At the Altar of America we have sworn ourselves to a single loyalty" (*Book of America's Making*, Foreword). African American leaders, although they acknowledged that they were not voluntary immigrants in the same sense as other participating groups, seized on the celebration as an occasion to promote black achievement and contributions to American society in economic growth, the military, and the arts (Ater, "Meta" 73.)

Du Bois initially had a different idea for the sculpture, as Ethiopia holding crystal globes marked "Music" and "Labor" (Du Bois, *Outline*). But Fuller went in a different direction to create "Ethiopia Awakening" for the exhibition, held at 71st Regiment Armory in New York.[14] The sculpture was "the focal point of the exhibit booth, which was designed to resemble an Egyptian temple" (Ater, "Meta" 58).[15] Du Bois also created an accompanying pageant, titled *The Seven Gifts of Ethiopia to America*, which he presented at the exhibition on November 11. Similar to *The Star of Ethiopia*, it featured a female Ethiopia; in this case, she is entombed in the pyramid, and emerges later in the pageant (Du Bois, *Seven*).

By the time Guinn wrote her pageant in 1924, "Ethiopia Awakening" was famous as an inspiring new work of art by an African American artist.[16] Fuller herself described the image as Ethiopia "awakening, gradually unwinding the bandages of [the] past and looking out on life again, expectant, but unafraid" (qtd. Kerr 261).[17] This unwrapping echoes the unveiling of Ethiopia in Du Bois's *The Star of Ethiopia* pageant. In Fuller's reference to "awakening," some scholars argue that the sculptor may have been directly addressing Daniel Chester French's sculpture "Africa" (1902), a symbolic rendering of the continent in the form of a sleeping female (in contrast to the alert figures of Asia, America, and Europe that complete the set) (Farrington 70–71; Wilson 69). Chester's vision of Africa draws on the image of the "sleeping continent"; Fuller seems to have wanted to wake her. The deathlike slumber from which Ethiopia is in the process of awakening echoes the title of Guinn's pageant: Ethiopia awakens, Africa comes out of the dark. These artistic creations by Fuller and Guinn display a parallel optimism.

The title of Frances Gunner's pageant *The Light of the Women* indicates a continuity with Guinn's *Out of the Dark*, and Gunner's pageant begins just the way Guinn's ends: with a rendition of the stirring "Lift Every Voice and Sing" (John Rosamond Johnson/James Weldon Johnson). Gunner was born in Kentucky and worked in the 1920s at the Brooklyn YWCA where the play was possibly performed (Corbould 85); an author's note on the frontispiece states that the piece is "adapted to the capacity of junior high and high school girls" (Gunner 333). *The Light of the Women*, subtitled "A ceremonial for the use of Negro groups," is an optimistic pageant that focuses solely on women;

its first half praises the achievements of black women of the past, while the second half presents the "Women of To-Day," mentioning recent service during World War I and climaxing when the allegorical Spirit of Service lights a torch for "all the girls of the world" (342). There are only five speaking characters: the Herald, the Spirit of Service (who has Beauty and Truth on either side of her), and Ethiopia. The rest of the women do not speak, but quite simply pass across the stage, while a group of girls sings or hums various tunes. Similarly to *Out of the Dark*'s device of opening a curtain to reveal (usually silent) historical tableaux, *The Light of the Women*'s narrator Ethiopia, who has the burden of lines in the play, details the accomplishments of each woman as she appears without speaking.

The lead characters have typical pageant woman costuming: Spirit of Service wears "flowing costumes, of light and color," Beauty wears "flowing robe shimmering with gold" and Truth is "in white, with a thin veil over her face" (334). In contrast, Ethiopia is in "royal robes, with just a touch of the barbaric" (334). Spirit of Service calls her a "dusky queen" (335) who has had much sorrow, and praises her courage. Ethiopia then states her purpose in the play: "I bring good news, news of light among the women" (336). She then proceeds to command the proceedings of the entire pageant, culminating by leading a Girl Reserve (a member of the YWCA club for girls) to the Spirit of Service, who gives her a lit torch "for all the girls in the world." In *The Light of the Women*, the slightly "barbaric" Ethiopia is active and vocal, taking charge of the pageant and its progression. She is the historian who speaks of and presents the heritage of African American women, in contrast to the silent Ethiopias of Du Bois and Guinn. In this way, Gunner's Ethiopia presages Du Bois's Witch of Endor, also a "barbaric" character who narrates the history of George Washington in quite her own way.

The final pageant in the anthology, *Ethiopia at the Bar of Justice* by Edward J. McCoo (an AME minister in Kentucky), puts Ethiopia on trial for excessive ambition, for "flying too high" (351). The play was privately published by the author (Gray xxxiv) and was produced in 1924 at the Quadrennial Conference of the A.M.E. Church in Louisville, among other occasions. Peterson states that it was frequently staged during Negro History Week (130). This allegorical courtroom drama, with numerous songs interspersed throughout its action, begins with children named Oppression vs. Leniency, whispering in the ear of Justice. Mercy, a young woman wearing clothes of "Greek style; soft, clinging material," quotes Portia's lines on mercy from *The Merchant of Venice* as she brings Ethiopia before the male Justice. The accuser Opposition is also female, a woman "quick in action and in speech" (McCoo 346). Opposition enters to ask for a judgment on Ethiopia; she argues that, "She is doing too much; she is becoming too ambitious [...] you must clip her wings" (351).

Justice later re-states the charge: "Opposition charges that you are drawing heavily upon the Bank of Civilization and that you have nothing on deposit there" (353). This reasoning is not stated in racial terms but is based on a monetary metaphor; neither is Opposition's race specified, although monochromatic illustrations by James Lesesne Wells [see Figure 6][18] published in the Richardson anthology indicate her whiteness in contrast to Ethiopia's blackness. Opposition's perspective on Ethiopia is that of Caucasian superiority and exclusionism: "I tell you she has gone without the bounds we set for her! She is building schools; she is building churches; she is buying farms; she is organizing wealth; she is operating banks; she is making great demands on a civilization which she did not produce!" (351)

Figure 6: "Ethiopia at the Bar of Justice" by James Lesesne Wells (Crisis Publishing Company).

To counteract this charge, the rest of the play presents opportunities to demonstrate African and African American contributions to world civilization (from the Ethiopian who bore Christ's cross to black soldiers at San Juan Hill to the Haitian revolution) via pageant format. Various others testify on Ethiopia's behalf. The female Haiti enters to the accompaniment of the Haitian National Anthem; Haiti's statement—"In my land Ethiopia reigns, and *Justice must and shall prevail!*" (366)—implies that Ethiopia is a pan-national monarch. Womanhood also testifies, with imagery recalling Gunner's play: she attributes to Ethiopia "a womanhood which has walked in darkness and yet has emerged, bringing with her a light that shines far and wide" (364). Most of these allegorical characters are bland and ahistorical, but the character Anti-lynch Law, costumed as a "rough and tumble type" (347), brings contemporary politics into the pageant in a more concretely critical way than do the characters of Burke, Gunner, and Guinn.

McCoo writes that his Ethiopia should be a "Young woman, regal bearing, not too fair of complexion; one who can sing well and act" (346). His insistence on her darkness, not visually indicative of racial mixture, suggests the importance of her purer African heritage. His description recalls Fuller's deliberate use of African physiognomy in her sculpture of Ethiopia. As with Du Bois's pageants, McCoo's musical choices offer clues to meaning. The script emphasizes the mandatory use of a single 1919 song by Hermes Zimmerman, "The Chief Corner Stone." The song, which draws on the Psalms verse "The stone which the builders rejected has become the chief corner stone," implies that Ethiopia (and therefore African American culture) is a dormant force that will rise to primacy. Despite this hint of the cultural rise of Ethiopia, in the pageant's conclusion (after he predictably rules in her favor), Justice descends to Ethiopia and proposes marriage. They "clasp hands," and as Wedding March plays, these two gendered allegorical characters are wed. Despite having offered the Haitian anthem earlier, the play ends with the "Star-Spangled Banner," a clear signal of the necessity and value of assimilation.

Although none of these four didactic pageants has the bold scope and imagination of *Star of Ethiopia* (Burke's play is tame throughout and McCoo's play ends that way), there are moments of power in each. Guinn's use of the Fuller sculpture is striking, and Gunner focuses on combating prevalent stereotypes as a means of inspiring her target audience of girls.

Du Bois's Anti-Columbia

In the quite bold *George Washington and Black Folk*, written in 1932 as a specifically African American response to the commemorations of the George

Washington Bicentenary, Du Bois again places a woman in a central role. The short unproduced play is a revisionist take on the historical events and persons surrounding Washington, contrasting his hypocritical slaveholding with the achievements of black artists, religious men, soldiers, and other leaders. Instead of relying on Ethiopia or abstracting a virtue or concept, however, Du Bois chose a Biblical character as his female narrator: the Witch of Endor. In the book of Samuel, the Witch is a necromancer who communicates, at the request of Saul, with the deceased prophet Samuel. Rather than triumphantly leading her audience through time as Ethiopia does in previous Du Bois pageants, the Witch presents dystopic scenes that subvert Washington's popular image, even as she raises the heroes of black achievement. As a powerful presence in contrast to the often passive Washington, she actively narrates, comments on scenes, and often provides voices.

Despite their surface differences, the Witch of Endor does have significant ties to Du Bois's earlier pageant women. Like his earlier Veiled Woman, the Witch *"is black and veiled and her grey robes flow down to the floor"* (121). Throughout his writing, the veil was a potent metaphor of the African American's separation and abjection; in *The Souls of Black Folk* (1903), he evokes "the Veil that hung between us and Opportunity" (50). But unlike his Veiled Woman, who appears unveiled with a bust of Lincoln, the Witch retains her veil as the play concludes with Washington's death, implying that Washington is no Lincoln. Like Ethiopia, the Witch is linked to Africa, because for Du Bois she had strong connotations of both Egyptian serpent worship and of the conjurers or obi-women of African and African American culture.[19] This Witch is not a black Columbia but an anti–Columbia, deconstructing closely held patriotic notions of the founding father.

Ethiopia(s) Awakening

In an era in which American women were making unprecedented ventures into the public sphere in education, politics, and business, the pageant woman character was an idealized marker of progressive change clad in ancient vestments. The African American counterpart to Columbia became Ethiopia, who would take on many of the former's quasi-Grecian traits, but would also connote Africa/Egypt, and suggest a regal power to be reclaimed. The 1915 D.C. *Star of Ethiopia* is to my knowledge the first stage use of Ethiopia as a female embodiment of—simultaneously—pan-African heritage and the African American experience. Du Bois's Ethiopia triumphs only after a scene in which she is burned alive (and in some versions, a graphic scene of rape); her degradation is violent and explicit. This first Ethiopia is forcefully anti-assimilationist;

she embodies and celebrates a glorious past but her resurrection has no relationship to a patriotic vision of America.

Burke's simplistic *Two Races*, although it has no Ethiopia character, represents the alternative strain of pageantry: assimilation. Two other women writers, Guinn and Gunner, each include an Ethiopia with stronger connections to Du Bois's vision. In Guinn's *Out of the Dark,* the female Chronicler is the "pageant woman" narrator, and her words emphasize the "rape of a continent" before describing later successes within the framework of American society. Guinn presents a silent and awakening Ethiopia in the form of a tableau of Fuller's sculpture. It is a tranquil and non-threatening image of unfolding, yet its Egyptian imagery supports a claim to ancient heritage. Gunner's *The Light of the Women*, whose all-woman cast is by its nature atypical and progressive, requests an Ethiopia with a touch of the "barbaric," but the script as a whole does not clarify whether this non-normativity is something to be celebrated or whether that barbarism is receding in assimilation to U.S. modernity. McCoo's Ethiopia seems less an African queen than the Ethiopias of Du Bois or Fuller/Guinn. She has a regal bearing, but his script specifies that she wear "modern dress" (347); there is nothing Grecian about her. This author's request for a dark-skinned Ethiopia stresses the connection to her African lineage, but the gendered marriage imagery of the conclusion tames the character by pairing her with the male Justice.

Finally, the Witch of Endor, in contrast to McCoo's Ethiopia, is not herself involved in the action. Du Bois describes her as a "colossal figure" (121). Although she is mentioned in the Bible, Du Bois's view of her connections to African/ Caribbean *obeah* worship emphasizes her non–Christian, non-normative nature. The Witch stresses blacks' roles in building Washington's America, and puts forward an alternative black history that stresses black superiority.

Because she was represented by a beautiful woman, Ethiopia was in some ways a palatable embodiment of cultural celebration. One can assume, in the age of lynching, that a powerful male performer in the role would have been a much more dangerous symbol. Yet Ethiopia's presence as an alternative black Columbia is still a striking subversion of white pageantry. The majority of pageant women in the United States were performed by Caucasian women; in pageants by Du Bois, Burke, Guinn, Gunner, and McCoo, these Spirits were to be portrayed by black women or girls, whose robes, crowns, and raised stars would create a message through iconography alone. These onstage women presented inspiring alternatives to prevalent negative portrayals of black women. As the black Columbia, the "dusky queen" with light-colored robes, Ethiopia employed the pageant woman's connotations of ancient Greece and patriotic America, yet transformed them to emphasize her own messages of cultural celebration.

UNIVERSITY OF HAWAI'I AT MĀNOA

Notes

1. In this essay, I will use the term Ethiopia to refer to a female character in an artistic representation. If I am referring to the country, I will specify that.

2. See Lumsden 103 for a full description of the costumes of all characters.

3. See Glassberg 286 for his theory on the reasons for the decline.

4. The version called *The People of Peoples* was printed in *Crisis* in November 1913 (Du Bois, "National"). Its introductory paragraph also titles it "Pageant of Negro History" (339). A substantial description of the 1915 D.C. performance was published in *The Washington Bee* ("Star of Ethiopia").

5. For example, in editions by Hatch and Shine, and Sundquist (Du Bois, *Star*, various).

6. This anonymous *Washington Bee* account ("Star of Ethiopia") exactly matches the last five pages of a draft typescript (Du Bois, *Star of Ethiopia, 1914*), indicating that the article was written by Du Bois himself.

7. Du Bois had this Ethiopia imagery in mind from the earliest drafts, which may date to 1911, when the pageant was called *The Jewel of Ethiopia*.

8. This typescript states that it was intended for the Women's Club of Xenia, Ohio, at the biennial meeting of the Federation (Du Bois, *Star of Ethiopia, 1914*). According to Rebecca Hewett, Du Bois melded his 1913 *People of Peoples* with this one to form the production script for the next large-scale incarnations in major cities (194).

9. All quotations from the W. E. B. Du Bois Papers are reproduced with permission from Special Collections and University Archives, University of Massachusetts Amherst Libraries.

10. In yet another version in the University of Massachusetts Amherst Du Bois archive (dated 1914) the closing scene features four Heralds, called in the cast list N, A, A, C, and P, who blow bugles to bring forth various river characters (Du Bois, *Star of Ethiopia: A Pageant*).

11. Katharine Capshaw Smith attempted more detailed investigation into Burke's career through the D.C. School System, with little success.

12. Guinn may have been a board member with the YWCA (Peterson 92). *Out of the Dark* (along with Gunner's *The Light of the Woman*) required that permission for production be sought from Womans Press, the New York publication department of the National YWCA.

13. I have not determined whether Fuller saw either of the *Star of Ethiopia* incarnations of 1915 (D.C.) or 1916 (Philadelphia).

14. See Ater, "Meta" 81 and Wilson 74 for accounts of the sculpture's various versions.

15. See Ater, "Meta" 74 for a full description of the exhibit from the records of the National Urban League.

16. See Ater, *Remaking Race*, 130 on Fuller's participation as "costume designer" for another pageant in 1921 that culminated with a tableau of the sculpture.

17. Kerr's source is a letter from Fuller to the art historian Freeman Murray (January 9, 1915) in the Freeman Murray Papers (Kerr 405).

18. The author wishes to thank to the Crisis Publishing Co., Inc., the publisher of the magazine of the National Association for the Advancement of Colored People, for the use of this image first published in the November 1928 issue of *The Crisis*.

19. For a fuller explanation of these connections, and a full analysis of the play, see my forthcoming article in *MELUS* (O'Malley).

WORKS CITED

Anonymous. "Review of *Plays and Pageants from the Life of the Negro* by Willis Richardson." *Journal of Negro History* 15.2 (1930) 264.

Ater, Renée. "Meta Warrick Fuller's Ethiopia and the America's Making Exposition of 1921." *Women Artists of the Harlem Renaissance*. Ed. Amy Helene Kirschke. Jackson: University Press of Mississippi, 2014. 53–84.

_____. *Remaking Race and History: The Sculpture of Meta Warrick Fuller*. Berkeley: University of California Press, 2011.

Banks, Ingrid. "Women in Film." *African Americans and Popular Culture*. Ed. Todd Boyd. Westport, CT: Praeger, 2008. 67–86.

The Book of America's Making Exposition. New York: City and State Departments of Education, 1921. Smithsonian Libraries. library.si.edu/digital-library/book/bookof americasma00amer. Web. Accessed April 14, 2015.

Burke, Inez. *Two Races. Plays and Pageants from the Life of the Negro*. 1930. Ed. Willis Richardson; Christine R. Gray. Jackson: University Press of Mississippi, 1993. 295–302.

"The Chinese Question." *Harper's Weekly* (February 18, 1871): 149. Library of Congress Prints and Photographs Division. www.loc.gov/pictures/item/2005696252/. Web. Accessed February 13, 2015.

Colbert, Soyica Diggs. *The African American Theatrical Body: Reception, Performance, and the Stage*. Cambridge: Cambridge University Press, 2011.

"Columbia Welcomes the Victims of German Persecution to "the Asylum of the Oppressed." *Frank Leslie's Illustrated Newspaper* 51 (January 22, 1881): 356. Library of Congress Prints and Photographs Division. www.loc.gov/pictures/item/20016 96516/. Web. Accessed January 15, 2015.

Corbould, Clare. *Becoming African Americans: Black Public Life in Harlem, 1919–1939*. Cambridge, MA: Harvard University Press, 2009.

Des Jardins, Julie. *Women and the Historical Enterprise in America: Gender, Race, and the Politics of Memory, 1880–1945*. Gender & American Culture. Chapel Hill: University of North Carolina Press, 2003.

Du Bois, W. E. B. "Criteria of Negro Art." *Crisis* 32.6 (October 1926): 290–97.

_____. *George Washington and Black Folk. Crisis* 41.4 (April 1932): 121–24.

_____. *The Jewel of Ethiopia*. Reel 87: Essays, Forewords, and Student Papers; Novels, Pageants, and Plays. *The Papers of W.E.B. Du Bois*. Sanford, NC: Microfilming Corporation of America, 1980. Frames 1415–1416. Microfilm.

_____. "The National Emancipation Exposition." *Crisis* 6.7 (November 1913): 339–41.

_____. *The Negro*. Home University Library of Modern Knowledge. New York: H. Holt, 1915.

_____. *Outline of Seven Gifts of Ethiopia, 1915?* TS. W. E. B. Du Bois Papers (MS 312). Special Collections and University Archives, University of Massachusetts Amherst Libraries. credo.library.umass.edu/view/full/mums312-b233-i044. Web. Accessed July 15, 2015.

_____. *The Seven Gifts of Ethiopia to America*. Reel 87: Essays, Forewords, and Student Papers; Novels, Pageants, and Plays. *The Papers of W. E. B. Du Bois*. Sanford, NC: Microfilming Corporation of America, 1980. Frames 1459–1464. Microfilm.

_____. *The Souls of Black Folk*. 1903. Rpt. Oxford World's Classics. Ed. Hayes Edwards. Oxford: Oxford University Press, 2007.

_____. "The Star of Ethiopia." *Crisis* 11.2 (December 1915): 91–94.

_____. *The Star of Ethiopia: A Pageant, 1914*. W.E.B. Du Bois Papers (MS 312). Special Collections and University Archives, University of Massachusetts Amherst Libraries. credo.library.umass.edu/view/full/mums312-b233-i083. Web. Accessed July 15, 2015.

_____. *The Star of Ethiopia*. *Black Theatre USA: Plays by African Americans*. Eds. James Vernon Hatch and Ted Shine. Rev. and expanded ed. 2 vols. New York: Free, 1996. I: 89–92.

_____. *Star of Ethiopia, 1914*. W.E.B. Du Bois Papers (MS 312). Special Collections and University Archives, University of Massachusetts Amherst Libraries. credo.library. umass.edu/view/full/mums312-b233-i017. Web. Accessed July 15, 2015.

_____. *The Star of Ethiopia*. *The Oxford W. E. B. Du Bois Reader*. Ed. Eric J. Sundquist. New York: Oxford University Press, 1996. 305–10.

Dunbar, Paul Laurence. "Ode to Ethiopia." *Oak and Ivy*. Dayton, OH: Press of United Brethren Publishing House, 1893. 5–6. catalog.hathitrust.org/Record/012348966. Web. Accessed March 11, 2014.

Farrington, Lisa E. *Creating Their Own Image: The History of African-American Women Artists*. Oxford: Oxford University Press, 2005.

"German Actress Hedwig Reicher Wearing Costume of 'Columbia' with Other Suffrage Pageant Participants Standing in Background in Front of the Treasury Building, March 3, 1913, Washington, D.C." 1913. Photograph. Lib. of Cong., Washington D.C. *Library of Congress Prints & Photographs Online Catalog*. www.loc.gov/pictures/item/975 10759/. Web. Accessed March 11, 2014.

Giguere, Joy M. *Characteristically American: Memorial Architecture, National Identity, and the Egyptian Revival*. Knoxville: University of Tennessee Press, 2014.

Glassberg, David. *American Historical Pageantry: The Uses of Tradition in the Early Twentieth Century*. Chapel Hill: University of North Carolina Press, 1990.

Gray, Christine Rauchfuss. "Introduction." *Plays and Pageants from the Life of the Negro*. 1930. Ed. Willis Richardson; Christine R. Gray. Jackson: University Press of Mississippi, 1993. vii–xli.

Guinn, Dorothy C. *Out of the Dark*. *Plays and Pageants from the Life of the Negro*. 1930. Ed. Willis Richardson; Christine R. Gray. Jackson: University Press of Mississippi, 1993. 305–30.

Gunner, Frances. *The Light of the Women*. *Plays and Pageants from the Life of the Negro*. 1930. Ed. Willis Richardson; Christine R. Gray. Jackson: University Press of Mississippi, 1993. 333–42.

Harris, Trudier. *Saints, Sinners, Saviors: Strong Black Women in African American Literature*. New York: Palgrave, 2001.

Hayford, J. E. Casely. *Ethiopia Unbound: Studies in Race Emancipation*. Cass Library of African Studies Africana Modern Library. 2d ed. London: Cass, 1969.

Hewett, Rebecca. "'Looking at One's Self through the Eyes of Others': Representations of the Progressive Era Middle Class in W. E. B. Du Bois's *The Star of Ethiopia*." *Theatre History Studies* 30 (2010): 187–201.

"The Historical Pageant of the Negro Race: Forty Maidens Dance Before the Enthroned Pharoah Ra, The Negro." Photograph. *Crisis* 7.2 (December 1913): 79.

Kerr, Judith Nina. *God-Given Work: The Life and Times of Sculptor Meta Vaux Warrick*

Fuller, 1877–1968 (Pennsylvania). Dissertation. University of Massachusetts Amherst, 1986.

Lumsden, Linda J. *Rampant Women: Suffragists and the Right of Assembly.* Knoxville: University of Tennessee Press, 1997.

McCoo, Edward J. "Ethiopia at the Bar of Justice." *Plays and Pageants from the Life of the Negro.* 1930. Ed. Willis Richardson. Jackson: University Press of Mississippi, 1993. 345–373.

McKinley, C. Alexander. *Illegitimate Children of the Enlightenment Anarchists and the French Revolution, 1880–1914.* Francophone Cultures and Literatures 53. New York: Peter Lang, 2007.

Nast, Thomas. "Franchise. And Not This Man?" *Harper's Weekly* (August 5, 1865): 489. Library of Congress Prints and Photographs Division. www.loc.gov/pictures/item/91705053/. Web. Accessed June 14, 2015.

"The National Emancipation Exposition: The Temple of Beauty in the Great Court of Freedom." Photograph. *Crisis* 7.2 (December 1913): 78.

O'Malley, Lurana Donnels. "The Witch of Endor Slept Here: Du Bois and the Crisis of the George Washington Bicentenary." Forthcoming in *MELUS: Multi-Ethnic Literature of the United States.*

Payne, F. Ursula. *The Vision of Columbus. Plays and Pageants of Democracy.* New York: Harper and Brothers, 1919. 1–30.

Peterson, Bernard L. *Early Black American Playwrights and Dramatic Writers: A Biographical Directory and Catalog of Plays, Films, and Broadcasting Scripts.* New York: Greenwood, 1990.

"The Philadelphia Pageant." Photographs. *Crisis* 12.4 (August 1916): 170, 172.

Richardson, Willis, ed. *Plays and Pageants from the Life of the Negro.* 1930. Jackson: University Press of Mississippi, 1993. Print.

Smith, Katharine Capshaw. "Constructing a Shared History: Black Pageantry for Children During the Harlem Renaissance." *Children's Literature* 27 (1999): 40–63.

"Star of Ethiopia." *Washington Bee* (October 9, 1915): 1, 6.

Ugonna, F. Nnabuenyi. "Introduction to the Second Edition." *Ethiopia Unbound: Studies in Race Emancipation.* J. E. Hayford. Cass Library of African Studies Africana Modern Library. 2d ed. London: Cass, 1969. v–xxxvi.

Veder, Robin. *The Living Line: Modern Art and the Economy of Energy.* Interfaces: Studies in Visual Culture. Dartmouth, NH: Dartmouth College Press, 2015.

Wallace, Michele. *Black Macho and the Myth of the Superwoman.* New York: Dial, 1979.

Williams, George Washington. *History of the Negro Race.* New York: G. P. Putnam, 1882. Hathi Trust. hdl.handle.net/2027/loc.ark:/13960/t57d2z146. Web. Accessed March 3, 2015.

Wilson, Judith. "Will the 'New Internationalism' Be the Same Old Story?" *Global Visions: Towards a New Internationalism in the Visual Arts.* Ed. Jean Fisher. London: Kala, 1994. 60–78.

Wintle, Michael. "Visual Representations of Europe in the Nineteenth-Century: The Age of Nationalism and Imperialism." *A Companion to Nineteenth-Century Europe, 1789–1914.* Ed. Berger, Stefan. Blackwell Companions to European History. Malden, MA: Blackwell, 2006. 11–30.

In Search of the Void: Metaphysical Theatricality in Giorgio de Chirico's *The Painter's Family* and Emptiness in the Arts

Davenne Essif

Abstract

Through an investigation of the metaphysical theatricality in de Chirico's The Painter's Family *(1926) this essay calls for an interdisciplinary approach to the study of emptiness as a creative strategy in the arts. While de Chirico's paintings of the 1920s, including the* The Painter's Family, *have often been discounted as "meaningless" and "lacking in artistic achievement," they are actually charged with theatrical enigmas that reveal metaphysical meaning. Working both alongside and directly with key theater figures, de Chirico explored theatricality and emptiness as strategies for communicating profound messages to his viewers. His paintings of the 1920s exhibit the meaningful results of this exploration. Compounded with his written texts on the subject, these paintings had an impact in both France and Italy, spreading the interest in emptiness beyond the geographical boundaries explored in theater scholarship to date. This essay thus argues that it is essential to both recognize the metaphysical theatricality of de Chirico's paintings and to explore the cross-disciplinary nature of the theoretical construct of emptiness.*

Giorgio de Chirico's *The Painter's Family* (1926) is a puzzling painting [see Figure 1]. At first, the title, family, and traditional triangular composition suggest a familiar drama—the biblical story of the Nativity. The sparse scene, moreover, underscores the sense of an underlying narrative. Emptied of the

154

Figure 1: Giorgio de Chirico (1888-1978) © Artists Rights Society (ARS), New York / SIAE, Rome. *The Painter's Family*, 1926. Oil on canvas, 1464 x 1149 mm. Tate Gallery (photograph: Tate, London / Art Resource, New York).

typical devices used to convey an entire story in one static image (for example, wise men and angels, barn animals, or manger), it seems to present just a moment, a "scene," of a much longer story. This, in turn, gives us the sense that we must wait for the "next" scene to reveal more of the plot. Yet the longer we study the painting and the more we wait for the familiar narrative to unfold, the more we realize there is no narrative, only theatrical enigma. Though the manger setting has been replaced with the small, confined space of the stage and living figures have been exchanged for non-living, marionette-like mannequins, there is no play. Though the canvas beside the family is not set up for a painter but for an audience, it impossibly dissolves into the background, reinforcing the sense of a surreal theatrical tableau.[1] Even the mannequins themselves resist logic with their disproportionately small legs and the abstracted architectural growths on their torsos. We are left wondering how this lifeless group of mannequins can possibly relate to the painter of the work's title let alone the Holy Family. Through this sense of confusion and mystery, the painting entices us and yet remains frustratingly empty of the logic, signs, figures, and events we expect to see.

To understand the complexities of what de Chirico is trying to achieve with these visual enigmas and this sense of theatricality, we must turn to theater studies. Research in this field has identified a nuanced, truly interdisciplinary definition of "theatricality" as a phenomenological strategy of spatial perception. Theater studies has also identified and begun to explore the artistic use of metaphysical emptiness, "the essential substance of the individual psychic space" within which primal, wordless awareness is formed (Essif 174). Both of these subjects, interdisciplinary theatricality and metaphysical emptiness, can help reveal deeper meaning in de Chirico's work that has yet to be fully explored in art historical scholarship. Completed in 1926, well into what a great majority of scholars have identified as the period of de Chirico's declining creativity and depth, *The Painter's Family* is generally considered part of a phase during which de Chirico began to go "too far" in emptying his paintings of logical sense.[2] Despite a recent interest in de Chirico's later work and the philosophies he borrowed from theater practitioners, no art historical study has explored what de Chirico called the metaphysical aspects of theatricality.[3] Instead, the scholars who have acknowledged a certain theatrical quality in de Chirico's work suggest that it is predominantly a matter of visual imagery; as if the theatricality in his work stems from a life-long interest in the theater that manifests as recognizable theatrical elements (stages, curtains, etc.) in his art.[4] Yet the theatricality within *The Painter's Family* goes beyond representations of stages or curtains. It is instead a much deeper metaphysical quality that de Chirico uses to evoke seemingly infinite layers of enigma, knowledge, and self-awareness. It also leaves viewers with a vast sense of absence. Thus while art historical sources have yet to recognize the tie, the metaphysical the-atricality in de Chirico's work is intellectually bound to a much larger, inter-disciplinary search for emptiness in the arts.

The wide scope of this search came, at least in part, from an early twentieth-century breakdown in the specificity of artistic mediums. During this time, key figures in various artistic fields began to pursue more cross-disciplinary approaches to their work; artists in the visual field experimented with theatricality and artists in the theater emphasized the visual images cre-ated in and by their plays. At the same time, key theater practitioners, theorists, and dramatists began to explore the possibility of emptying their art of con-ventional signs, props, characters, and narratives in order to reveal a profound mental and spiritual void. In the case of Giorgio de Chirico and his work, a pursuit of such goals both sprang from and generated a complex web of the-atrical and artistic influence. Like key theater figures such as Edward Gordon Craig, Maurice Maeterlinck, Antonin Artaud, Tadeusz Kantor, and Samuel Beckett, de Chirico adopted aspects of theatricality and emptiness into his work that help him to achieve an "alogical plurality of possible senses" (Bal-dacci 96). The resulting metaphysical art, in turn, influenced theater figures such as Italian playwright and theorist Massimo Bontempelli. De Chirico's work thus stands as evidence that this interest and practice was not limited to the theater. Rather the metaphysical nature of the search for emptiness led to deeply interdisciplinary art.

In the twentieth century, artists in both the theater and visual arts under-took a search for inspiration that led them to identify theatricality as a con-structive element capable of heightening the creativity and deepening the meaning in their work. Looking back on the first half of the twentieth century in a discussion of the theatrical art of the 1980s, Josette Féral identifies this as a moment when theatricality was "systematically re-examined" and ultimately lost its former distinction as a "strictly theatrical phenomenon" (99). As a result, she observes, theatricality can no longer be conceptualized as a concrete property identifiable beyond a shadow of a doubt. Instead, theatricality is a process. The spectator, Féral explains, plays a crucial role in initiating this process through the act of watching. He perceives the events, acts, or tableaux presented to him as part of an "'other' space, no longer subject to the laws of the quotidian, and [...] where he has no place except as external observer" (105). Building on this expanded notion of theatricality, William Egginton also ties his definition of theatricality to spatiality, basing his explanation on the concept's use as a "phenomenological notion." He explains that while there remains a distant connection between theatricality and the theater, "the 'the-ater' in this formulation [...] has become *that medium of interaction whose con-ventions structure and reveal to us our sense of space or spatiality.*" He concludes,

"The spatiality so revealed is theatricality" (Egginton 3; author's emphasis). Anne Britt-Gran adds yet another layer to this perspective by emphasizing fiction as key to the perception of theatricality. This process, she argues, is distinct from performance or performativity because in its spatiality and conception it exists only outside the realm of reality. Because of this, theatricality can be understood as the "victory of representation" (221). For these scholars, such "victories of representation" and fully fictional spaces are the constructive results of theatricality which can be employed in a variety of media both in and beyond officially sanctioned theater venues.

Recent art historical studies have also begun to explore more specifically the ways in which visual artists use theatricality creatively and intentionally to evoke particular viewer responses to their works of art. Caroline van Eck and Stijn Bussels argue that the use of theatrical elements in a painting is much more than a simple matter of borrowing costumes, gestures, or compositional features.[5] Rather, such elements evoke a theatricality that changes the way viewers approach the work of art. These elements act as "signals to the viewer that he or she should look at what is represented as a viewer of a play" (10). In other words, the viewer is asked to approach the artwork as if the tableau presented were an unfolding drama not anchored in time but continuing beyond the artwork itself. Furthermore, art historian Kati Rötger, much like Féral, views theatricality as a process tied to the perception of a fictional "other" space. It is capable, she writes, of complicating and transforming viewers' typical faith in and relationship with awareness by "inserting a gap between beholder and beheld that pervades their relationship with alterity" and "suspends the fundamental constituents of the belief in perception" (183). She argues that theatricality asks us to adopt a different perspective by holding truth and deceit, reality and illusion in equal suspension (182). Finally, many of these art historical sources agree that "one element remains constant: that of duplication and self-referentiality, self-consciousness or even an infinite regress" (van Eck and Bussels 21). In other words, theatricality can give artwork "meta-" qualities that can suggest seemingly infinite layers of meaning, knowledge, and self-awareness.

While such recent sources have thus begun to approach theatricality as a creative and useful element in visual art, many art historians have previously explored this topic in negative terms, particularly so in relation to de Chirico's oeuvre. As early as 1914, reviewers of the Salon des Indépendants dismissed de Chirico's entries as "amusing, slightly literary theater sets" (Vauxcelles 2).[6] Since then, despite de Chirico's published rebuttal to this "misunderstanding," many, if not most, scholars and critics have continued to perpetuate such ideas. In 1925 and 1926, the surrealists André Breton and Max Morise wrote of a severe "lack" in de Chirico's painting. While Morise declares, "I cannot resign myself to not understanding" de Chirico's "unintelligible signs" (32), Breton laments the loss of the artist's "greatness," writing that "we do not want to follow him to his substandard conclusions, of which the least we can say is that spirit [*l'esprit*] is totally absent" (4). Compounded with the 1914 classification of de Chirico's work as stage sets, such assessments made de his art seem like a failure: not only because it was like a "set" or background (of lesser importance) but also because it seemed to prove that de he did not have the talent or the intelligence to achieve profound, decipherable messages on his canvases.

Since such reviews in the early twentieth century, scholars interested in connecting de Chirico to the theater have continued to perpetuate this dismissive approach to theatricality by discussing it in very basic terms. This has in part stemmed from the influence of one of the most famous rejections of the theatricality in art. In the 1970s, art historian Michael Fried defined theatricality as "an artificial construction in which persuasiveness was sacrificed and dramatic illusion vitiated in the attempt to impress the beholder and solicit his applause" (100). Responding to this superficial definition, as well as Fried's lengthy critique of its use in art, many critics and scholars writing on the theatricality in de Chirico's work have since adopted the same attitude. As a result, theatricality becomes an element used to attack his art as lacking convincing dramatic illusion as well as sincere depth or meaning. Even scholars attempting to shed more positive light on the theatricality of de Chirico's work often identify or define theatricality in overly simplistic terms that do not help reveal any greater depth in his art. Francesco Poli, an Italian scholar who insists on a close relationship between the artistic goals of de Chirico and Edward Gordon Craig, locates the theatricality of de Chirico's paintings in their scenographic qualities. He writes that "de Chirico's pictorial vision derives from the *definition of a stage set*—architectural figurative space with boundaries of appearance that are well-traced out, but unstable" (136; my emphasis).[7] Similarly, other sources often pinpoint in his paintings certain lighting effects, the shallowness of the space, the placement of figures, and other such theatrical elements without exploring any deeper connections the work might have to the theater world or its many philosophies, theories, or practices. Together, such assessments of this artistic element either insist or imply that for art in general and for de Chirico's art in particular theatricality is an often undesirable quality which does not affect viewer perception and cannot create profound meaning within or elicit profound understanding from an artwork.

The theatricality in de Chirico's work is, however, calculated to evoke a viewer response that moves toward a deep and metaphysical meaning. In 1921, de Chirico wrote an essay defending German symbolist painter Max Klinger's *Crucifixion* (1890), which had been criticized for its overt theatricality. Within his defense of this painting, de Chirico reveals his belief that theatricality can actually *validate* a work of art. "In this painting," de Chirico writes, "[Klinger] has sought to exploit a certain bizarre and metaphysical appearance that actors assume upon the stage. [...] The whole picture is *theatrical*, but not in the way usually connected with this word." The usual connotations of "theatrical," de Chirico admits, make it an undesirable quality that diminishes both the aesthetic and spiritual value of a work of art, particularly when "the theatricality of the work is an element that creeps in without the intervention of the artist's will." He does not, however, see this involuntary aspect in Klinger's *Crucifixion*. Here, de Chirico argues, "the theatrical aspect is *desired* and *conscious* since only the metaphysical side has been used, and, as I mentioned, this element, rather than diminishing the spiritual power of the work, augments it" (133). Unfortunately, de Chirico never describes precisely what makes the desired and conscious use of theatricality metaphysical nor does he give a very descriptive account of the ways in which it augments the spiritual power of the work.[8] This he leaves up to the reader to surmise, as he leaves it up to the viewer to decipher the metaphysical meaning in his paintings. Still, it is evident in this essay and many of his other writings as well as his artwork, that de Chirico is concerned with something far deeper than the scenographic qualities and lack of "spirit" identified by his critics.

To get at this deeper theatricality we must start, as art historian Marianne Martin encourages, by examining the more basic and visible theatrical elements of de Chirico's work. Following such an approach, we can identify the aspects of de Chirico's paintings that initially ask viewers to approach this work as a theatrical composition. From there, we can begin to unravel the subtleties through which metaphysical meanings are ultimately revealed and explore the overlapping philosophical ideas and visual devices that connect de Chirico to a larger web of artists in the theater. Initiating such an investigation herself, Martin locates the origins of his more overt theatricality in his use of compositional elements (curtains, stages, placement of objects and figures, etc.) to evoke "his particular brand of quasi-illusionism," in his tendency to conceptualize his life as a drama, and in the inspiration he drew from his many theatrical collaborations with his brother Alberto Savinio and other theater figures of the time (81). Though she does not discuss *The Painter's Family* specifically, Martin's ideas can be applied to this painting as a starting point for this investigation.

In this painting, not only does de Chirico allude to an autobiographical element in the work but he also employs a number of contradictory theatrical elements to create his "quasi-illusionism." Though it defies logic, the title *The Painter's Family* suggests a personal narrative, corroborating Martin's insistence on de Chirico's tendency to theatricalize his life story in in his art. Moreover, this family becomes the medium through which de Chirico urges us to see this composition as a theatrical tableau. The compositional elements of spotlighting and delimited space (both of which Martin generally traces to the influence of stage designer and theorist Georg Fuchs) present the mannequin figures as if they are on stage. Here the orange background seems to be a backdrop, lowered to create a tight space in which there is insufficient room for an artist to work on the unfinished canvas in the background. The spotlight, which comes from above and highlights the family, focuses our attention on their triangular tableau in which even the baby seems to "cheat out" toward an "audience." At the same time, such highlighting draws our attention to the many contradictions in this work. In addition to the tension created between the lifelessness of these mannequins and our expectations that they have something to do with a living painter, many other contradictions occur within his use of theatrical elements: between the convincing lighting effects and the dissolving easel; between the evocation of an actual stage space and mannequins and the absurdity of the scene; and between the fleshiness of the figures and the inexplicable architectural growths on their torsos.[9] Through such incongruities as well as allusions to autobiographical elements, de Chirico builds up what Martin identifies as "his particular brand of quasi-illusionism," which here creates a scene with life-like elements that ask us to see this surreal tableau as simultaneously truth and fiction. The complexities of de Chirico's metaphysical theatricality begin to unfold.

Beyond the lighting, shallow space, and other compositional effects, the mannequin figure itself acts as an important theatrical element, one that not only draws on the brotherly inspiration identified by Martin but also one that presents us with a deepening concept of theatricality. Despite its growing popularity in the theater of the time, such a figure had few, if any, contemporary equivalents in the visual arts. It thus first entered de Chirico's painting directly from the theater, specifically from Savinio's play *Les chants de la mi-mort*.[10] De Chirico had long been struck by the mannequins and tailors' dummies displayed in stores where "whole scenes, dramas of modern life, are reconstructed in the small space of the shop window-theater" ("Vale Lutetia" 495). This interest, however, did not translate into his paintings until the figure was further developed in Savinio's play. Once he did adopt the mannequin into his art, de Chirico transformed it into his own unique figure but never removed it from its theatrical context, continuing to produce images and set designs that overtly connected the mannequin to the theater.[11] He even wrote about his mannequins as theatrical "characters" who had an enigmatic effect on the "spectators" of his scenes ("Birth" 282). The mannequin's form, however, did change, eventually becoming like the mannequins in *The Painter's Family*: seated and with abstracted architectural growths, featureless ovate heads, and completely disproportionate legs. In this form, de Chirico wrote, the figures were more "mysterious" than their standing counterparts who seemed able to "get up, walk around [...] enter life's grand illusion, in short, live!!" (283). By maintaining their status as theatrical elements and developing them further to create a more enigmatic effect, de Chirico was able to use his mannequins to reinforce the division between the viewer's quotidian space and the painting's metaphysical reality. Like his counterparts in the theater who turned to mannequin-like figures to stress the boundary between reality and theatricality, de Chirico's emphasis on the division between the quotidian and the metaphysical was central to his art.

In this function, as deeply theatrical figures, de Chirico's mannequins particularly link his work to that of Craig and Bontempelli.[12] Working at the same time as de Chirico and similarly rejecting realism, Craig invented a figure he called the "über-marionette." This figure, he hoped, would "[not] compete with life—rather will go beyond it" (146). In his 1907 treatise on this figure, Craig explains, "Do away with the actor, and you do away with the means by which a debased stage-realism is produced and flourishes." (144).[13] By contrast, Craig believes, the über-marionette will point spectators beyond notions of reality or fiction and to the mysterious spirit beyond. According to Poli and Ara Merjian, Craig's published work on this figure helped de Chirico, who was familiar with publications like *The Mask*, develop the philosophical ideas behind his marionette-like mannequins. The resulting visual and textual exploration of this figure, in turn, directly shaped Bontempelli's work. Inspired specifically by what de Chirico named metaphysical art, Bontempelli used life-size puppets to address epistemological issues such as questions of language and knowledge creation as well as distinctions between fiction and reality (Storchi 301).[14] Thus, all three men turned to marionette-like figures in order to take viewers out of standard systems of meaning in which man is the measure of all things. Rather than replacing human beings, their mannequin-like figures ask viewers to question human beings.

In addition to finding inspiration in mannequin-like figures, Craig, Bontempelli, and de Chirico were greatly influenced by their personal interpretations of Nietzschean philosophy. Guided by works like *The Birth of Tragedy*, de Chirico, like Craig, felt his eyes had been opened to the spirit beyond "debased realism." This not only led him, as Merjian has argued, to a visual and verbal rehearsal of Nietzsche's "theatre-eye" but it also defined the philosophical messages put forth in his publications and paintings, which ultimately drew Bontempelli toward metaphysicality (132). Central to the metaphysical was de Chirico's belief that Nietzschean philosophy pointed past the unstable, flawed, and relative systems of language, truth, and knowledge and toward a profound meaning lying behind or beyond the physical world. This separate state of awareness, according to de Chirico's interpretation, could be revealed only in visual images which strike us in moments of pure non-sense. Thus, he aimed for the "deletion of the logical sense in art" and instead emphasized "the deep significance of the non-meaning of life," which ultimately formed "the inner skeleton of an art really new, free and deep" ("Noi Metafisici"). In an attempt to capture such ideas in paint, de Chirico began to work toward an approach that would allow him to reveal a world beyond discursive meaning and fabricated systems of signs and symbols. This world, he wrote, "excludes a priori every logical possibility of visual or psychic education" ("Metaphysical Art" 89).[15] By exposing viewers to this world apart, de Chirico hoped to communicate, and ultimately share, the artist-philosopher's experience of the "senseless and quiet beauty of the material" and the "terrible emptiness" of the infinite ("Noi Metafisici").

This philosophical underpinning to his continued development of the mannequin figure is paramount to a deeper understanding of the overlap between de Chirico, Bontempelli, and Craig as well as de Chirico's eventual move toward emptiness. As Poli observes, the essential element that imbues de Chirico's art with its signature "disturbing and alienating tension" is "the [imminent and pressing] absence of the human presence, or of living beings." He adds that, rather than human beings, de Chirico's paintings "are inhabited only by simulacra of the human figure and shadows, in a triumph of absence, the void, and the double" (137). Despite Merjian's recent insistence that the "simulacra" within de Chirico's work ultimately remain wed to language's "invisible filaments," the "triumph of absence, the void, and the double" that Poli observes actually points us through such ties to language and to the metaphysical emptiness beyond (Merjian, 261). By keeping his figures within the "self-imposed limits of language" and by refusing to "liberate" his paintings from "the prison-house of figuration," de Chirico gives viewers a point of entry into his work (274–75). From there, however, he denies any solid connections to conscious logic or meaning. Instead, the painting's simultaneous accessibility and enigma, what Merjian calls its "twofold disingenuousness," points us not back to language's "invisible filaments" but to the primal, wordless meaning that emerges in the emptiness of his figures and composition.

We can see this process clearly in de Chirico's *The Painter's Family* which presents viewers with what seems like an understandable system of visual representation only to contradict and dismantle any such logic or candor. Though the title promises us a family, we are confronted by a lifeless grouping of mannequins, who so nearly embody the traditional figures of a family that they ultimately further underscore its absence. These figures cannot have the bodily organs, human emotions, or knowledge of a "real" human family; they are empty of those elements we might otherwise assume to be present inside of human figures. Beyond these figures, the background further accentuates a sense of empty space. A mesmerizing series of orange and gray brushstrokes, this background seems in suspension between shallow and deep space; at the same time that the backdrop delimits the mannequins' space, it also draws us in, inviting us to get lost in its seemingly endless organic patterning. Riccardo Dottori has observed that in a number of de Chirico's other metaphysical paintings "our gaze goes steadily further from the earth and gets lost in the infinity of empty space, the symbol of metaphysical nothingness" (130). In *The Painter's Family* we are not presented with the cloudless, starless skies that Dottori gives as examples of this phenomenon, but de Chirico has given us something even more removed from reality and consequently even more empty. In search of an enigma that could heighten his own painting to the profound level he sought, de Chirico charges the theatrical elements of his art with emptiness in order to reveal the metaphysical essence of his work to viewers. Moreover, the sense of empty space he evokes can further solidify our sense of this painting's theatricality in terms of its spatial and phenomenological qualities. Like the metaphysical qualities that Craig's über-marionette and Bontempelli's puppets project, the theatricality of de Chirico's mannequins thus connects work and viewer to the void.[16]

The "absence" in de Chirico's metaphysical art must be further explored through theater studies in order to better understand the complexities of this strategy, which is part of a much larger movement in history. According to Jean-Pierre Sarrazac, "At the turn of the twentieth century, the theater, along with the other representational arts, gradually became aware of its inner emptiness and began to project this void outwards" (58). In other words, as artists searched for inspiration within the recesses of their minds, they encountered a profound abyss. This then led them, like de Chirico, away from a simulation of "reality" and toward a rejection of conventional, surface-level illusions that had previously filled the arts with narrative, characters, props, and scenery. Writing in the same year that de Chirico completed *The Painter's Family*, Antonin Artaud explains, "We do not seek [...] as has always been characteristic of the theater, to give the illusion of what is not, but on the contrary, to present to the eye certain tableaux, certain indestructible, undeniable images that will speak directly to the mind" (160). To make this vital connection, Artaud argues, we must find a way to move beyond constructed reality and meaning. Joining this move away from realism and toward a more metaphysical interest in the recesses of the human mind, de Chirico published an essay in the Italian theater periodical *Il dramma* in which he denounced realism and all realist tendencies in theatrical performance (qtd. in Gigli 71). Yet it is not within his work for the theater but in his paintings of the 1920s that his art moves away from reality by moving toward the void. By removing the human figure from his canvas, much like Craig removed actors from his stage, de Chirico moves toward what Sarrazac identifies as "the revelation of theatricality through the emptying of theater" (59).

Other theater figures pushed toward this same strategy. Investigating emptiness more in depth than Sarrazac, Les Essif reveals still more of the complexities this element can bring to a work. According to Essif, key twentieth-century theater figures, much like de Chirico, believed that while the origin and the vital depth of human consciousness is non-referential, our "referentially conditioned thought processes" and the "web of signification" they have created render us unable to connect to such awareness (Essif 198, 35). Because of this, we cannot conceive of the extralinguistic or invisible world of the non-representational and non-referential except through "a unique, creative manipulation of language and the apparently 'real' world" (7). This belief led a number of artists to create in their art "a psychic space within which our concrete ideas are suspended" (16). The resulting "empty" space allowed influential theater figures such as Antonin Artaud and Samuel Beckett to move toward a suppression of both man and language as a point of reference. As in de Chirico's paintings, this empty space is therefore "metaphysical," transcending conventional systems of logic and understanding and conflicting with our desire to understand and establish reality. With the theater figures of his day, de Chirico shares in the idea that emptiness could free artists from "the web of signification" and allow them instead to search for the profound awareness that lies beyond conditioned thought.

The natural outgrowth of such a search was, as Essif and Sarrazac agree, an "emptying" of the theater. Naturalistic and representational illusions so central to realism could not operate as a metaphor for the non-representational, extralinguistic void that the artists discovered in the depths of their minds. So dramatists, practitioners, and theorists focused on a single, introspective character in whom essential elements of the work were concentrated, including its metadiscourses, or self-consciousness (Essif 45). Such a character Essif calls "hypersubjective," explaining that "one solitary and introspective dramatic character becomes the overdetermined focal point (*mise en abyme*) of a theatrical metadiscourse based on an image of empty space" (45). As a "hypersubjective" figure, this marionette-like character thus becomes the representative of both the work's infinite layers of meaning and its empty space. Looking inward at the wordless theater of their own minds, these "self-sufficient protagonists" draw us with them into a supra-referential space beyond conditioned thought and referential constructions. Within this process, these figures take on a profound spatial dimension as their empty minds elide with the empty space of the stage around them (8). Rendered less human by this spatial dimension, these figures also become more of an image than any earlier theatrical characters. Moreover, as Martin Green and John Swan have argued, a marionette amplifies "human meanings [which] reverberate and swell to thunder" inside the "hollow space" of the figure. In this way, such complex, yet empty figures, allowed artists not only to point spectators and viewers toward extra-linguistic thought but also to amplify such awareness to the point that the audience "feels those meanings become larger than life" (Green and Swan 20). Ultimately, according to Essif, such visually profound, marionette-like characters, emptied of language and filled instead with empty space, allowed theater practitioners like Craig, Artaud, and Beckett to achieve a deeply complex "meaninglessness" (or "emptiness") in their work (175).

Though de Chirico's inclusion of multiple figures in *The Painter's Family* diverges from the work of dramatists like Beckett who focused on the solitary hypersubjective marionette-like character, this painting and his figures still adhere to a great number of hypersubjective characteristics. De Chirico has brought our focus to rest intently on a few figures in a tight, relatively bare space. He is not interested in surrounding architectural spaces or the audience. Instead there is an intensification, a focalization on the stage image. He not only uses highlighting and color to draw our attention to the mannequins, but also includes their image doubled on a canvas. This is a painting of a painting, its self-consciousness shows through. With their heads bent down away from our gaze, these characters have an air of introspection, but as faceless, non-living mannequins their heads are empty—of language, of thought, of feeling. This contradiction further reminds us that no painted figures, intentionally inanimate or otherwise, are truly "real" or "living." The objects and figures in a painting are not real; they are painted representations that can only evoke a sense of reality and trick us into suspending our disbelief. Finally, these characters are, in fact, images but they have also become more spatial than other figures, as the architecture of their torsos makes apparent.[17] Springing, it seems, from the mannequins themselves, the archways and tunnels open into a deeply shadowed interior. At the same time that the architecture acts as a fortress-like barrier between viewers and mannequins, the openings within it seem to invite us in, but to what? Furthermore, they trigger us to ask more questions of this painting. Are these mannequins on a stage or are they, in fact, stages themselves? Are they empty, inanimate objects or are they the ultimate example of philosophical meaninglessness with their attention focused completely on the metaphysical void?

By eliciting such questions, *The Painter's Family* encourages viewers to break free of the ingrained laws of the quotidian and instead enter into the metaphysical. This family is both inviting, with their warm skin tones and fleshy curves, and startling, with their empty faces and cold lifelessness. The small space represented is both cozy, as it seems to safely contain the family, and oppressive, as it traps them within a tight space and denies us the narrative information we may seek. The mannequins seem solid enough to touch and yet the easel and the orange background seem to shimmer on the verge of dissipation. Through these contradictions, de Chirico confounds our sense of expectation and logic. Then, once we are initially confused, our sense of fiction and reality suspended, de Chirico's painting confronts us with even more challenges. Suddenly, we find our expectations about familial relations and roles as well as the fundamental nature of human relationships questioned. Do these mannequins represent the meaninglessness of concepts like "mother," "father," "son," "daughter"? Are the foundational relationships in our lives as enigmatic as these mannequins? Are we, ourselves, filled with emptiness? Despite whether we choose to embrace or reject such enigmas, we, like the Surrealist critics discussed above, cannot ignore them; de Chirico confronts us with a "family" that will not let us avoid irreconcilable contradictions or uncomfortable illogical questions. As Green and Swan observe of marionette-like characters in general, their hollowness amplifies human meanings to larger-than-life proportions. Yet when we are given questions instead of answers, it is the mystery of the contradictions that becomes overwhelming. They outgrow any system of logic in which we might be able to resolve them and are instead turned into metaphysical enigmas—questions beyond answers, puzzles beyond solutions—intended to point viewers to a new experience of awareness.

Like his counterparts in the theater, de Chirico profoundly challenges the supremacy of representation and concrete meaning. All of these men turned to the metaphysical, which rejects the tenants of realism and instead evokes a mystery that allows us to see through reality and toward a profound spiritual realm. Through his intentional and targeted use of theatricality, de Chirico points to the fabrication and fiction, the non-reality, of art and then uses this to elicit a deeper response in his viewers than any illusionistic painting or play was thought capable of achieving. By using mannequins to create what he suggests is a family portrait, he confuses our expectations that lifeless mannequins and living genealogies are mutually exclusive. Asking us in his title to approach these figures as a family, he simultaneously uses architectural growths to build both literal and figurative barriers between viewer and mannequin. By thus eliciting our world of defined human relationships only to confound our expectations of this world, de Chirico pushes us to constantly ask questions. In what way, for example, do these mannequins and human beings share common ground? Do they embody our habit of developing and performing fabricated identities to the world around us? Or do they represent something even deeper, the profound, wordless void inside us? Is it emptiness we share?

To date, critics and scholars have generally refused to follow de Chirico into the confusing and illogical void he creates in these images. They have instead identified the extremity of de Chirico's enigmas as an artistic failure. His endless puzzles frustrated the Surrealists who lamented the lack of concrete meaning in his metaphysical mannequin paintings. The boundless mystery and "meaninglessness" have since created difficulties for scholars who try to prove that there is "something" there. Yet if we turn to theater studies to help identify the complexities of this work, great possibilities open up for interpretation. We not only begin to recognize the deeply interdisciplinary nature of the search for emptiness in the arts, but we also begin to grasp the complexities of de Chirico's metaphysical theatricality. When we embrace this understanding we see that this painting is not devoid of meaning but full of emptiness.

UNIVERSITY OF NORTH CAROLINA AT CHAPEL HILL

NOTES

1. A comparison with de Chirico's *Comedy and Tragedy* (1926) can help us to see the stage space that de Chirico may have had in mind when composing *The Painter's Family*. In the second painting, it is as if de Chirico has given us a wider view of the same space. Here the theater figures of Comedy and Tragedy are perched on a sort of mini-stage. Behind them, we can make out an arena of spectators—extremely distant, but nevertheless present. This overtly theatrical painting can tell us three things about *The Painter's Family*. To begin with, much like the marionettes of the theater, mannequins are figures whose bodies are designed for show or spectacle and de Chirico sees these figures with their architectural growths, short legs, and classical drapery as having a home in the theater. Second, wooden planking of the stage can help to corroborate a reading of the floor in *The Painter's Family* as a stage. Third, the mannequins' small stage in *Comedy and Tragedy* is quite shallow, like the space we see in *The Painter's Family*.

2. Two major sources in particular insist on this perceived trajectory in de Chirico's work: J.T. Soby, *Giorgio de Chirico* (New York: MoMA, 1955), and Paolo Baldacci, *De Chirico: The Metaphysical Period, 1888–1919* (Boston: Little, Brown, 1997). But, as Juliet Bellow pointed out as recently as 2013, scholars "still tend too often to dismiss most of the artist's postwar output as overly nostalgic, insufficiently critical, and just plain kitschy" (212).

3. Bellow and Ara Merjian stand out as art historians who have recently published on de Chirico's work and his involvement in the theater world of his time. While Bellow reveals the meaningful complexities in de Chirico's set designs for the Ballet Russe's 1929 production of *Le Bal*, Merjian explores the influence of Edward Gordon Craig's philosophies on de Chirico's early metaphysical painting. Yet they are primarily interested in themes of "ruin" and "recurrence" and do not consider emptiness.

4. There are a few exceptions. Matthew Gale's essay on the connections between de Chirico and Luigi Pirandello allow him to touch on the metaphysical aspects of the theatrical elements in de Chirico's work. Marianne Martin's work suggests that there is something deeper than we can see in the visual signs of theatricality in his paintings. Francisco Poli and Ara Merjian have argued for an important link between de Chirico and Edward Gordon Craig. Merjian even goes as far as to connect the theatrical aspects of de Chirico's work to Nietzschean philosophy and the metaphysical (something argued

later in this article as well). None of them, however, explore what de Chirico calls the "metaphysical side" of theatricality. Nor do they consider the artist's work in terms of empty space.

5. Egginton's own assessment of theatricality not only sustains this conclusion but also takes it one step further. He writes, "Theatricality, on the other hand, should not be understood as the quality of engaging in overt performance, or as emotiveness, or as being self-conscious of one's status as actor. Nor [...] should it be equated with the notion in art criticism of the overflowing of borders (although it is deeply connected with this artistic effect). And though still maintaining some of its root meaning, 'of or having to do with the theater,' it departs from this definition insofar as it is used as a *phenomenological* notion" (3).

6. All translations from the original French and Italian are mine unless otherwise noted.

7. Poli's approach to the work of both of these men draws parallels between them in terms of scenography rather than a deeper metaphysical theatricality. This is not an uncommon interpretation. Critics of both men have frequently discussed their work in such terms. Christopher Innes addresses this issue in the reception of Craig's work, writing, "This tendency to see Craig solely as a scene designer and therefore to dismiss his vision as an attempt to substitute visual spectacle for drama, is an all-too-common-error. Even [his partner and inspiration] Isadora Duncan ... referred to his work only as 'the perfect setting'—which led Craig to exclaim that 'even after 20 years ... she thought I was thinking of scenery!'" (Innes 4).

8. This is not wholly surprising as de Chirico seems to have also been unable to explicitly define his concept of the "metaphysical." This is, in great part, because, in pointing beyond reality to a realm of non-referential consciousness, the metaphysical is an inherently extra-linguistic concept.

9. Though these architectural growths seem to be an important theatrical device in this image, there is not space to fully explore them in this article. That said, Merjian's recent book on the subject focuses on de Chirico's metaphysical architecture more generally, observing that in his later work the mannequin's bodies and their surrounding architectural environments become nearly indistinguishable.

10. For more on the collaborative development of this figure see Willard Bohn, "Apollinaire and de Chirico: The Making of the Mannequins," *Comparative Literature* 27 (1975): 153–165.

11. I am thinking specifically of *Comedy and Tragedy*, his work for Massimo Bontempelli's play *Siepe a nordovest* (1919), and his essay "The Birth of the Mannequin" (1928). For a description of *Comedy and Tragedy*, see note 1.

12. The use of mannequin-like figures also links de Chirico to later figures such as Tadeusz Kantor, a Polish theater and visual artist, who was also inspired by Craig and also employed these types of figures to achieve similar goals in his work. As we will see with de Chirico, Kantor was also interested in capturing emptiness in his art. He wrote that "'What matters most for art is poverty, and not riches. [...] A hollowing-out, an inner void—this is, as it were, the first step towards removing the spell (qtd. in Fazan et. al 382). For more of his writings see Michal Kobialka, *Further on, Nothing: Tadeusz Kantor's Theatre* (Minneapolis: University of Minnesota Press, 2009).

13. The similarities between de Chirico's ideas and Craig's are astounding. Among other similarities, both men took inspiration from and worked in the two fields of visual

art and theater and both were even criticized and "misunderstood" for producing surface-level scenographic images with no deeper theatricality.

14. In her assessment of the links between de Chirico's and Bontempelli's work, Simona Storchi argues for closer attention to the "parallel developments in literature and the visual arts ... a common discourse transcending the specificity of the two artistic media" (300). Similarly, such connections and discourses should be established in scholarship on theater and the visual arts.

15. While visual artists do not deal directly in written language, throughout history the art world has pushed toward work that can be "read." The historical development of "iconography," the study of subject matter that leads to classification of themes, motifs, symbols, etc. as well as the standardization of image formulas, has enabled viewers to "read" familiar stories, commonly held beliefs, and other clearly defined information in visual art. So while de Chirico's work does not deal directly with semiotics and semantics, it still addresses and rejects the supremacy of a conventional system by moving away from narrative, illusionistic techniques, and subject matter. Working in pictorial form, de Chirico thus attempts to destabilize what we see in order to point us toward something more profound.

16. Bontempelli has never been considered in terms of emptiness, but Craig has. Not only do both Les Essif and Jean-Pierre Sarrazac place Craig in the lineage of key theater figures moving toward emptiness during the twentieth-century, but other scholars as well have noted the importance of emptiness to his work. Innes, for example, cites Isadora Duncan on this subject, writing that "If so many of Craig's ideas seem negative, it is because his concept of what theater might become could not be realized [...] until 'the great incubus of the present theater is destroyed [...] leaving CLEAR SPACE" (6; author's emphasis).

17. This is further supported in Merjian's recent work. Though concerned almost exclusively with paintings from the 1910s, he writes that the "Metaphysical city" and the mannequin bodies of de Chirico's paintings "appear increasingly indistinguishable" in de Chirico's later metaphysical work (257). Merjian's overarching argument, however, contradicts a truly "metaphysical" definition of de Chirico's work, insisting that the Metaphysical city "enthrones meaning again [...] as much as it deals it a blow" and ultimately "offers something intractably, indissolubly physical still" (274, 275).

WORKS CITED

Artaud, Antonin. "Manifesto for a Theater That Failed." *Selected Writings*. Ed. Susan Sontag. New York: Farrar, Straus and Giroux, 1976: 159–62.

Baldacci, Paolo. "De Chirico: The Metaphysical Period, 188–1919." Boston: Little Brown, 1997.

Bellow, Juliet. *Modernism on Stage: The Ballets Russes and the Parisian Avant-Garde*. Burlington, VT: Ashgate, 2013: 209–45.

Bohn, Willard. "Apollinaire and de Chirico: The Making of the Mannequins." *Comparative Literature* 27 (1975): 153–65.

Breton, André. "Le Surréalisme et la Peinture." *Révolution Surréaliste* 1926, no. 7: 3–6.

Britt-Gran, Anne. "The Fall of Theatricality in the Age of Modernity." *SubStance* 31.2 (2002): 251–64.

de Chirico, Giorgio. "Birth of the Mannequin." *Metafisica* 1–2 (2002): 282–83.

_____. "Letters by Giorgio de Chirico, Gemma de Chirico, and Alberto de Chirico to Fritz Gartz, 1908–1911." *Metafisica* 2008, 7–8 (2008): 561–62.

_____. "Max Klinger." *Il Convegno*, May 1921. *Metaphysical Art*. Ed. Massimo Carrà. New York: Praeger, 1971. 97–100, 133–37.

_____. "Metaphysical Art." *Valori Plastici* April-May, 1919. *Metaphysical Art*. Ed. Massimo Carrà. New York: Praeger, 1971.

_____. "Noi metafisici." February 15, 1919. "Cronache d'attualità." *Fondazione de Chirico*. Rome: Fondazione Giorgio e Isa de Chirico. www.fondazionedechirico.org/scritti/consultazioni/saggi/noi-metafisici/. Web. Accessed May 28, 2015.

_____. "Vale Lutetia." *Metafisica* 7–8 (2008): 494–97.

Craig, Edward Gordon. "The Actor and the Über-marionette." *The Twentieth-Century Performance Reader*. Ed. Teresa Brayshaw and Noel Witts. 3d ed. New York: Routledge, 2014: 144–50.

Dottori, Riccardo. "From Zarathustra's Poetry to the Aesthetics of Metaphysical Art." *Metafisica* 7–8 (2008): 117–38.

Egginton, William. *How the World Became a Stage: Presence, Theatricality, and the Question of Modernity*. Albany: State University of New York Press, 2003.

Essif, Les. *Empty Figure on an Empty Stage: The Theatre of Samuel Beckett and His Generation*. Bloomington: Indiana University Press, 2001.

Fazan, Katarzyna, Ana Róza Burzunska and Marta Brys. *Tadeusz Kantor Today: Metamorphoses of Death, Memory and Presence*. New York: Peter Lang, 2014.

Féral, Josette. "The Specificity of Theatrical Language." *SubStance* 31.2 (2002): 94–108.

Fried, Michael. *Absorption and Theatricality: Painting and Beholder in the Age of Diderot*. Berkeley: University of California Press, 1980.

Gale, Matthew. "De Chirico and Pirandello." *Pirandello Studies* 19 (1999): 18–29.

Gigli, Elena. "De Chirico and Performance." *Sipario/Staged Art*. Milan: Charta, 1997: 71–77.

Green, Martin, and John Swan. *The Triumph of Pierrot: The Comedia dell'Arte and the Modern Imagination*. University Park, PA : Macmillan, 1993.

Innes, Christopher. *Edward Gordon Craig : A Vision of the Theater*. Amsterdam: Hardwood, 1998.

Martin, Marianne. "On de Chirico's Theater." In *De Chirico*. New York: MoMA, 1982: 81–100.

Merjian, Ara. *Giorgio de Chirico and the Metaphysical City: Nietzsche, Modernism, Paris*. New Haven, CT: Yale University Press, 2014.

Mories, Max. "A propos de l'Exposition Chirico." *Révolution Surréaliste* 4 (1925): 31–32.

Nietzsche, Friedrich. "The Birth of Tragedy." *The Complete Works of Friedrich Nietzsche*. Vol. 1. Ed. Oscar Levy. Trans. WM. A. Haussmann. New York: Macmillan, 1909.

Poli, Francesco. "Statues, Shadows, Mannequins." *Nature According to de Chirico*. Ed. Achille Bonito Olivia. Milan: Federico Motta Editore, 2010: 136–41.

Röttger, Kati. "'What Do I See?' The Order of Looking in Lessing's *Emilia Galotti*." *Theatricality in Early Modern Art and Architecture*. Eds. Caroline van Eck and Stijn Bussels. Malden, MA: Wiley-Blackwell, 2011: 178–89.

Sarrazac, Jean-Pierre. "The Invention of 'Theatricality:' Rereading Bernard Dort and Roland Barthes." *Theatricality* Spec. issue of *SubStance* 31.2 (2002): 57–72.

Soby, J. T. *De Chirico*. New York: MoMA, 1955.

Storchi, Simona. "Massimo Bontempelli between de Chirico and Nietzsche: Mannequins, Marionettes, and the De-Humanized Subject in *La scacchiera davanti allo specchio* and *Eva ultima*." *Romance Studies* (2009): 298–310.
van Eck, Caroline, and Stijn Bussels. "The Visual Arts and the Theatre in Early Modern Europe." *Theatricality in Early Modern Art and Architecture*. Eds. Caroline van Eck and Stijn Bussels. Malden, MA: Wiley-Blackwell, 2011: 178–89.
Vauxcelles, Louis. "Le Salon des Indépendants." *Gil Blas* (February 28, 1914): 1–2.

Archives of an Ironic Film Fan: The "Tony" Drafts of *The Glass Menagerie*

Jeffrey B. Loomis

Abstract

Considerable debate has frequently been roused concerning which of two early published versions of Tennessee Williams's The Glass Menagerie *is the more definitive text. Evaluators often choose the 1945 "reading version," an utterance of the Wingfield family's tale which includes within it the use of a Brechtian screen device, making ironic commentary on characters' sometimes-excessive emotions. Other students of the play favor the 1948 "acting version," which seems to emphasize more sympathy for the onstage personages, and even to make them quite clearly deserving of sympathy. However, examination of Williams's quite early "Tony" drafts of the* Menagerie *scenario seems to reveal that the playwright was always dialogical about this particular drama's tone. Thus, neither the "reading version" nor the "acting version," as a published play script, should be taken to be any more definitive than the alternative published text in its tonal approach.*

Considerable debate has been voiced over whether or not the 1945 "reading version" of Tennessee Williams's *The Glass Menagerie* is the play's ideal text, or whether the 1948 "acting version" proves superior. The 1945 "reading version" includes within it Williams's inserted and controversial Piscatorean/ Brechtian "screens," on which are etched cajolingly playful images and words (many of them in some way designed seemingly at least to josh, and maybe at times to barb with a slight sting, the characters and their tendencies to excessive, even obsessive, sentimentality).[1] While casting an ironic glance at the play's moments of surplus pathos,[2] these screens (through their silent images and terse words of wit) also demonstrate how often Williams must truly have gone to the movies (especially, before the late 1920s, to quite melodramatic silent ones). His moviegoer experience evidently led him to feel tinges of sympathy, but also a definite reserve, toward heady sorts of cinematic-styled emotion.[3] It seems no wonder that his character Tom eventually wanted to counter the passivity of a mere moviegoer's existence with a decision actively to pursue the "adventures" possible to one who dared actually to "*move*" (*TGM [RV]* 79).

Some critics who favor the later "acting version" of *Menagerie* judge it, because of its place in his lifetime's chronology, obviously to represent Williams's "final intentions" for the script (Beaurline 142–143). It does not include the "screens," and it focuses on characters, especially the mother Amanda Wingfield, who for some readers now appear, in contrast with earlier versions, "more gentle, more loving and understanding" (Rowland 68). Yet archival research shows that, as far back as the late 1930s or early 1940s, Williams had almost always blended apparent pity for the Wingfields' travails with light (or even heavier) mockery of their occasionally histrionic tendencies. Thus, one cannot help but wonder if Williams could even conceivably have had "final intentions" which eradicated that irony, or whether (as I fully believe) irony and sympathy were, in his work, always in resonant tension.[4]

In keeping with Williams's usual approach, the esoteric early "Tony" script, as an intriguing antecedent of the eventual *Glass Menagerie*,[5] shows much sympathy for beleaguered characters. Yet it surely also ironizes them. It is named (at least by me) for socialist street singer Tony, presented as a buddy to both the protagonist Tom and to Tom's somber sister Laura—a girl who indeed seems romantically inclined toward this fellow, despite her mother's contempt for him. The script reveals a Wingfield family beset by poverty, caused both by a Great Depression and by a father's desertion of his official "dependents." But the plan of Tony and Tom soon to abscond from the premises, and thus to reject any further struggles with familial strife, approximates (and fairly harshly so) the effect of *Menagerie*'s sardonic 1945 "screens." This "Tony" drama, in any case, clarifies how Williams's dialogical equipoise of moods characteristically (and, in the writing of *The Glass Menagerie*, almost always) combines pity for human suffering with a contrasting quest for a balancing emotional detachment.

*   *   *

A letter sent October 9, 1937, to his theatre director friend Willard Holland, found Williams already contemplating, if not yet composing, a middle-class "family drama," set in an average St. Louis "apartment" (*SL,* 1, 108).[6] The

"Tony" draft, although it cannot have been fully written before 1939 or 1940,[7] does contain many hints of Williams's mid–1930s St. Louis life,[8] as well as reflecting a brief 1935 summer sojourn that he spent in Memphis, where this script takes place.[9]

The Tony character in particular could derive some characterization details from multiple 1930s St. Louis associates of Williams. One of these, the eventual American poet laureate William Jay Smith, has pondered whether he himself might have partly modelled Tony.[10] Yet Smith obliquely may, in some *published* comments, make us sense Tony, more strikingly, as a close analogue to Williams himself. Smith reports that Williams could in this 1930s era vary wildly in his mood swings, from brashly cackling to quasi-catatonic and somber (72). Likewise, Tony is a creature of widely diverse moods. Indeed, Tony is assigned lines and topics to prate about (the coming world war, for instance) that would in the more finalized *Menagerie* be assigned to the central protagonist, the quasi-autobiographical Williams character of Tom (Texas 17.2/ 5). Whenever Tony is onstage, Tom is basically silent; and Tony sometimes speaks, quite simply (and seemingly inappropriately), to Amanda Wingfield as "Mother" and to her daughter Laura as "Sister" (Texas 17.2/A7-A8).

While Williams's official *alter ego* character Tom, in this early script, alternates some sympathy for his mother and sister with caustic derision of them, the Tony character is also split in his attitudes. He is often very sympathetic with Laura, but usually (quite like the 1945 "screens") contrastingly teases, and often a little snidely, mother Amanda Wingfield's preening puritanical poses of social superiority and pseudo-graciousness. To support these binary emphases, Tony is often depicted as if he were schizoid or bipolar. His morose depression especially emerges in a short script called "The Poetry Club Meeting," where Amanda castigates him harshly for reciting, in her presence, a seemingly vulgar poem (Texas 17.2/B21-B25). Then, in the script called "The Night of the Gentleman Caller," which is a more direct ancestor for *The Glass Menagerie*, Tony is contrastingly frisky or manic. He even demonstrates tinges of actual vengefulness toward Amanda, whom he boisterously addresses as "Mother Wing" (in a spate of illogical dinnertime comments, as if he sneers a bit while forcing her to acknowledge him).[11] He also appears quite anxious to shock her by bantering casually about his frequenting of whorehouses and nighttime courtrooms (Texas 17.2/A9-A11). Still, Tony is ever supportive of and appreciated by Amanda's two children. In particular, the romantically smitten Laura (Texas 17.2/A14–15) repeatedly admonishes her mother to stop desecrating either Tony's name or his slovenly physical appearance.[12]

Tony also seems fully invested in Laura's brother Tom's scheme to escape St. Louis, a plan being instigated so that young Mr. Wingfield can, as Tom himself declares, elude any further plaguesome "responsibility" (Texas 17.2/B66) for his mother, his sister, and what he calls, somewhat deprecatingly, their ongoing "festival of women" (Texas 17.3/B16). According to the implications of this particular "Tony" manuscript, Tom ostensibly feels a need for Tony's support as a projected traveling companion sharing his venture into escape. Tony is, after all, another self-declared "Dreamer Type": someone who claims that he "c[ould]n't be driven" overmuch by others (Texas 17.2/A19). Tom surely feels maligned by his mother's imposing "parentification" complexes upon him. She stridently seeks to make him feel born to serve as the duteous, and evidently eternal, Wingfield breadwinner (Single 76–77). Still, Tom also feels plentifully guilty about any attempt to escape these burdens. Hence, he seems to require Tony's boosterism and companionship before he dares to vacate his niche in the family home.

It is important to realize that this "Tony" script does not utter incontrovertible misogyny. After all, Tom at least understands Amanda's desire to find her daughter a beau (Texas 17.2/B66, B16). He also acknowledges some of Amanda's other impressive traits. For example, he notes that she can amazingly replace store-bought furniture, which had recently been "repossessed" by retail credit managers, with vibrantly transformed boxes and stitched-together flour sacks (Texas 17.2/B65).[13] Tom does eventually desert this woman and his sister, too, apparently leaving them as likely prey to a far more extreme poverty than even what they have heretofore known. But his doing so does not appear to mean that he *hates* them.

Indeed, in the "Tony" dramatization, as in all scripts previewing *The Glass Menagerie*, Williams clearly still pities the two central women characters. Critic Masami Usui finds plenteous pathos in the standard *Menagerie* portraits of Laura's and Amanda's economic and psychological impoverishment, and she compares their pathetic situation with that exposed in Virginia Woolf's *A Room of One's Own* (Usui 21). Actually, in all variations of the Wingfield family's drama, echoes of Woolf seem persistently present,[14] for Williams nicknames his male protagonist "Shakespeare" and has Jim express shock that Tom has a "sister" (Texas 17.2/D1; Texas 16.1/96; Delaware 1.23/89–90; *TGM [RV]* 76). His play text thus reminds any Woolfians who also encounter Williams's work that Woolf had postulated Judith Shakespeare, imaginary *sister* of dramatist William, to have fled Stratford-upon-Avon for London, hoping there to become a stage actress. But she would, Woolf says, most likely have become, instead, the sexual prey of a theatre director—who would probably have impregnated and then abandoned her, driving her to desperate suicide (*Room* 46–48). Woolf, of course, uses that hypothesis about imaginary Judith's fate as a cue for protesting a long history of patriarchal abuse toward women.[15]

The "Tony" script makes the playwright's awareness of Woolf seem especially likely. After all, in that script Laura is portrayed, like Woolf's Judith Shakespeare, as a girl with ardent thespian ambitions. She fantasizes herself as "Duse! Bernhardt! Duncan!," "Pavlova! Cornell! Garbo!," and "Maude Adams! Jane Cowl! Hepburn!" To her mind, all of these stage or film performers could "stand alone—and [yet] gather the richness in them to give to the world!"[16] Already active in local amateur theatrics, this version of the Laura character tells her mother that "On the stage ... my nerves, my skin—come ... alive! I—tingle! Oh, I'm an instrument, ...—an instrument—for poets!" (Texas 17.2/D43). After reading such lines, one could surely sympathize with Laura, and even want especially to cheer her on. Allusions to theatrical ambitions like those that once might have helped to victimize a Judith Shakespeare make Laura's fight for a more powerful resilience in life seem increasingly poignant.[17] The Wingfield tale begins to seem primarily character-driven, and, even more primarily, feminist.

Yet our reaction probably would become once again complicated upon learning that Williams supposedly claimed that he could not "digest" Virginia Woolf's writing at all (Brown 272). I do believe that he was here acting somewhat as a *poseur*, overstating his disdain for Woolf or for feminism such as hers. At the same time, however, his refusal to give Woolf unlimited encomiums may explain why he has painted Laura as a girl who would like to flaunt herself before stage footlights, even while he also has made her sound so emotionally shrill as almost to guarantee her later onstage public failure.

Contradistinctively, we can recall that in the "Tony" draft the character of Laura does, nevertheless, dare to defy some of her mother's derisive scorn.[18] She thus proves herself not altogether wrong when she claims to possess both "feelings" and "intelligen[ce]" (Texas 17.3/B4-B5). But she also sounds, still, dangerously naïve (and thus probably more dominated by her "feelings" than by her braininess) when she seems to ignore the many likely obstacles that can interfere with her theatrical pipe dreams. The "Tony" compilation of scenes even includes a rather trenchant moment of analysis, when her brother Tom, more acerbic than he has generally been earlier, thoroughly debunks all her ambitions for an acting career. He now declares her doomed to an almost certain "long, hard drop," during which "there [would be] bound to be some glass broken!" (Texas 17.2/D49).

Through Tom's wry spoofing of Laura's excessively earnest theatrical fantasies in this early "Tony" draft, Williams already seems to be previewing his silent-film-spoofing commentary screens of 1945 (e.g., "Annunciation!," "Terror!," "Not Jim!"—*TGM [RV]* 38, 56, 54). In 1945, the screens project no deep animosity, but at least raise eyebrows, toward the melodrama inherent in Amanda Wingfield's Gentleman Caller plot: her reverie of finding, almost miraculously and overnight, a fitting beau (and even maybe a future husband) for her physically and emotionally challenged daughter. Williams's 1945 Brechtian *Verfremdungseffekt* screens actually probably mock mother Amanda's emotional excesses more fully than they tease Laura. On the other hand, Williams did, in some other early script sketches, treat the much maligned Amanda as actually a largely virtuous exemplar of daring pioneer "heroic, fighting spirit" (*SL*, 1, 463 [letter to Audrey Wood of June 18, 1943]). And the "Tony" script perhaps argues better than any other text for Amanda's versatile indomitability as a would-be survivor: it has her boast that she has alternately worked as both an artist's model and as a model for matron's fashions. She has also been employed as a high school cafeteria cook, as a clerk in retail store bargain basements, and as a magazine-selling telemarketer (Texas 17.2/D17; HNOC MSS 562 365.74/17; Texas 16.5/M8; Texas 17.4/D4; Texas 17.1/F7; *TGM [RV]* 38).

In the 1948 "acting version" Williams does somewhat soften Amanda's self-flaunting pushiness (Rowland 68). In contrast to these later modifications, her abrasiveness (or just plain obtuseness) is quite often on display in the "Tony" script. For instance, she regards a long and self-indulgent litany of her past sufferings to be a fitting topic for mere introductory conversation with the Gentleman Caller Jim (Texas 17.2/D17). She also rather ridiculously blurts out the words "A man!" as her goofily punning response to the closing word of Jim's table grace, "Amen" (Texas 17.2/A11). Nevertheless, Williams always, and not only in 1948, viewed Amanda at least as an earnest would-be caregiver. Her *"silliness"* eventually was superseded by her *"dignity and tragic beauty"* (*TGM [RV]* 114). For such reasons, it does not appear particularly surprising that Williams, at least in one early manuscript, makes Amanda herself the self-sacrificial family member forced to sleep in the family's living room (Texas 16.1/D4).

Actually, if he were fully obeying the paradigms raised by Woolf's *A Room of One's Own*, Williams would doubtlessly make Laura, his play's "Judith Shakespeare" analogue, into the character who has to sleep in the Wingfield apartment's exposed living room space. Laura does lack her own personal bed chamber in one manuscript version of *Menagerie* (Texas 16.5/P1, C1). Yet it seems telling that the character who is said, in multiple drafts, to be forced to sleep in the apartment living room is actually her brother Tom (Texas 15.8/303; Texas 17.1/C7, J1, K2; Texas 16.10/58).

One might speculate that such a detail about Tom reflects only borrowing of a motif from Clifford Odets's 1935 play *Awake and Sing!*, where the young male protagonist Ralph also must sleep on a living room cot (Odets 26). Yet it remains true that Williams's *Glass Menagerie*, along with many of its preparatory scripts, views Tom as the true central character. However spiritually unresolved the gesture may ultimately prove to be, he does still perform the play's central dramatic act—when, by not paying the family's electric bill, he marshals the funds to finance his escape from St. Louis. He simultaneously "[b]low[s] out [the] candles" (*TGM [RV]* 115) of what to him are old and perhaps dysfunctional social rites.

Some critics sense Tom as principally wanting, in a sort of exorcism, to use this entire "memory play" as a means for "blow[ing] out" all "candles" that illumined his birth-family life. To these critics he also, at the end, commands the stubbornly lingering wraith of remembered Laura to extinguish those wicks of memory, too—thus asking her to absolve him of all guilt for what even the early "Tony" script showed us was his long-plotted desire to reject, as merely temporary, a Wingfield homestead (Scheye 207–211). At the same time, however, the "Tony" script portrays Laura as herself having *some* propensity for self-assertion, ambition, and defiance of her mother's naysaying. That part of the "Tony" draft might appeal to a different sort of reader: one speculating that when Tom eventually tells Laura in *Menagerie* to extinguish *her* candles, he actually, from some subconscious depth of his own being, still urges *her* to rebel valiantly against society's various deadened rituals (*TGM [RV]* 115).[19] Surely Tom, looking a lot like a quasi-Nietzschean rebel, would concur with a Nietzsche quotation that Williams once copied down: "To accept a belief simply because it is customary implies that one is dishonest, cowardly, and lazy" (*N* 54–55).

At the same time, it must be admitted that neither the theatrical character Tom nor the authorial Tennessee would have refuted some contrasting, but still very real, Nietzschean *pessimism*. The German philosopher believed, as Williams so often does, that anti-social defiance very likely destroys any rebel—for "life's inexhaustibleness," in Nietzsche's terms, often requires the "*sacrifice*" of life's "highest types" (qtd. in Morgan 308). Concurring with such analyses of human fate, most readers usually interpret the end of *The Glass Menagerie* as basically lugubrious. Tom, in a reading that is now more *Othello*-like, here just commands Laura, quite resignedly and even quasi-mortally, to "blow out [*her*] candles" (*TGM [RV]* 115).

I offer that last interpretation, however, without insisting that it be the only one which can mark our final response to Williams's play. Even today, critics can be far too insistent about reading literary texts in only one single way. They may thus either want staunchly to define Williams as only the 1948 "acting version" heart-stringer or else as only the 1945 man of the ironic Brechtian screens. I personally respect, and see operating almost always in Williams's writing, both sympathetic and ironic approaches. After all, both were composed by the same man, and that man, with his constant tendency to revision, proved to be an ever-*dialogical* draftsman. The Williams who writes of Tony and the Wingfields is, yes, like the 1948 "acting version" scribe, quite sensitive to human suffering, both the suffering of *women* and the suffering of *men*. Yet, in the early "Tony" pages, he also questions the common sense of some of our pity, as he later continues to do in the emotion-needling silent-film-imitative screens of the 1945 *Menagerie* "reading version." To deny Williams his full *dialogism*—his capacity to appreciate complicated variations of tone in our responses to both life's pain and its more jocose absurdities—is, in the end, to deny him some of that very complex humanity about which he himself always so compellingly writes.

NORTHWEST MISSOURI STATE UNIVERSITY

NOTES

Manuscripts from the many repositories holding Williams's archived writings are each cited with, first, the encompassing information for the entire collection; then a box number, followed by a period; a folder number; and, after a slash, any sub-folder indication [A, B, C, D, for instance, according to the sequence of any sub-folders within the larger folder], and then page numbers.

1. Pictures on Williams's screens of young swains with bouquets of flowers look a little silly as they suggest mere maudlin and cutesy courtship practices. Blazonry borrowed from church ritual, like the terms "AVE MARIA" or "Annunciation," appears to nudge characters to acknowledge that their struggles do not quite turn them into figures so fraught with cosmic significance as the Virgin Mary. Quotations from Villon ("Où sont les neiges [d'antan]?") hint that Amanda Wingfield misses the robust dating life of her youth, but also that life's winters and their snows are inevitable, even if one grew up in Mississippi. Laura's recalled nickname, "Blue Roses," itself a silly mistaken ear-memory of the name of her declared illness "pleurosis," also hints at impossible reveries that now demand correction. The term "Blue Roses" hearkens back to the German Romantic poet Novalis and the impossible aspirations of his hero Heinrich von Ofterdingen—who dreamed of finding, on some transcendently sweet day, the supreme *blue flower* of all-surpassing romantic love. Williams's proposed screens may thus not be bitterly satiric, but they do seem motivated to tease the overly heated emotions of the play's fretful Wingfield family. See *TGM [RV]* 9, 17, 19, 38.

2. It may be true that Williams briefly tried to suppress the screens' irony somewhat. Two archived manuscripts at the University of Virginia appear to show him cutting some of that irony out, when he excised some sardonic lines ("GONE UP THE SPOUT!," "THE CRUST OF HUMILITY," and "AFTER THE FIASCO")—even though he re-inserted those screened declarations into his scenario evidently only one revision later (Virginia MSS 6694: Earlier Bound Draft: 20, 21, 24; Virginia MSS 6694, Donald Windham Bound Gift Copy: 20, 24). Williams may thus have been trying out the blander approach to his "legends" which he seems to pronounce as his purpose both in the later draft at Virginia (the Windham gift copy) and also in the 1945 "reading version" of *Menagerie*. In those two transcriptions, he asserts that his screen device has as its design merely "to give accent to certain values in each scene," revealing "primary point[s]" with "emotional appeal" (Virginia MSS 6694: Donald Windham Bound Gift Copy, iii; *TGM [RV]* 8). The later Windham gift draft, nonetheless, has returned to the script

most of the barbed tone of the "legends." In a still earlier version of the text which still has not totally disappeared from the first of the two Virginia-archived scripts, Williams had his narrator Tom write onto a giant onstage slate, rather than to have them projected on screens.

3. In an article which proves throughout to be solid and wise, Geoffrey Borny writes that even though "neither the acing style nor the conventions of silent film titles were originally meant to be funny, time has made them so" (111).

4. Williams appears to have created the "acting version" as a particular response after Eddie Dowling and company staged the play so successfully on Broadway, where they did not use the "reading version" screens (Parker 417). Even while reporting this fact, however, Brian Parker, with scholarly thoroughness, does not ignore (as do both Beaurline and Rowland) the full, and largely irony-laden, manuscript history of the *Menagerie* scripts. Beaurline does not seem even to have known of any earlier (and ironic) previous treatments of the Wingfields' drama than the 1943 "Portrait of a Girl in Glass" short story, with its "fragile pathos" (Beaurline 142). Rowland makes quite a case for the admirably softer Amanda who appears in the 1948 "acting version," but he does not even try to understand why the "reading version" tensions of mood might have a different sort of value, and one which Williams often had emphasized. Parker, by contrast, makes a very salient point when he notes that "it [specifically] was because" Laurette Taylor, the original Amanda, "could balance" a wry and mordant "black comedy" against Amanda's partially quite "sympathetic qualities" that Williams so much admired her performance in the dialogical maternal role (Parker 416).

5. The "Tony" script only appears as part of the Harry Ransom Center University of Texas archive. It is a group of sheets filed loosely, even at times haphazardly, in just a pair of folders. The logical scene sequence can be fairly easily reconstructed, however, given the well-known chronology of the eventual *Menagerie*, and the "Tony" materials do shed light on what *Menagerie* became. Unfortunately, no Williams correspondence or journal entries specifically tell us what he thought of his brief foray into imagining the character Tony.

6. Influences from Clifford Odets seem likely upon this planned script—and, indeed, the "Tony" script that I examine has the young character Tony (Texas 17.2/A5) discuss the future development of television, as Gus Michaels does in Odets's *Paradise Lost* of 1935 (Odets 143), and as Jim O'Connor will in the completed *Glass Menagerie* (*TGM [RV]* 82).

7. I make this estimate of its dating because Williams quotes within the "Tony" pages from his play *Battle of Angels*, a work that was evidently begun around 1938–1939. He has his character Laura claim to have starred on a community theatre stage as a woman (*Battle of Angels*' Myra Torrance) who waxes ecstatic over having once elegantly danced while wearing "mousseline de soie" (Texas 3.3/1–26).

8. I say this because the socialist street singer Tony, present only in this rendition of *Glass Menagerie* motifs and themes, recalls Williams's 1930s St. Louis cronies who were inclined toward socialism. One of these, at least to some degree, evidently was the poet Clark Mills McBurney, to whom Williams dedicated a different *Menagerie* precursor script with, as its epigraph, the Marxist adage "Capitalistic Society is a pyramid of boxes" (Texas 16.10/Aiii).

9. The street singer Tony, for instance, reports "[p]an-handling" on Memphis's famed Beale Street (Texas 17.2/A10). For more information on Williams's Memphis summer, see Leverich 149–50 and Lahr 607.

10. Smith suggested as much to me in a telephone conversation during February 2006.

11. Some of his rather indecorous and nearly taunting lines are among his first ones: "I'm hongry!"; "Feed me!"; "Ain't I presentable, Mother Wing?" (Texas 17.2/A9, A11). He raucously tries to convince her to say a table grace that he claims to have learned at Alice Reagan's cathouse (A11), then later bursts out regularly with guffaws of laughter (A12, A19). When the favored official Gentleman Caller, Jim, is invited by a charmed Amanda to come and actually live with the Wingfields, Tony ripostes "Hey now! Mother Wing! You never made me a proposition like that!" (A6).

12. Protesting that she will "walk out!" if her mother cannot stop "get[ting] started on Tony," Laura calls him a "brilliant" possessor of "very sensitive feelings," a "cavalier" in some ways, and just as "clean" as Amanda (who sees him as someone very much in need of "Dutch Cleanser" [Texas 17.2/D40, A15]).

13. True enough, he tempers this praise of Amanda by ambiguously labelling her a "witch" of "arts and crafts" (Texas 17.2/B65).

14. I cannot help but surmise that Williams ran the risk of being accused of borderline plagiarism when he wrote a story description for the pre-*Menagerie* prose sketch "Portrait of a Girl in Glass." It seems to me almost patent that he must have read Woolf's novel *Mrs. Dalloway*, and its passage about the advertising "aeroplane [...] curving up and up, straight up, like something mounting in ecstasy" as it wrote "a T, an O, an F" in the sky (Woolf *Mrs. D.* 41–42). This Woolfian *leitmotif* surely seems remarkably similar to Williams's inscribed declaration, in a "Portrait of a Girl in Glass" draft, that a plane flew overhead ("way, way up") and "began to trace [...] messages," like a "reply from God"— only later to reveal that its revelation was no more than "a tremendous capital C. Then O. Then C again. Then A" (Texas 17.7/B8).

15. Its sincerity seems easy to call into question, but Williams in the 1930s did write one sonnet of supposed lamentation for the neglected "women poets of this land," most notably Elinor Wylie and Edna St. Vincent Millay, who had now joined, or soon would join, older women writers of European lands, like Sappho and Elizabeth Barrett Browning, in being sadly "sheeted in their graves" (qtd. in Smith and Marrs 89).

16. By including Garbo and Jane Cowl, this list of actresses from a distance seems to prefigure the use of silent-film-imitative screens in the actual *Glass Menagerie* script of 1945.

17. Even more surprising to us than the portrait of a somewhat self-assertive Laura in the "Tony" draft is Williams's treatment of her in a screenplay where he looks at her as having enough "strength and character" to lead her tired mother back to Amanda's childhood hometown—Blue Mountain, Mississippi—after years of defeat in St. Louis (Texas 17.4/C8).

18. She even becomes pretty brazenly scornful of her mother's own human faults, when she mocks that woman's "screaming hyena" laughter from the audience during a Little Theatre performance in which Laura had acted (Texas 17.2/D41).

19. This interpretation makes even more sense when applied to the "Tony" draft than the later *Menagerie* compositions. After all, in the "Tony" text Laura is still somewhat feisty and independent, even though she also remains markedly frail and naïve.

WORKS CITED

Beaurline, Lester A. "*The Glass Menagerie*: From Story to Play." *Modern Drama* 8 (1965): 142–49.

Borny, Geoffey. "The Two Glass Menageries: Reading Edition and Acting Edition." *Modern Critical Interpretations: "The Glass Menagerie."* Ed. Harold Bloom. New York: Chelsea House, 1988. 101–17.

Brown, Cecil. "Interview with Tennessee Williams" (1974). *Conversations with Tennessee Williams*. Ed. Albert J. Devlin. Jackson and London: University Press of Mississippi, 1986. 251–83.

Lahr, John. *Mad Pilgrimage of the Flesh: A Biography*. New York: Norton, 2014.

Leverich, Lyle. *Tom: The Unknown Tennessee Williams*. New York: Crown, 1995.

Morgan, George A. *What Nietzsche Means*. New York, Evanston, and London: Harper, 1941.

Novalis, Friedrich. *Henry von Ofterdingen [Heinrich von Ofterdingen]*. Trans. Palmer Hilty. Prospect Heights, IL: Waveland, 1990.

Odets, Clifford. *Six Plays*. New York: Grove, 1979.

Parker, Brian. "The Composition of *The Glass Menagerie*: An Argument for Complexity." *Modern Drama* 25.3 (1982): 409–22.

Rowland, James L. "Tennessee's Two Amandas." *"The Glass Menagerie": A Collection of Critical Essays*. Ed. R. B. Parker. Englewood Cliffs, NJ: Prentice-Hall, 1983. 62–74.

Scheye, Thomas E. "*The Glass Menagerie*: 'It's no tragedy, Freckles.'" *Tennessee Williams: A Tribute*. Ed. Jac Tharpe. Jackson: University Press of Mississippi, 1977. 207–13.

Shakespeare, William. *Othello*. Ed. Norman Sanders. Cambridge: Cambridge University Press, 1985.

Single, Lori Leathers. "Flying the Jolly Roger: Images of Escape and Selfhood in *The Glass Menagerie*." *The Tennessee Williams Annual Review* 2 (1999): 69–85.

Smith, William Jay. Telephone interview with Jeffrey B. Loomis. February 2006.

_____. "'Tom': The Making of 'The Glass Menagerie.'" *The New Criterion* 14.7 (1996): 72–77.

Smith, William Jay, and Suzanne Marrs. *My Friend Tom: The Poet-Playwright Tennessee Williams*. Jackson: University Press of Mississippi, 2012.

Usui, Masami. "A World of Her Own in Tennessee Williams's *The Glass Menagerie*." *Studies in Culture and the Humanities (Hiroshima University)* 1 (1992): 21–37.

Williams, Tennessee. Delaware 1.23. *The Glass Menagerie*—[film—shooting script]. Tennessee Williams Collection, Morris Library, University of Delaware.

_____. *The Glass Menagerie*. New York: Dramatists Play Service, 1999. ("Acting Version")

_____. *The Glass Menagerie*. New York: New Directions, 1945. ("Reading Version") [*RV*]

_____. Historical New Orleans Collection [HNOC], The Fred W. Todd Collection, MSS 562, 365. 74—*The Glass Menagerie*.

_____. *Notebooks*. Ed. Margaret Bradham Thornton. New Haven and London: Yale University Press, 2006. (*N*)

_____. *Selected Letters, 1 (1920–1945)*. Ed. Albert J. Devlin and Nancy M. Tischler. New York: New Directions, 2000. (*SL, 1*)

_____. Texas Tennessee Williams Collection, Harry Ransom Humanities Center, University of Texas, TXRC-C99-A14, Series 1 (Works): Texas 3.3—*Battle of Angels*: Full Script, 1939 [November]; Texas 16.1—*The Glass Menagerie*: Motion Picture Script, n.d.; Texas 16.5: *The Glass Menagerie*: Typescript Fragments, 1943, n.d. [A]; Texas 16.10—*The Glass Menagerie*: Early Drafts, n.d.; Texas 17.1—*The Glass Menagerie*:

"The Gentleman Caller": Draft Fragments, n.d. [A]; Texas 17.2—*The Glass Menagerie*: "The Gentleman Caller": Draft Fragments, n.d. [B]; Texas 17.3—*The Glass Menagerie*: "The Gentleman Caller": Draft Fragments, n.d. [C]; *The Glass Menagerie*: "The Gentleman Caller": Motion Picture Treatment, 1943, n.d.; Texas 17.7—*The Glass Menagerie*: *Portrait of a Girl in Glass,* 1941–1943, n.d.

_____. Virginia Tennessee Williams Collection. MSS 6694. *The Glass Menagerie*, or *The Gentleman Caller*. Original ms., inscribed in the author's hand, Provincetown, MA, August 1944. Copy of Donald Windham, acquired December 14, 1961. Clifton Walter Barrett Library of American Literature, Albert and Shirley Small Special Collections Library, University of Virginia. [Donald Windham Bound Gift Copy]

_____. Virginia Tennessee Williams Collection. MSS 6694. *The Glass Menagerie*, or *The Gentleman Caller (A Play)*. Clifton Walter Barrett Library of American Literature, Albert and Shirley Small Special Collections Library, University of Virginia. [Earlier Bound Draft]

Woolf, Virginia. *Mrs. Dalloway.* 1925. London: Harcourt, Brace, 1989.

_____. *A Room of One's Own.* London: Harcourt, Brace, 1929.

"Bring Your Own Translator": Communication and Changing Business Paradigms in David Mamet's *Glengarry Glen Ross* and David Henry Hwang's *Chinglish*

MARTHA JOHNSON

Abstract

David Henry Hwang's 2011 play Chinglish *responds to David Mamet's 1983 play* Glengarry Glen Ross. *Both deal with anxieties in American business.* Glengarry Glen Ross *portrays a landscape of increasingly ruthless management and competition for a group of real estate salesmen. In* Chinglish, *a naive American businessman travels to China for an extended stay in the hopes of securing a large contract to save his floundering family company. Both plays focus on failed communication, questions of ethics, and use dialogue to expose competing agendas and power dynamics in the business dealings they portray. But while Mamet's salesmen overtalk, argue, and boast, Hwang's characters struggle with language barriers and translation nuance. In both cases, true motivations, egos, and alliances are at play and are ultimately exposed. In this essay, I will analyze, compare, and contrast the structure of the scenes, the construction of language and dialogue, and place both in the context of the American business.*

In the opening scene of David Henry Hwang's *Chinglish*, Daniel tells us the most important thing to know about doing business in China is to "bring your own translator" (8). But isn't that always the case? And what does that imply? A purely linguistic function? Or someone to tell you the rules of the game? In very different ways Hwang's *Chinglish* and David Mamet's *Glengarry Glen Ross* consider the role of language in transaction and negotiation. If language is the currency of the salesman, both expose the inevitable failure of words to truly encompass meaning, in business and in life. As Xi warns Daniel, "Use at your own risk" (43).

American playwrights love salesmen—in part, surely, because salesmen are actors. The stories are told in different locales and contexts, but for generations of playwrights, the iconic American businessman has embodied the human manifestation of capitalism, reflecting and responding to societal change and anxiety. At the 2014 Comparative Drama Conference, I asked playwright David Henry Hwang what work his 2011 play *Chinglish* responds to, as he tends to take inspiration from specific works in the drama canon. He replied that it was David Mamet's 1983 play *Glengarry Glen Ross*. Both plays seek to expose individual anxieties during times of economic crisis in the U.S., and both confront changing paradigms in the very way that business "is done." As Patrick Healy pointed out in his review of *Chinglish* on Broadway, "Americans and Chinese are united in capitalist greed but divided by their cultural sensibilities."

In *Chinglish* a naïve American businessman travels to China, in the hopes of securing a large contract that will save his almost bankrupt, third generation, family-owned company in Cleveland. He is forced to depend on a series of cultural mentors, translators, and a lover, and is drawn into a web of complex, nepotistic relationships and dynamics. In *Glengarry Glen Ross,* fast-talking, hardworking salesmen chase down "leads" in an environment of increasingly disconnected management and brutal sales competition. Both plays focus on language, power, and communication, and use dialogue to simultaneously conceal and expose competing agendas and desires. While Mamet's salesmen overtalk, argue, distract, badger, bluster and boast, Hwang's characters struggle with literal language barriers, cultural codes, basic word meanings and translation nuance.

David Mamet's 1984 Pulitzer prize-winning play *Glengarry Glen Ross* tells the story of a group of small-time real estate salesmen in Chicago. A sales competition will result in the top salesman winning a Cadillac, and the bottom performer losing his job. Mamet spent part of 1969 working in what he has described as "a fly-by-night operation" trying to sell "worthless land to elderly people who couldn't afford it" (Nightingale 92). The experience was formative. The play is a dialogue-driven study of Reagan-era, hyper-competitive, sales culture. As Anne Dean points out, "here, the term *cutthroat* takes on a new significance; it is no coincidence that the second prize in the salesroom competition is a set of knives" (47). His ethically challenged salesmen "sell" to customers, sell to management, and sell to each other. No one is honest or trustworthy as they compete for the top spot on "The Board," using any means necessary to get the coveted "best" leads.

David Henry Hwang's 2011 play *Chinglish* tells the story of an American ex–Enron executive going to China in a last-ditch effort to save his almost bankrupt family business, and marks a subtle, but noteworthy, shift for the playwright. While he has always been interested in cross-cultural communication—or miscommunication—he now takes on more directly the inherent challenges involved in inter-cultural communication. While his previous works had maintained a U.S.-centric cultural focus, here he moves the conversation beyond the boundaries of the U.S. In *Chinglish*, the specific experience of the American seeking to do business in China exposes disparate cultural practices and juxtaposes values for comedic effect.

While the dynamic between modern American and Chinese culture would seem to be obvious territory for Hwang, it's actually complicated and new, as Hwang is Chinese-American, not Chinese. While his personal experience and upbringing have clear influences from his Chinese immigrant parents, his first-hand knowledge of Chinese cultural dynamics, particularly in contemporary China was, and is, limited. His personal experience of China came later in life. His first trip was at the age of thirty-six, in 1993, on a family "heritage" trip. In recent years, however, he has travelled to China frequently, and learned something of business practices. As Mamet was inspired by his experience in the sales office, so Hwang draws on these visits (Johnson). He began to note and track issues having to do with translation, and communication. He cites one experience, in particular, as being influential: "I visited a new cultural center in Shanghai in 2005 that was pretty much perfect, except for the really badly translated Chinglish signs: a handicapped restroom that said 'Deformed Man's Toilet,' that kind of thing. And I began thinking of using the signs as a jumping-off point to write a play that would deal with doing business in China but would also tackle the issue of language, which I'd never seen any play or movie attempt to do" (Zimmer). The result was the first bilingual production to be staged on Broadway.

In structural terms there are similarities and differences between *Glengarry* and *Chinglish*. The latter takes place in a series of public and private spaces. Two early scenes take place in restaurants and are, in fact, reminiscent of *Glengarry*. When asked what elements of *Chinglish* are most inspired by *Glengarry*, Hwang responds that he "started out being influenced by Mamet's pace and style, which is reflected in *Chinglish's* first scene, which like *Glengarry*, is also a two-hander set in a Chinese restaurant" (Johnson). In contrast to Mamet's Chinese restaurant, however, Hwang's restaurant is *in* China. An analysis juxtaposing the opening scenes in the two plays is instructive. Both intentionally locate themselves in the restaurants. In *Glengarry* the "real" business takes place in the restaurant. In *Chinglish* Daniel develops his closest local relationships and is indoctrinated into the complexities of Chines culture in the restaurant. Both *Glengarry* and *Chinglish* use their respective Chinese restaurants as neutral, public, yet oddly more intimate spaces, to locate the negotiations, manipulations, and the "off the record" conversations. The established rituals and process of selling high investment purchases increasingly require the illusion of relaxation and interpersonal relationships; the "casual" meal or drink becomes an expectation. The restaurants serve as a heterotopia of sorts, or a liminal space. The comparison suggests that, while the rules of business may be different in China and the U.S., there are fundamental similarities. Important dynamics, subplots, and plans to undermine or betray supervisors and colleagues are revealed in the nether space of each restaurant. The opening restaurant conversations in both are also ultimately revealed to be false and duplicitous.

Glengarry has two acts and five scenes. All of Act One takes place in the familiar Chinese restaurant frequented by the salesmen. All of Act two takes place in the sales office. As the play opens, Mamet denies us context or exposition, choosing instead to throw us immediately into the action, or more accurately in this case, the conversation. Levene opens the play:

> John…. John…. John. Okay, John. John. Look: (*pause*) The Glengarry Highland's leads, you're sending Roma out. Fine. He's a good man. We know what his is. He's fine. All I'm saying, you look at the *board,* he's throwing … wait, wait, wait, he's throwing them *away,* he's throwing the leads away. All that I'm saying, that you're wasting lead. I don't want to tell you your *job.* All that I'm saying, things get *set,* I know they do, you get a certain *mindset.…* A guy gets a reputation. We know how this … all I'm saying, put a *closer* on the job. There's more than one man for the…. Put a … wait a second, put a *proven man out* … and you watch, now *wait* a second—and you watch your *dollar* volumes…. You start closing them for *fifty* 'stead of *twenty five* … you put a *closer* on the … [15].

We are rudely thrust into a barrage of words, arguments, sales lingo, and fast, incomplete dialogue between characters we know nothing about. The pairings in the restaurants suggest alliances and relationships, but the dynamics at play are not discernible, and many of our first impressions are wrong. The dialogue is exhausting and, in David Worster's words, "salesmen talk about talking" endlessly (65). The competition that accelerates the action has already been announced, inhibiting our understanding of the central dramatic complication driving the plot. We "overhear" the conversations, a tour-de-force of the rhetoric of manipulation and coercion. Mamet barrages us "with the sounds of linguistic warfare" (Dean 49), but provides very little upon which to stabilize our perspective or comprehension.

Chinglish has two acts with thirteen scenes. It opens with the principal character, American businessman Daniel Cavanaugh, directly addressing the audience. In contrast to Mamet, Hwang assigns the audience a specific identity as the Commerce League of Ohio. The story is being presented in retrospect. Given that Daniel is an invited speaker, it would seem he has achieved some level of success in China. So in contrast with *Glengarry*, where the outcome of the action is not revealed until the end, Hwang chooses to open *Chinglish* by positioning Daniel as already successful. In other words, while *Glengarry's* interest is in the sales competition's outcome, the focus in *Chinglish* is not on *if* he succeeded, but rather *how*.

In *Glengarry*, Mamet largely denies his characters a personal life. As Benedict Nightingale points out, "They are never seen in their domestic environment, and so have even less chance to engage our sympathies" (90). On the other hand, Hwang develops our bond with Daniel by repositioning him beyond public settings. As his relationship with Xi evolves, they gravitate toward increasingly intimate spaces. Their first meeting is in the restaurant, the second in Daniel's hotel bar, and the rest of their scenes take place in his hotel room, culminating in an affair. This is a noteworthy departure from the trope. The very presence of a woman in the business dynamic undermines traditional masculine power structures. The sexual liaison adds a level of complexity and has broad implications for the genre.

What Christopher Bigsby writes of *Glengarry* can be said of *Chinglish* as well: "Within the apparent harmonics of conversation are dissonances that suddenly expose the extent of alienation, the nature and profundity of personal and social anxieties" (44). Both of these plays are heavily, and *Chinglish* perhaps uniquely, reliant on performance to demonstrate the exhaustion of communication. And while all plays are written ultimately to be performed, some make performance and, indeed, language, central subjects. Glengarry's dialogue is rife with fragments and unfinished sentences. *Glengarry* in performance is frustrating and fatiguing. Nightingale suggests,

> Always you feel Mamet is trying to replicate the minutiae of speech, with its unfinished sentences, its twists, its redundancies, its emphases, its muddles. Thus, Levene, exhilarated by an improbable sale responds: "And, and, and, and I did it. And I put a kid through school. She ... and cold calling fella. Door to door. But you don't know. You don't know. You never heard of a streak." The speech reflects the vindictive triumph of the moment, but also reflects Levene's impulsive, erratic character and chaotic state of being [101].

In *Chinglish* Hwang's constant interface between Chinese and English creates a similar dissonance. Because of the constant use of translations, an upstage screen is prominent throughout. The use of the subtitles serves a dual purpose. The first is simply functional, in that they translate in both directions

(Chinese to English and English to Chinese). This provides an ongoing illustration of what can happen when language is translated. By translating both directions, Hwang attempts to create a linguistically level playing field. Neither language is entirely dominant, although technically only one quarter of the lines are in Mandarin. In either case, he is ambitious in his attempts to change some of the paradigms of traditional stage dialogue. The script requires several actors to be capable of delivering lines in both languages, and the subtitles demonstrate the nuances of idiom and limitations of literal language translation.

For example, in the initial meeting with the Minister of Culture for Guinyang, Daniel's crucial "sales pitch" is translated by the first in a series of truly disastrous translators. The result is a humorous and awkward attempt at compliments and sales points, literally misinterpreted and lost in translation. "We're a small family firm" becomes "his company is tiny and insignificant" (12); and "here is why we are worth the money" translates as "He will explain why he spends money so recklessly" (20). Ironically, he is selling translated signs. The danger of poor translations, and examples from venues in China, are at the heart of his pitch. As David Worster points out in his essay "How to Do Things with Salesmen," "sales talk expresses the salesman's vision of reality, transferring the most obvious and urgent needs from the salesman to the customer and the power from the customer to the salesman" (69). Daniel needs them to need his signs. But the constant disruption of flow, interruptions, and translation corrections keep his critical initial sales pitch from ever gaining any real verbal momentum.

If *Glengarry* focuses on the use of language to persuade and manipulate, perhaps *Chinglish* is best understood as a study in the impotence of persuasion in the absence of a common language and lexicon. American salesmen, from Willy Loman to Henry Hill and the *Glengarry* sales force, live and die by their words. Hwang, conversely, denies his salesman the most basic tool Mamet's characters wield so brutally. We are mesmerized by Roma's monologue in the Chinese restaurant in *Glengarry*, along with the unsuspecting patsy, Lingk, long before understanding Roma's intended endgame. The result is a "uniquely detailed account of the language of manipulation" (Nightingale 93) in "a linguistic environment created by the need to gain capital" (Greenbaum 4).

For theatregoers used to hearing dialogue exclusively in English, the constant need to read the translations in *Chinglish* is slightly disruptive, reminiscent of a classic Brechtian alienation technique. The subtitles contribute to a disruption of the fourth wall and the audience is required to engage with both the screen and the action simultaneously. Here language is being played against itself. Meaning is an approximation, always open to misunderstanding. It is potentially dangerous. If it can generate humor, it can equally cause anxiety.

Communication always offers this potential. What Hwang does is to stage a conversation in which language is not fully transitive. There are some things, it seems, this resist language—some secrets best not fully decoded.

When Daniel and Xi begin an affair, we see two people trying to communicate across a linguistic barrier who discover the plasticity of language, its specificities and evasions. In an early conversation, he finally comprehends her treasonous revelations, including humorous references to using the minister's wife's back door, and the two share a celebratory "high five." Daniel admits the conversation "was exhausting" to which Xi responds, "I am sleeping with you" (46), instead of the intended statement that he is tiring her. The limitations are both liberating and frustrating. Xi admits, "This is exactly what I need right now ... to forget everything," but only in Chinese (103). We, in turn, are made voyeurs to their most intimate dialogue, confessions spoken in the safety of incomprehension.

The characters in both plays share ethical challenges. Hwang chooses to enhance the farcical elements, satirizing the absurdities of the postmodern global business landscape. Mamet's moral and ethical concerns in *Glengarry* are more serious. He suggests there will be casualties and consequences of the corporatization of traditional sales ideology and methodology, manifested in the cut-throat competition imposed by the never seen but omnipresent Murray and Mitch from "downtown." We know instinctively (or perhaps because of his more apparent desperation) that, in the tradition of Willy Loman, Levene will be left behind. This is an environment where past successes mean nothing. However, none of Mamet's characters are heroes, or even anti-heroes. They are self-serving, backstabbing con men.

The contest presents as an epic battle, but these warriors are corrupt charlatans selling worthless swampland. We sympathize with their situation and desperation, but none of them are particularly sympathetic. All are dishonest and duplicitous to varying degrees. And Mamet's denial of relationships or the domestic lives that might provide a tragic element to their decay leaves us with little sympathy for their plight. Mamet's primary concern is with the system he faults for forcing increasingly amoral choices and practices, resulting in the characters' collective ethical deterioration. Mamet has said,

> The code of an institution ratifies us in acting amorally ... as any guilt which might arise out of our acts would be borne not by ourselves but shared out through the institution. [...] If they are done in the name of some larger group, a state, a company, a team, those vile acts are somehow magically transformed and become praiseworthy. [...] If you don't exploit the possible opportunities, not only are you being silly, you're being negligent [qtd. in Nightingale 95].

In other words, amoral sales techniques have become an imperative. In the end Levene takes the blame for the burglary, but we never know who else was, or was not, involved. Are any of them truly *not* guilty? Does it matter? As the play closes, Roma laments the loss of the "old ways." His nostalgia positions their dishonest, hard-sell tactics as less reprehensible than the bureaucratic, competition-oriented "machine" of the future.

While Mamet's concerns are specific to business in the U.S. context, Hwang shifts the focus to the new frontier: China. The same ethical concerns can be applied to the machinations in *Chinglish*, but there is a critical difference in the tone. Mamet's characters are not likeable, and any humor to be found is very dark. The brutality of the sales competition, and their consequent desperation, underscores an anxiety about changing American business values, indeed American values in general. Hwang maps the anxieties and moral questions his context will create, but he sees the humor and humanity as well. Daniel is told at his first meeting with his British consultant that while China has no justice system, it does have "predictable outcomes" (9). As the story evolves, the complex dynamics influencing the contract are slowly divulged, including undisclosed favors owed, nepotism, and "Quingi," the Chinese concept of face. We also learn that Daniel's business is little more than a website and cell phone.

As in *Glengarry*, the competing agendas are revealed incrementally, as characters betray and mislead each other. In contrast, Hwang seems to embrace the possible validity of the Chinese system: corrupt, amoral, and disorganized on the surface, but with its own code of honor and rules. He suggests that ethics and morality may be culturally relativistic, as demonstrated both in business dealings and interpersonal relationships. Daniel's history as an Enron executive makes him a pariah in the U.S. but a celebrity in China. Xi ends their relationship when she fears it will damage her unhappy marriage, and she admits she began the affair to help her husband advance in politics.

The list of *Chinglish's* characters' ethical compromises is exhaustive. Hwang's characters are seriously flawed but somehow still sympathetic. It is also a critical distinction to note that what Daniel is selling is a real product and not a swampland con. We can see Daniel's success, despite his past transgressions, as offering the hope of redemption. As William Boles points out in *Understanding David Henry Hwang*, "Daniel learns from his mistakes and comes away from the experience an educated and successful man" (122). This ending suggests an alternative discourse to Mamet's doomed salesman character left behind by progress.

Perhaps the most striking difference between the two is Mamet's dogged pessimism in contrast to Hwang's realism, bordering on optimism. Mamet fears the art of the "cold call" and "soft pitch" have become irrelevant and language is increasingly impotent. Hwang suggests that words are only as powerful as their comprehension and context, so it does not necessarily matter.

UNIVERSITY OF EAST ANGLIA

WORK CITED

Bigsby, C. W. E. *The Cambridge Companion to David Mamet.* New York: Cambridge University Press, 2004.

Boles, William C. *Understanding David Henry Hwang.* Columbia: University of South Carolina Press, 2013.

Dean, Anne. "The Discourse of Anxiety." *David Mamet's* Glengarry Glen Ross*: Text and Performance.* New York: Garland, 1996. 47–61.

Greenbaum, Andrea. "Brass Balls: Masculine Communication and the Discourse of Capitalism in David Mamet's *Glengarry Glen Ross.*" *The Journal of Men's Studies* 8 (1999): 33–43.

Healy, Patrick. "Do You Know What I Mean? Probably Not." *New York Times* (October 20, 2011). Web.

Hwang, David Henry, *Chinglish.* New York: Theatre Communications Group, 2012.

Johnson, Martha. Personal correspondence with David Henry Hwang, 2014–2015.

Mamet, David, *Glengarry Glen Ross.* New York: Grove, 1982.

Nightingale, Benedict, "*Glengarry Glen Ross.*" *The Cambridge Companion to David Mamet.* Ed. C. W. E. Bigsby. New York: Cambridge University Press, 2004. 89–98.

Worster, David. "How to Do Things with Salesmen: David Mamet's Speech Act Play." *David Mamet's Glengarry Glen Ross: Text and Performance.* New York: Garland, 1996. 63–79.

Zimmer, Ben, "*Chinglish* Playwright David Henry Hwang on Bringing Mandarin to Broadway, Growing Up Chinese-American, and Translation Fails." www.vulture.com. October 27, 2011. Web.

Sympathetic Curiosity, Not Voyeurism: David Lindsay-Abaire Takes Up Joanna Baillie's Abandoned Grief Project

Amy Muse

Abstract

In 1798 Joanna Baillie conceived of a massive project for an intimate theatre: A Series of Plays: In which it is Attempted to Delineate the Stronger Passions of the Mind—*plays designed for a small theatre in which audiences could witness the unfolding of a self on stage. The plays allow us to exercise what Baillie calls our "sympathetic curiosity": the "natural desire we have to look into the thoughts, and observe the behavior of others." Her plan included plays on love, hate, ambition, fear, hope, remorse, jealousy, pride, envy, revenge, anger, joy, and grief. She never wrote the one on grief, though. This is where David Lindsay-Abaire steps in. As Baillie noted, grief is a complicated passion, intricately bound up with anger, despair, revenge, and hope. By sitting us down in the dark to listen to Becca work through the full range of grief, Lindsay-Abaire's* Rabbit Hole *teaches the audience to be the friend a grieving person sorely needs.*

I'm at the corner table, so engrossed in my chai and the reading of a play that I hardly notice the two people who've slid in to the table across from me until I sense unhappiness. What clues me in is something in the air around them more than the fragments of dialogue—"How's your soup?" "I can't have this talk"—that I catch. On the page in front of me I've just underlined "People get weird, you know that" (36), and I hear it in my head as if it's the voiceover of this scene. I glance up as casually as I can to see a man hunched warily over

194

his potato and bacon chowder; the woman with him has her back to me but I assume she's his wife since he's wearing a wedding ring and they're speaking to one another with a distinctive taken-for-grantedness. It feels like more than just everyday inattentiveness, though. There's something hanging, unsaid, as they struggle to make conversation. Although my ears must now strain to catch specific words, my gaze returns to my play, for if they sense I'm listening they will switch abruptly into public mode and let me know what I'm already aware of: that what I'm doing is rude.

Unless I were in the theatre. Then it would be ok.

In the theatre my looking would be invited, even courted. I wouldn't need to feel guilty for invading their privacy. My longing to look, my innate attraction to people whose masks have slipped, is a sign of my "sympathetic curiosity," according to playwright and theatre theorist Joanna Baillie (1762–1851). She gets me. Baillie may be in 1798 Glasgow, I in 2015 St. Paul, but we're excellent theatre companions. Both of us love nothing more than peering into others' windows and eavesdropping on their conversations, feeling like we're seeing into their souls. "What human creature is there," Baillie asks, "who can behold a being like himself under the violent agitation of those passions which all have, in some degree, experienced, without feeling himself most powerfully excited by the sight?" (72). She understands why I gravitate to intimate theatre (indeed, she invented it). I'm not a voyeur in my desire to feel what they're going through, she assures me. I'm not vampirically feeding on this couple's unhappiness. I want to learn how to help.

Maybe I'm so sensitive to this conversation because the play I'm reading is David Lindsay-Abaire's *Rabbit Hole*, about a couple grieving the loss of their four-year-old son, Danny, who ran out into the street chasing his dog and was killed by a teenage driver. During the course of the play we witness two very different grieving processes, Becca's and Howie's, so astute they've been touted as essential viewing for both therapists and patients. (Barry Scott Kaufman in *Psychology Today*: "a strikingly authentic portrait of what it's like to cope with unimaginable loss." Michael Blumenfield on the blog *Psychiatry Talk*: an "excellent teaching" opportunity "for mental health professionals who are studying manifestations of grief.")

It's a quiet play and, prior to *Good People* (2011), Lindsay-Abaire's first foray into a kind of kitchen-sink realism, although the "type of truthfulness" it tells has "nothing to do with running water" (Evans 134). Some critics wrote it off as untheatrical ("thin gruel," "too compassionate," "you might as well watch TV"),[1] especially fans of Lindsay-Abaire's highly stylized earlier plays *Fuddy Mears* and *Kimberly Akimbo*. But quiet and realistic don't mean unimaginative. What is most powerful in *Rabbit Hole* is what is unseen, and what it needs its audience to see.

Becca and Howie need a live audience. They need listeners. They need friends. As painful as their grieving is, it is worsened by their isolation, David Cox writes in *The Guardian* (reviewing the film version of *Rabbit Hole*). The couple are left to "grapple with their loss in a state of claustrophobic reclusion. The problem is theirs and theirs alone to solve, as is emphasised by the conclusion, which shows them facing their uncertain future together but alone." Because there's no collective grief in modern society their "mourning has been privatized." Becca in particular is lonely and mourns not just the loss of her son but of her best friend, Debbie, who hasn't called once since Danny died. It's as if their friends are afraid of getting too close, of having the misfortune rub off on them. Becca, feeling this, wants to "drop her a note" saying "Dear Debbie—just so's ya know, accidents aren't contagious" (36).

Over two hundred years earlier Joanna Baillie coined the term "sympathetic curiosity" to describe the natural desire we have to know what others are thinking and feeling. Perhaps *diagnose* is a better word than merely *describe*, since this is not merely a desire but an overwhelming urge, and what we are most drawn to watch is people in distress. "How sensible are we," Baillie writes, "of this strong propensity within us, when we behold any person under the pressure of great and uncommon calamity!" Don't try to deny it. The propensity is "universal," Baillie insists. We may try to restrain ourselves but "even the smallest indications of an unquiet mind," such as "the restless eye, the muttering lip, the half-checked exclamation, and the hasty start, will set our attention as anxiously upon the watch, as the first distant flashes of a gathering storm" (73). What wouldn't we give for an invisibility cloak at these moments so that we could follow the person into, as Baillie puts it, his "lonely haunts," into "his closet, into the midnight silence of his chamber?" (73). She goes so far as to declare that "there is, perhaps, no employment which the human mind will with so much avidity pursue, as the discovery of concealed passion, as the tracing the varieties and progress of a perturbed soul" (73).

If this curiosity sounds a bit unseemly, especially in Baillie's Gothic language of spying another's "muttering lip," perhaps it is. Critic Barbara Judson is skeptical whether sympathetic curiosity (to her a "speculative fiction") can truly develop "moral feeling" when it grows out of bad soil: a "passion for spectatorship, particularly a lust to view human suffering" (50). While we might discipline that passion into a moral sympathetic curiosity, it begins its life as "mere scopophilia" (52). Thus she finds Baillie's theory morally ambiguous, if not downright dangerous, emerging "as a drive for knowledge of human suffering and as a pleasure, both voyeuristic and sadistic, in observing that suffering" (56). Judson insinuates that Baillie has more in common with the Marquis de Sade than she might like to admit. Her "fascinated scrutiny of the mind and body is accompanied by a certain amount of heavy breathing on Baillie's part" (55).

Victoria Myers tempers Judson's qualms. Whereas *mere* curiosity is, to Baillie, "impersonal and analytical," *sympathetic* curiosity is committed to the "fellow-feeling" and "predisposition to benevolence" that Francis Hutcheson identified as an "innate sixth sense in humankind" (Myers 89). Baillie was steeped in the eighteenth-century theories of sympathy of fellow Scots Hutcheson, David Hume, and Adam Smith. Her motive is educational: sympathetic curiosity is "our best and most powerful instructor. From it we are taught the proprieties and decencies of ordinary life, and are prepared for distressing and difficult situations" (74). "Unless when accompanied with passions of the dark and malevolent mind," which Baillie finds are far outweighed by kindness, "we cannot well exercise this disposition without becoming more just, more merciful, more compassionate" (74).

Sympathetic curiosity can be seen as Baillie's psychological counterpart to her brother Matthew's work on the physical anatomy of humans. Matthew Baillie, named "Physician Extraordinary" to George III, wrote in *Morbid Anatomy of Some of the Most Important Parts of the Human Body* (1793) that his "principal motive" was to "render the morbid structure of parts more accurately and generally known, as one of the best means of advancing our knowledge of diseases" (qtd. McMillan 68).[2] To put it in medical terms, Baillie believed that the stage could work as a kind of operating theatre to examine the passions, isolate the diseased element, and get the patient on the road to recovery. It was why she chose drama instead of the more interior novel form for her project, believing that "the passions must be fully embodied to be understood, the course of the disease followed and if possible cured" (McMillan 77). As Dorothy McMillan puts it, Baillie "imagines herself entering those privacies that are available only to the priest and the doctor" to know the secrets of a soul; yet she is not "bound by the oaths of the professions to keep her discoveries secret: to be a writer is to be empowered to reveal what the doctor is sworn to conceal" (78). The playwright, then, usurps the role of physician as well as priest. Baillie travels into the "dark side" of the eighteenth-century moral philosophers, and in Victoria Myers's words, "elicits from their studies not so much potential lessons on morality" as "disturbing ambiguities in the moral role of the spectator/judge" (88). Judson goes further: "Baillie unabashedly places voyeurism at the heart of moral inquiry, arguing that because people habitually wear masks in everyday commerce, knowledge of another's heart may at times call for a culture of the keyhole" (54).

This is what I fear as I watch that couple pick at their soup and strain to make conversation with one another. What is my moral role as spectator and, inevitably, judge? I want to think my curiosity is sympathetic because my compassion is aroused, but I know it's pleasurable to my mind to detect subtext in the terse conversation, to interpret from the guarded body language and defeated sighs whether they're simply irritated that they arrived at a late lunch hour and had to take the table by the restrooms, or are feeling the gnawing emptiness of the chair between them that used to be filled and the loneliness of having to go at this alone.

Highly respected and popular in her own day—they called her "the female Shakespeare"[3]—and fully resurrected and regularly researched now by Romanticists, Joanna Baillie deserves to be better known and more widely studied and taught by theatre scholars. In 1798 she launched what would become her magnum opus, *A Series of Plays: In which it is Attempted to Delineate the Stronger Passions of the Mind*. Between 1798 and 1836 she would publish a three-volume set of twelve plays, each of which isolated one emotion and traced its "rise and progress in the heart" (91).[4] Her grand plan was to write two plays each—a tragedy and a comedy—carefully disclosing the passions of love, hate, ambition, fear, hope, remorse, jealousy, pride, envy, revenge, anger, joy, and grief.

Although several of these *Plays on the Passions*, as they're known, have been reissued in modern editions for the classroom,[5] we are still learning how to read and appreciate them. Jeffrey Cox, now one of the preeminent scholars of Romantic drama, argued in 1992 that Baillie's plays "participate in the confusions of psychological analysis with moral judgement that led Coleridge to condemn the Gothic drama" (*Seven Gothic Dramas* 52). In 2004 he regards them more highly, pointing out that the plays "return from melodrama to tragedy" when we stage them and can hear and see their "tragic richness" ("Staging Baillie" 147). Her use of the stage language and dramaturgy of the theatre of her day, including "deliberately fragmented, nonsequential utterances to communicate inchoate or incoherent thought" (Judson 57), allows Baillie to focus on "investigating" the characters' "inner struggles" (Cox, "Staging Baillie" 150). Gothic language is "appropriately ambivalent" as it is "given to serious exploration of the dark side of life" (Judson 54), but it can take some getting used to for readers unfamiliar with its conventions—readers who can no longer hear its freshness in contrast to earlier heroic drama.[6] Her works fit into the category Peter Brook called "The Theatre of the Invisible-Made-Visible," or Holy Theatre, in their attempts to stage consciousness, or "unveil the human mind" (Baillie 91).[7] And, as we have with other works in that dramatic mode, we need to learn how to read Baillie's plays.

The theatre theory that prefaces the first and third volumes of her plays, however, needs no learning curve and will strike theatre scholars as eerily familiar—as a call they heard a century later by Strindberg: "seek the intimate, a small theme exhaustively treated, few characters, big viewpoints, free imagination, but built on observation, experience, closely studied" (qtd. Meyer 475–76). Baillie's design for intimate theatre created a socially-sanctioned way of peering into windows and souls. Her ambition, in Dorothy McMillan's lovely phrase, is "no less than an attempt to know the whole of human affective life" (76).

The "Introductory Discourse" to the first volume (1798), where she presents her theory of sympathetic curiosity, mounts a defense of the theatre as a place of feeling. Baillie understands that, as Erin Hurley puts it in *Theatre & Feeling* (though Baillie appears nowhere in Hurley's book) "feeling is the core of the theatre. It furnishes theatre's reason for being, cements its purpose—whether such purpose is construed as entertainment or instruction—and undergirds the art form's social work and value" (77). One of the reasons we go to the theatre is "to experience an expanded, more expressive, and nuanced range of feeling imaginatively and viscerally with the aid of another person or agency" (77); in other words, to exercise our sympathetic curiosity.

By 1812, when Baillie releases her third volume of plays on the passions, she has grown tired of being relegated to the closet—that is, to being considered a writer of closet dramas by critics who don't understand how her plays work—and so in the preface "To the Reader" unfurls her manifesto for the theatre needed to animate her drama. The patent theatres of Covent Garden and Drury Lane swelled to seat over 3,000 spectators in Baillie's lifetime, putting enormous constraints on actors to be seen and heard. Her chief battle cry is "Reduce the size of those cavernous halls!" Following Samuel Foote's declaration in *A Treatise on the Passions* (1747) that the face was the "index of the Mind" (qtd. Duthie 37), she envisions a lighting design that "would allow audiences to read the psychological shifts being performed by actors" (Burroughs 87).[8] Instead of light "cast up from lamps" on the bottom front of the stage, which disfigures actors' faces and leaves them "less capable of any expression, unless it be of the ludicrous kind," have light be "thrown down" upon them, which will present "a varied harmonious mass of figures to the eye, deep, mellow and brilliant" (qtd. Cox and Gamer 377n136).

The "department of acting" suffers most in these circumstances, particularly soliloquies, which spotlight the unfolding of passions. Imagining the fine variations of vocal intonation her work calls for, she questions rhetorically, "what actor in his senses" would, on those bloated stages,

> think of giving to the solitary musing of a perturbed mind that muttered, imperfect articulation which grows by degrees into words; that heavy, suppressed voice as of one speaking through sleep; that rapid burst of sounds which often succeeds the slow languid tones of distress; those sudden, untuned exclamations which, as if frightened at their own discord, are struck again into silence as sudden and abrupt, with all the corresponding variety of countenance that belongs

to it;—what actor, so situated, will attempt to exhibit all this? [qtd. Cox and Gamer 375].

None, Baillie concludes. No actor will even bother trying to work against such obstacles. Instead, "he will be satisfied, after taking a turn or two across the front of the stage, to place himself directly in the middle of it; and there, spreading out his hands as if he were addressing some person whom it behoved him to treat with great ceremony, to tell to himself, in an audible uniform voice, all the secret thoughts of his own heart" (qtd. Cox and Gamer 375).

Baillie's examination of human affective life was so finely observed as to be "anatomical," an 1818 reviewer for the *Edinburgh Magazine* determined. "No one," the reviewer claimed, except Baillie, ever thought of giving, in dramatic form, "an anatomical analysis, a philosophical dissection of a passion" (qtd. Cox and Gamer 381). Her plays work as a kind of "microscope," he added, "by means of which she seems to think that she has brought within the sphere of our vision things too minute for the naked intellectual eye" (381–82). To the reviewer this is a problem—he finds it the "radical defect" of her plays— but today it is considered her most brilliant endeavor, an innovative theatrical experiment; in the words of Aileen Forbes, it is a "proto-psychoanalytic theater" that "begins to articulate the theatrical structures that will shape psychoanalysis in the following century" (33).

In the end, Baillie never wrote the play on grief. She gave up on it, concluding that grief is "generally of too transient a nature" and "too frequently the attendant of all our other passions to be made the subject of an entire play." She was right: grief is a complicated passion, intricately bound up with anger, despair, revenge, and hope. I like to think of *Rabbit Hole* as David Lindsay-Abaire's completion of Baillie's abandoned grief project. It's my own fantasy, of course; Baillie's been resting in her grave at St. John's Hampstead since 1851 and Lindsay-Abaire had never heard of her when I asked. On the surface no one would put them in the same dramatic lineage: their styles are radically different, as suits the theatre of their eras. Yet the impulse they share to invite us into the intimacy of an unveiling of grief, moment by moment, connects them. Ben Brantley's review of *Rabbit Hole* for the *New York Times* echoes Baillie's *Edinburgh Magazine* reviewer in calling the playwriting "anatomical" in its own way, yet in this case it's a compliment. "The sad, sweet release of *Rabbit Hole* lies precisely in the access it allows to the pain of others, in its meticulously mapped empathy. This anatomy of grief doesn't so much jerk tears as tap them, from a reservoir of feelings common to anyone who has experienced the landscape-shifting vacuum left by a death in the family."

Reminiscent of Baillie's design, which was to show the "thousand delicate traits" (91) that make up an emotion, Lindsay-Abaire doesn't reduce grief to a single image. There's no character in a heap on the floor, weeping, signifying "grief." There might have been, immediately after the event. But the play shrewdly opens eight months after Danny's death. Grief is not a short-lived passion; it overstays its welcome and continues to haunt in all manner of ways. Between Becca and Howie we'll see moments of rage, melancholy, paralysis, envy, nostalgia, accusation, guilt, longing, defensiveness, helplessness, fear, and inklings of hope.

Recall that Baillie abandoned the grief play because grief is such a "transient" emotion: fleeting, on the move, unpredictable. In *Rabbit Hole* we know Becca is grieving because of her ferocious attempts to displace it. Because, in other words, of how hard she tries *not* to show that she's grieving. Lindsay-Abaire traces the "rise and progress in the heart" of Becca's grief through a winding path. It surfaces at the opening of the play as envy and resentment of her irresponsible sister Izzy's pregnancy, which feels like a cosmic injustice since Izzy has never shown maternal instincts and has gotten accidentally knocked up through messing around with another woman's boyfriend. It's hard for Becca to move beyond "oh my god, Izzy" (repeated three times, 20, 22). "I hope it's a girl," Izzy says (26). "Me, too," Becca responds, followed by the stage direction "*(Beat.)*," signaling space in which both of them want no reminder or replacement of Danny.

The subsequent scene reveals Becca's grief in the form of resistance to intimacy with her husband. It's been almost eight months since they've been intimate, we learn. Howie tries to set the mood with wine, dimmed lights, and Al Green on the stereo. Becca's response is complicated, and it takes the entire scene's full unfolding to show her fear of taking pleasure; her fear of being emotionally vulnerable with Howie, who's experienced everything she has; her apprehension of possibly becoming pregnant and caring so intensely all over again; and sheer lack of physical arousal because of those fears and apprehensions. Entwined in all of this is blame and guilt: twinges of blame that her husband insisted upon the dog who ran out into the street; twinges of guilt that she was the one who didn't check to see that the gate was locked.

Add to that the grief experienced as scorn toward those in the therapy support group who take comfort in stock phrases such as "God needed another angel"; defensiveness toward her mother, Nat, who wants to equate her own loss of a son, Becca's brother Arthur, a heroin addict who committed suicide as an adult, to Becca's pain over losing Danny; and unbridled rage against another mother at the supermarket who refuses to give her child a fruit rollup, and whom Becca slaps. At the same time, demonstrating the wondrous complexities of grief, she is the one who wants to remove daily evidence of life with Danny: pictures on the refrigerator, clothes, the dog, even the house. She has lost herself in the object that was lost: when Danny was born she quit her job and was completely absorbed in being a mother. Now she doesn't know who she is.

Howie's grief, while somewhat less fully fleshed out, is still multidimensional.[9] We see him reaching out to make intimate contact with his wife but also seeking comfort in what could become an affair with another grieving parent from the support group to which Becca has refused to return. Late at night he takes joy in watching the last remaining presence of Danny, a video, and breaks down in tears when Becca erases it, accusing her of doing so on purpose.

In this intimate theatre, "a theatre that attempts to exteriorize and hence to visualize a hidden interiority, to act out and hence to make sense of what is most unintelligible, secretive, and essential about us" (Forbes 45), nuanced body language, facial expression, gesture, and vocal intonation are as essential as dialogue. *Rabbit Hole* is a "delicate play tonally," Lindsay-Abaire warns in his Author's Note; it "can be easily thrown out of whack." If the play lurches into sentimentality it will "flatten out and come across as a bad movie-of-the-week" (159). "If the stage directions don't mention tears, please resist adding them," he urges actors and directors. "I'm pretty sure Izzy doesn't need to cry in this play. And I *know* Jason shouldn't cry, ever. (Yes, he's haunted by the death of Danny, but his emotions aren't especially accessible to him.)" (159).

Echoing this in his keynote discussion at the Comparative Drama Conference in March 2015, Lindsay-Abaire noted that "if executed properly," Becca should not show tears until the middle of the second act when she meets with Jason, the boy who killed their son. Howie refuses to talk with or absolve him, but Becca invites him over, makes him lemon squares and listens to him tell the story of the fateful day. Becca knows Jason needs to unburden himself and yet understands the adolescent state of development that holds him back from being able to fully acknowledge what he did: "I might've have been going too fast. That day," he tells her. "I'm not sure, but I might've been. [...] It's a thirty zone. And I might've been going thirty-three. Or thirty-two. [...] I might've been going a little over the limit. I can't be positive either way, though" (137). She shows sympathetic curiosity for Jason, and grants him what *she* has wanted: someone to listen to her story, even as it causes pain.

Becca has "compartmentalized everything in her life, including her grief," Lindsay-Abaire explained to the CDC audience. She has come to some terms with grieving the loss of her four-year-old son, but has not reckoned with the loss of a twelve-year-old, a seventeen-year-old, a son she would have seen going to his own prom. "That loss is so enormous" at this moment with Jason that she breaks down, which should be the climax of the play, Lindsay-Abaire pointed out. If the performers are "quivery" in the first act there's "no dramatic event in the second act." We're focused on the boy and his tale of his prom and Becca's gulf of tears seemingly comes out of nowhere. The passion in this climactic scene is indicated entirely in the stage directions, not the dialogue. A reader might easily skim over the intended dramatic intensity of this moment. For an actor, though, the stage directions are carefully detailed. They read, "*Becca has been tearing up while listening. And with little warning, she is crying. A lot. It goes on for a few beats. Jason just sits, not sure what to do*" (140).

Sympathetic curiosity gives us a vicarious experience of another person. It arouses our attention to the other, takes us out of indifference, builds empathy.[10] Theatre answers the "human needs, regulated by both curiosity and fear, to experience the world vicariously as well as directly," as Joseph Roach has put it (121). We want it so much people "will part with good money to experience experience (by living through someone else's performance of it)" (121). Using today's neuroscience to explain theatre's effect, Erin Hurley explains that "witnessing another's actions and emotional experiences can create the same neurological imprint as doing or feeling them oneself" (76).

Some plays are designed to give audiences a vicarious experience of the thing itself—in this case, of what it's like to experience grief. But David Lindsay-Abaire isn't writing *4:48 Psychosis*. While *Rabbit Hole* pulls on our sympathetic curiosity to know just what a grieving couple—and grieving individuals—experience, we remain onlookers. Caring onlookers, but onlookers just the same. John Cameron Mitchell's film version, for which Lindsay-Abaire wrote the screenplay, tries to thrust us into the thing itself. With its mono-mood direction, flattening sentimental flashbacks of life with Danny, and melodramatic musical scoring signposting "sadness," it runs counter to the playwright's wishes for his stage script and presses hard for tears. Reviewing it for *Psychology Today*, Jeremy Clyman observes that "as viewers our mirror neurons are firing to such a degree that the sense of empathy and helplessness becomes exhausting." This is decidedly not the case onstage or in reading the play, in my experience. Which is not a criticism of Lindsay-Abaire's script. Instead, I find it an appealing and, in the end, wise playwriting decision.

The play puts the audience in the position not of Becca, engulfed in grief, but of Debbie, her friend standing apart not knowing what to do about her friend who's engulfed in grief. Put differently, we are not having the vicarious experience of going through the grief; we are having the vicarious experience of being a friend watching a friend go through grief. But because this is theatre rather than life, we are put in the position Debbie would *want* to be in—able to peer into the window and listen in to know what her friend is going through so she might know what to say and do to comfort her.

This is also where Lindsay-Abaire not only completes Baillie's grief project but takes it a step further. Baillie was fascinated with the anatomical dissection. Lindsay-Abaire moves toward putting the patient back together. What

Becca needs is what she gave Jason: someone to tell her story to. Howie recognizes this; it's why they had gone to group therapy. He suggests "a psychiatrist then. Someone to talk to" (45). Howie is too entangled in the grief himself. Any talk they have is just reliving the story, reopening the wound. Izzy is too caught up in her own dramas, and Nat in comparing her own grief. Becca needs a friend.

Debbie, though an unseen character, is one of the first we're introduced to, in the opening of the second scene of the play. Howie and Debbie's husband Rick see one another regularly for squash games as they always had in the past but Becca and Debbie haven't spoken since the funeral. Becca misses her friend, wants to know how she is, how her kids are. She sorely wants to reconnect but feels forsaken by Debbie, who has "vanished" (36). "I don't wanna call her," Becca explains to Howie (35); Debbie may feel awkward and uncomfortable but she needs to recognize that "it's her job to call me" (36). As we see in Becca's grief expressed elsewhere in the play, her sorrow over the estranged friendship is also multi-faceted. It surfaces as a snarky vision of revenge when, cleaning out Danny's room with Nat, she discovers an irritating battery-operated yippy-dog toy and remarks slyly, "Debbie's kids might like that. We should save it for *them*. That'd show her." "Still haven't heard from her?" Nat asks. "Nope," Becca responds (120).

It is Becca and Debbie's relationship that is given the real dramatic arc in *Rabbit Hole*. The play resists any releasing scene of healing between Becca and Howie—"avoid resolution at all costs," Lindsay-Abaire advises directors. "I don't ever want a moment (not even the very end) where the audience sighs and says, 'Oh good, they're gonna be okay now'" (*Rabbit Hole* 160). But we *are* given a compensating resolution in the friendship of Becca and Debbie. In the closing scene we learn that Becca has called Debbie and been invited over for a family cookout. Debbie, Becca tells Howie, was surprised to be called, "cried,"

> then apologized about sixty times, and then cried some more. [...] She said she kept meaning to call, but she felt freaked-out about everything and so she kept putting it off, and before she knew it months had gone by, and so then she *really* couldn't call because she felt like such an asshole, and assumed I hated her, so it just seemed easier to not pick up the phone [153].

Pick up the phone, the play tells us. The grieving person needs to tell her story. But only if you are listening; otherwise it doesn't feel safe to unveil the messy, ugly, many-sided faces of grief.

Intimate theatre creates the conditions that help us learn how to listen. In the theatre you have to put away your cell phone and hold yourself back from interrupting. (I am tempted to say *only* in the theatre, as it sometimes seems about the only place left in our society—"the last human venue," as Alan

Read has called it—where people are expected to turn off their phones and tune in to another, but even that is eroding. You can tune out, or fall asleep, or rudely look at your phone anyway, or climb up on the stage to recharge it.[11]) In the theatre you can nod; you can, quietly, express sympathetic utterances; but you're not expected to say anything or do anything but listen to the other's story. This is "not voyeuristic," Lindsay-Abaire insisted in his talk to the Comparative Drama Conference. We go to the theatre not to peer without consequence but because "we want to connect [...]. We want to feel less alone." By sitting us down in the dark to listen to Becca work through the full range of grieving the death of her son, *Rabbit Hole* teaches the audience to be the friend a grieving person sorely needs.

University of St. Thomas

Notes

Acknowledgements: Many thanks to David Lindsay-Abaire, Kelly Younger, Chelsea Dove, Martha Johnson, and Doug Phillips for their conversation and comments, and to the two anonymous reviewers for *Text & Presentation* for their probing questions.

1. Howard Kissel (*New York Daily News*) called it "thin gruel"; Michael Feingold (*Village Voice*) labeled it "too compassionate"; Jeremy McCarter (*New York Magazine*) complained that it "belongs to a swollen class of plays that have all sorts of storytelling virtues but no particular theatrical virtues. You might as well watch TV."

2. As many scholars have noted, Baillie came from a medical family—"the most famous medical family of the period, perhaps of all periods in the history of British medicine," as Dorothy McMillan puts it in "'Dr.' Baillie" (70). In addition to her brother Matthew Baillie, her uncles William and John Hunter were a renowned anatomist and obstetrician and one of the greatest experimental surgeons.

3. See Fiona Ritchie, "Joanna Baillie: the Female Shakespeare," *Women Making Shakespeare: Text, Reception, Performance*, eds. Gordon McMullan, Lena Cowen Orlin, and Virginia Mason Vaughan (London & New York: Bloomsbury, 2014), 143–52.

4. Thanks to the work of feminist scholars, the Introductory Discourse was excerpted in *The "Other" Eighteenth Century: English Women of Letters 1660–1800*, eds. Robert W. Uphaus and Gretchen M. Foster (East Lansing, MI: Colleagues, 1991), and a somewhat longer chunk of it, along with her preface to the 1812 *Series of Plays* was excerpted in *Women Critics 1660–1820: an anthology*, ed. Folger Collective on Early Women Critics (Bloomington: Indiana University Press, 1995). Thomas Crochunis supplies a history of Baillie scholarship in "Introduction: The Case of Joanna Baillie" in his *Joanna Baillie, Romantic Dramatist* (1–7). While there have been articles on Baillie in *Theatre Journal* and *Theatre Survey*, the overwhelming majority of scholarly studies have been published in journals of Romanticism or women's studies.

5. *Plays on the Passions*, ed. Peter Duthie (Broadview, 2001), includes *De Monfort, Count Basil,* and *The Tryal*—the three plays in Baillie's first volume of the plays on the passions in 1798. *Seven Gothic Dramas*, ed. Jeffrey N. Cox (Ohio University Press, 1992) anthologizes *De Monfort* (the most famous of Baillie's plays because of all the contextual

material we have from its premiere production in 1800 starring Sarah Siddons and John Philip Kemble). The *Broadview Anthology of Romantic Drama* (2006), eds. Cox and Michael Gamer, includes *Orra*. Adrienne Scullion included Baillie's *The Family Legend* (not one of the Plays on the Passions) earlier in *Female Playwrights of the Nineteenth Century* (Everyman, 1996).

6. Jeffrey N. Cox points out that Baillie positions herself opposite "the tradition of the heroic drama" from Beaumont and Fletcher and Dryden; she "contends that in such plays the psychology of the tragic hero is lost because, in their focus on action, they are not concerned with investigating his or her inner struggles" ("Staging Baillie" 150). "At times, she seems to be calling for an intimate theatre of subtle psychological exchanges that would lead to a reasoned, moral response. However, in that her tragedies are filled with hatred, murder, ritual violence, witchcraft, and supernatural fears, they at times seem closer to Artaud's theatre of cruelty" (Cox, "Staging Baillie" 154).

7. Peter Brook, *The Empty Space* (New York: Atheneum, 1968), 42. See also Amy Muse, "Lifting the Painted Veil: Romantic Drama as Holy Theatre," in *Teaching Romantic Drama: Special Issue of the Romantic Pedagogy Commons*, ed. Thomas C. Crochunis, *Romantic Circles* (May 2011). Web.

8. Peter Duthie adds that "it is understandable, then, that any audience seeking the rewards of serious drama would struggle with the physical conditions of the contemporary stage" (37). Alan Richardson explains that "early facial expression theory was being developed in tandem by neurologists and literary artists alike" and credits Baillie for anticipating Charles Bell's "physiological," "neuroscientific" approach in his *Anatomy and Philosophy of Human Expression* (1806), which "for Darwin marked the beginning of a legitimately scientific approach" (68, 73).

9. At the Comparative Drama Conference, Lindsay-Abaire noted that the play was written as a study of one woman's grief, while the film version of *Rabbit Hole* opened up the perspective to examine the grief of the couple.

10. Building empathy is not all that theatre is good for, of course. Palgrave Macmillan's "Theatre &" series showcases theatre's long reach and many missions, from *Theatre & Feeling* to *Theatre & Human Rights, Theatre & Nation, Theatre & Politics, Theatre & Prison, Theatre & Ethics, Theatre & Sexuality* & etc.

11. In a now-infamous incident, nineteen-year-old Nick Silvestri jumped up onto the set of the Broadway production of *Hand to God* in an attempt to charge his cell phone. This incited debate on *American Theatre*'s website www.americantheatre.org over whether it brought a much-needed "charge" to live theatre, or was a "dickish move." www.americantheatre.org/2015/07/10/the-infamous-iphone-incident-at-hand-to-god-theatre-could-use-a-charge-like-that/

WORKS CITED

Allard, James Robert. "Joanna Baillie and the Theater of Consequence." *Staging Pain, 1500–1800*. Ed. James Robert Allard. Burlington, VT: Ashgate, 2009. 169–183.

Baillie, Joanna. *Plays on the Passions*. Ed. Peter Duthie. Peterborough, Ontario: Broadview, 2001.

Blumenfeld, Michael. "The Rabbit Hole—Complicated Grief." *Psychiatry Talk*. www.psychiatrytalk.com/2010/12/the-rabbit-hole-complicated-grief/. Web. Accessed August 25, 2015.

Brantley, Ben. Review of *Rabbit Hole*. *New York Times* (February 3, 2006). Web. Accessed May 25, 2015.

Burroughs, Catherine B. *Closet Stages: Joanna Baillie and the Theater Theory of British Women Romantic Writers*. Philadelphia: University of Pennsylvania Press, 1997.

Carney, Sean. "The Passion of Joanna Baillie: Playwright as Martyr." *Theatre Journal* 52.2 (2000): 227–252.

Clyman, Jeremy. "Rabbit Hole: Treatment for Grief." *Psychology Today* (April 21, 2011). Web. Accessed August 25, 2015.

Cox, David. "Rabbit Hole Burrows into Our Ideals." *The Guardian* (February 7, 2011). Web. Accessed August 25, 2015.

Cox, Jeffrey N. *Seven Gothic Dramas: 1789–1825*. Athens: Ohio University Press, 1992.

Cox, Jeffrey N., and Michael Gamer, eds. *The Broadview Anthology of Romantic Drama*. Peterborough, Ontario: Broadview, 2003.

Crochunis, Thomas, ed. and intro. *Joanna Baillie, Romantic Dramatist*. New York and London: Routledge, 2004.

Evans, Rachel. Review of *Rabbit Hole*. *Theatre Journal* 59.1 (2007): 134–135.

Forbes, Aileen, "'Sympathetic Curiosity' in Joanna Baillie's Theater of the Passions." *European Romantic Review* 14.1 (2003): 31–48.

Hurley, Erin. *Theatre & Feeling*. Basingstoke: Palgrave Macmillan, 2010.

Judson, Barbara. "'Sympathetic Curiosity': The Theater of Joanna Baillie." *Tulsa Studies in Women's Literature* 25.1 (2006): 49–70.

Kaufman, Scott Barry. "Peering through the Rabbit Hole." "Beautiful Minds" column. *Psychology Today* (December 20, 2010). Web. Accessed May 21, 2015.

Kissel, Howard. Review of *Rabbit Hole*, *New York Daily News* (February 3, 2006). Web. Accessed September 1, 2015.

Lindsay-Abaire, David. *Rabbit Hole*. New York: Theatre Communications Group, 2006.

McCarter, Jeremy. "Offstage Drama." *New York Magazine* (February 13, 2006). Web. Accessed September 1, 2015.

McMillan, Dorothy. "'Dr.' Baillie." *1798: The Year of the Lyrical Ballads*. Ed. Richard Cronin. New York: St. Martin's, 1998. 68–92.

Meyer, Michael. *Strindberg*. New York: Random House, 1985.

Myers, Victoria. "Joanna Baillie's Theatre of Cruelty." *Joanna Baillie, Romantic Dramatist*. Ed. Thomas Crochunis. New York and London: Routledge, 2004. 87–107.

Read, Alan. *Theatre, Intimacy, and Engagement*. Basingstoke: Palgrave Macmillan, 2008.

"Remarks on the Plays on the Passions, by Joanna Baillie." *Edinburgh Magazine* 2 (June 1818): 517–20. Rpt. *The Broadview Anthology of Romantic Drama*. Eds. Jeffrey N. Cox and Michael Gamer. Peterborough, Ontario: Broadview, 2003. 380–83.

Richardson, Alan. "Facial Expression Theory from Romanticism to the Present." *An Introduction to Cognitive Cultural Studies*. Ed. Lisa Zunshine. Baltimore: Johns Hopkins University Press, 2010. 65–83.

Roach, Joseph R. "Vicarious: Theater and the Rise of Synthetic Experience." *Theorizing Practice: Redefining Theatre History*. Eds. W. B. Worthen and Peter Holland. Basingstoke: Palgrave Macmillan, 2003. 120–35.

Review of Literature: Selected Books

Paul Elsam. *Stephen Joseph: Theatre Pioneer and Provocateur*. London: Bloomsbury, 2013. Pp. 202+xvi. Hardcover $112. Paperback $29.95.

Stephen Joseph (1921–1967) founded theatre-in-the-round in England. He opened two such theatres at a time when established theatre critics preferred more conventional proscenium stages and were hostile to Joseph's experiments. Joseph designed the first professional theatre-in-the-round for his newly founded Studio Theatre in an upper room of the library in Scarborough, a town on the North Yorkshire coast, in 1955. He created the second—and first permanent—theatre-in-the-round, the Vic at Stoke-on-Trent, Staffordshire, for his touring company in 1962, again choosing a theatrically underserved location away from the centers of theatrical prestige, where it was still possible to create democratized theatre for new audiences.

In *Stephen Joseph: Theatre Pioneer and Provocateur* Paul Elsam seeks to undo half a century of critical neglect and to establish Joseph's importance and influence on British theatre in the middle years of the twentieth century and beyond. Joseph was a teacher (at the Central School of Speech and Drama and the University of Manchester), an author of books on theatre, notably *Theatre in the Round* (1967) and *New Theatre Forms* (1968), and a designer of and consultant on theatrical spaces, for example, the Nuffield Theatre in Lancaster. Elsam charts Joseph's lasting influence on open stage theatres in England, on individual theatrical practitioners, and on the democratization of theatre.

Joseph's most important and lasting contributions to theatre in England are the growing number of open stage theatres in the country today, especially the Stephen Joseph Theatre in Scarborough (1996), located in an old cinema building, and the New Vic in Stoke-on-Trent (1986), the first purpose-built theatre-in-the-round in Europe. Performance in-the-round encourages the democratization of theatre through its egalitarian use of space. Sitting on four sides of the stage, audience members are in a close intimate relationship with the actors, and they can also see each other across the stage. No seat is better or more expensive than another, and sightlines are equally good for all. Through his emphasis on informality and new plays Joseph aimed to develop new audiences. In Scarborough, for example, holiday-makers as well as local enthusiasts found their way to the library theatre.

Joseph was adamant in his support of new playwriting. Elsam describes his influence on dramatists James Saunders, Alan Plater, David Campton, and especially Alan Ayckbourn, who got his start as a stage manager and actor and then, with Joseph's encouragement, dramatist at Scarborough's theatre-in-the-round, which he eventually went on to direct. In Stoke-on-Trent Joseph brought in Peter Cheeseman as the first director of the Vic. Cheeseman became important in the development of documentary theatre: both musical community theatre and verbatim theatre (in which plays are constructed from people's actual words). Elsam describes, too, how Joseph was instrumental in jumpstarting the career of Harold Pinter. After the first failed production of *The Birthday Party* in 1958, Joseph invited Pinter to direct the play himself for Studio Theatre. Pinter's production achieved critical success in Birmingham in 1960, and Joseph then initiated an equally successful production by Independent Television.

A more diffuse influence was on Ben Kingsley, who acted at the Vic in Stoke-on-Trent under Peter Cheeseman in the early 1960s but never actually met Joseph. In an interview with Elsam, Kingsley affirmed Joseph's influence on his own work, noting that performing in the round requires actors to act truthfully, without "tricks," because, as Joseph emphasized, there is "no hiding place"; further, "[y]ou must have the energy in your body language and your vocal range to include the people sitting behind you" (116). Joseph himself distinguished between the "linear" projection actors use in proscenium theatres and the "organic" projection required in "three-dimensional space" (17). The 2008 interview with Kingsley exemplifies how Elsam has been at pains to explore even indirect traces of Joseph's impact on theatre and theatrical practitioners and to demonstrate the effects of his work into the present century. If sometimes Elsam seems to stretch what counts as influence to document Joseph's significance, it is well to remember that the impact of one individual on his milieu often is dispersed or implicit but nonetheless important for all that.

In tracing the various strands of Joseph's work in theatre, Elsam draws on published and unpublished sources, reviews, archives, interviews, and a huge amount of correspondence. He arranges his material topically according to the different kinds of influence that Joseph had—on playwrights, on theatrical structures—and the means by which he achieved such influence—by encouraging company members to write plays, by teaching, and so on.

He controls his material, however, via a disconcerting degree of enumeration (1a, Case study 4). Elsam's organizational choices entail both skipping back and forth between Stoke-on-Trent and Scarborough and going over the same few years again and again, without quite providing as clear a sense of the history of each theatre as one might wish. Though Elsam mentions some of the plays that were performed at the two theatres, he does not give us much sense of their overall seasons or of how the productions were received by the local communities (for example, by the local press). A second unfortunate consequence of his choice of organization is that, in trying to account for all of the strands of Joseph's influence, Elsam actually fragments his subject's work.

On the positive side, Elsam does, however, clearly demonstrate Joseph's originality in theatrical activities ranging from stage design to acting theory and his energetic activism on behalf of his ideas for a more democratic theatre. Elsam provides substantial information, much of it drawn from letters, about Joseph's efforts to find support for his experimental work and about his quarrels with established theatre critics such as W. A. Darlington and Kenneth Tynan. Sometimes Joseph would sign his letters "R. Heath Block," under which name he occasionally wrote satiric attacks on himself. Writing of Joseph the man, Elsam notes, too, and speculates about Joseph's strange habit of disappearing at times from his theatre in Scarborough, supposedly to engage in manual labor, such as delivering coal. I had no idea.

The son of publisher Michael Joseph and actress Hermione Gingold, Stephen Joseph was a larger-than-life presence in many aspects of theatre in the 1950s and 1960s. Certainly he seemed so to this stage-struck Scarborough schoolgirl who handed out free programs in exchange for a free seat. (I learn from Elsam's book that free programs were also one of Joseph's innovations.) After half a century I still remember vividly Stephen Joseph standing in the entranceway to the stage at the interval, announcing to audiences in his deep sonorous voice, "Coffee is now being served in the exhibition room." I later met Joseph as we kneeled side by side taking the theatre apart at the end of one summer season. He was charming. I am glad to have the opportunity in this review to express my gratitude to him for creating in a small seaside town a theatre that inspired at least one professor of dramatic literature. I recommend Paul Elsam's book to anyone interested in what else was going on in English theatre, outside George Devine's Royal Court and Joan Littlewood's Stratford East, in the heady experimental years of the mid-twentieth century.

VERNA A. FOSTER
Loyola University Chicago

J. Chris Westgate. *Staging the Slums, Slumming the Stage: Class, Poverty, Ethnicity and Sexuality in American Theatre, 1890–1916.* Palgrave Studies in Theatre and Performance History. New York: Palgrave Macmillan, 2014. Pp. 278+xii. Hardcover $90.

Never has the inherent voyeurism of standard fourth-wall realism been more apparent than in the "slumming" plays that are documented in J. Chris Westgate's remarkable feat of theatrical archaeology titled *Staging the Slums, Slumming the Stage: Class, Poverty, Ethnicity, and Sexuality in American Theatre, 1890–1916.* Respectably bourgeois-to-upper-class theatregoers, being affluent enough to afford a Broadway "good night out," could gaze from their (more or less) comfortable seats upon the artfully impersonated lives of New York's destitute citizen-slum-dwellers whose real-life counterparts lived only blocks away in the Bowery and other such refuges of the down-and-more-or-less-out. Secure in their knowledge that the ever-so-protective "invisible fourth wall" would never be breached to disrupt their physical and psychological class-based comfort, they could partake in the vicarious thrills afforded by sensational plots that could involve scenes in gaudy brothels, nefarious gangland hideouts, disreputable saloons, and Chinese opium dens. Those patrons who had enough courage could, for slightly more money, sign onto escorted tours of *actual* slums after the performance—All-American Entrepreneurial Spirit at its finest, thriving back in those mythic "Good Old Days"—though of course *actual* slum-dwellers and their tourist-voyeurs would be far less reliably ready to burst into song on cue. The ostentatiously over-dressed man and woman on the cover of Westgate's book, who look imminently ready to burst into song, are just such slum-tourists [see Figure 1]. They were in fact "The Bowery Burlesquers, presenting an original *burletta* on the latest New York craze, 'Slumming.'" Behind them to their left, a shadowy silhouetted figure lurks in a lighted doorway, ready to entice passers-by into a den of iniquity. Only the unusually brave or the unnaturally depraved would undertake such a journey solo—or so proper, prosperous, propriety-loving middle-class theatre-goers of the time would have presumed.

Nevertheless, "slumming" plays offered "a thrill a minute" for the mere price of a ticket. The most thrilling and/or appalling of these was *The Bowery after Dark* (1899) which "shows you how the lower world lives [...] depicting the pleasures, misery and crime on the Bowery at night, when all the city is asleep and the Bowery is in full blast" (48). Its *Indiana Jones*–worthy plot included multiple abductions, "white slavery" [i.e., forced prostitution], an opium den known as Lee's Chinese Joint, an attempted poisoning, a pit full of snakes into which the hero gets hurled, a threatened child-strangulation, and a woman's hand being nailed to a chair onstage—the brutality of which

Figure 1: Slumming. 1898. H. C. Miner Litho. Co. Photograph from the Library of Congress, Prints and Photographs Division. This was used as the cover image for J. Chris Westgate's *Staging the Slums, Slumming the Stage: Class, Poverty, Ethnicity, and Sexuality in American Theatre, 1890-1916* (reproduced with permission of Palgrave Macmillan).

"violate[d] theatrical decorum, which mandated that violence occur offstage, [...] [a]lthough the horror of this scene may have been mitigated by the fact that [the victim] is Chinese and not white" (49). The first act also included a visit inside a tavern modeled after John McGurk's Suicide Hall, a notorious Bowery saloon whose "clientele was sailors who would enjoy drinks, music, and prostitution [...] [and which] 'was nearly the lowest rung for prostitutes [and] became a favorite location for committing suicide, generally by drinking carbolic acid. [...] [The scholar Luc] Sante estimates that in 1899 there were at least six [suicides there], as well as more than seven attempts" (50). Amid such extravagant perils in such lurid venues, when the beleaguered heroine and her companions eventually find time to "kneel down to pray and [heroine] Flora touches [the] cross, it 'shines radiantly' [...] and shocks [the villainous] Lee into leaving them alone—yet another instance where *The Bowery After Dark* confirm[ed] middle-class values" (48)—and, no doubt, that (especially with theatrical special effects) The Lord worketh in truly wondrous ways.

By the early twentieth century, however, social reformers of various types realized that slum-set plays could in fact be used not as mere entertainment but as vehicles for the advancement of a "new social conscience, which would significantly change the way class and poverty, charity and capitalism, amusement and responsibility were understood in the United States" (54). What Westgate terms the "sociological narrative" thus supplanted the earlier "tourism narrative" with its sensationalism, entertainment value, and exhibitionism. Accordingly, these playwrights "privileged the problems from slum life, from tenement neglect to ethnic prejudices to the social evil of prostitution" and set forth drama that "became less about the settings of the slums, like tenements and saloons, and more about the struggles of characters with[in] the slums, like impoverishment and addiction" (55). No longer merely gaping at their seemingly not-so-*semblables* and less-than-*freres*-and-*soeurs*, playwrights deliberately provoked bourgeois theatregoers into thinking about large and complex issues of social and moral responsibility for the status quo. In short, American slum-set theatre aligned itself with the then-shocking ethos of Ibsen, Strindberg, and Zola—more willing to discomfit and provoke its audiences rather than merely to entertain and amuse.

Westgate then provides separate chapters on distinct varieties of "slumming" plays based on their particular settings: tenements, immigrant neighborhoods, and "red light districts." The latter proved to be the most controversial, of course, as critics and theatregoers debated whether such spectacles encouraged or discouraged patronage of the real venues; there were "brothel tours" available at the time as well as guidebooks intended to advise the unwary of places to avoid—though they *could* be used for exactly the opposite purpose by those who were otherwise inclined. Once again, verisimilitude and authenticity were an extraordinarily high priority for theatrical impresarios, not least among them the director David Belsaco (after whom a Broadway theatre has been named). Dissatisfied with the initial stage set for Eugene Walter's *The Easiest Way* (1909), Belasco found the Tenderloin district's shabbiest boarding house and "bought the entire interior of one of its most dilapidated rooms—patched furniture, threadbare carpet, tarnished and broken glass fixtures, tumbledown cupboards, dinghy doors and window casings, and even faded paper on the walls" and reassembled them all on his Stuyvesant Theatre stage, to overwhelming critical acclaim and box office success (150). It was and is, Westgate claims, "the best known of any slum play considered in this study," which number into the dozens. Readers of his volume may well feel like Keats's "stout Cortez" (née Balboa) gazing out from that famous peak in Darien.

My sole caveat about *Staging the Slums, Slumming the Stage* is that, by stopping his coverage in 1916, Westgate necessarily excludes the most interesting—and most infamous—of the "red light district" slumming plays, whose renowned author and actress was tried for obscenity, convicted, and jailed in a workhouse: none other than the iconic Mae West, whose play titled *Sex* ran for over a year in 1926–27.[1] With lots of her inimitable double entendres and song-and-dances routines (the "shimmy dance" among them, though not, she insisted, the "shimmy shewabble," which she deemed vulgar), and more than a little justification of her character's occupation, West starred as an unrepentant prostitute who rescues an upper-class female slum tourist from peril but later learns that the woman's son, a client of hers, wants to marry her. Without the context newly provided by Westgate's book, *Sex* seems preposterously contrived and a mere vehicle for the musical numbers and jokes. Post-Westgate, however, it can be understood within the context of a long-lost tradition in popular theatre.

A more astonishing, revelatory, and entertainingly written volume of literary history than J. Chris Westgate's *Staging the Slums, Slumming the Stage* would be very hard to find.

Note

1. For further details, see my essay, "Mae West as Playwright: Broadway's *Sex* Scandal of 1926–27," *Text & Presentation: Journal of the Comparative Drama Conference* 21 (2000): 101–15. The long-suppressed text of the play was first published in *Three Plays by Mae West*, ed. Lillian Schlissel (New York: Routledge, 1994), 33–92.

WILLIAM HUTCHINGS
University of Alabama at Birmingham

Gwendolyn Compton-Engle. *Costume in the Comedies of Aristophanes*. Cambridge: Cambridge University Press, 2015. Pp. 210+31 illus. Hardcover $99.

Since Oliver Taplin's *The Stagecraft of Aeschylus* (Clarendon, 1977) opened the door to scholarship on the performance of Greek drama, with a few exceptions (the work of J. R. Green, Eric Csapo and Peter Wilson in particular) the study of Greek drama has clung to its philological roots, taking the text as the blueprint for all discussion of performance. As a result, while there has been much scholarship on significant actions and objects and entrances and exits, guided by the principle that these must be indicated in the text, there has been much less work on the conditions of performance.[1] Compton-Engle's book is a welcome addition to the growing bibliography on physical aspects of performance, focusing on the use of costumes in the plays of Aristophanes, incorporating and building on her excellent articles on the use of costume in Old Comedy.

This book will largely replace Laura Stone's *Costume in Aristophanic Comedy* (Arno, 1981), which has long been limited in its usefulness, since it was published before the proliferation of research on ancient Greek drama in performance, before gender and performance, and before the identification of the Wurzberg Telephus vase as an depiction of a scene from Aristophanes' *Thesmophoriazusae* (see Compton-Engle 5), which decisively linked the so-called phlyax vases and Athenian Old Comedy, providing visual evidence for various aspects of performance. All of these scholarly developments serve as a foundation for this book. This volume forms a obvious counterpoint volume to Rosie Wyle's recent *Costume in Greek Tragedy* (Bristol Classical, 2011) and deserves to find a wide readership not only among scholars of Old Comedy, but also scholars working on the history of theatre costumes, graduate students and senior undergraduates.

There are five chapters and a short conclusion: 1. Comic costume in Action; 2. Comic Body as Costume; 3. Cloaks, Shoes, and Societal Redress; 4. Disguise, Gender, and the Poet; and, 5. Animal Costumes and Choral Spectacle. In the introductory chapter, Compton-Engle sets out her approach, which is a modified form of Taplin's "significant action hypothesis," positing that significant stage action is always marked by the words of the characters on stage. She argues that costumes that deviate from the norm will receive comment—the Eye of the King in *Acharnians* or Agathon's effeminate clothing in *Thesmophoriazusae* for example—and that an absence of comment on a costume is indicative of a "normal" comic costume. The introduction also sets out Compton-Engle's basic categories for understanding costume manipulation, which will be applied to various plays in later chapters. She identifies four basic types of costume change: (1) voluntary stripping in which characters or, more often, chorus members, remove some elements of their costumes (for characters, this is concentrated in *Lysistrata*); (2) involuntary stripping, with verbal or physical force used to remove costume elements, leading to a loss of status for the stripped character (the stripping of Strepsiades, for example, as he prepares to enter Socrates' Thinkery in *Clouds*); (3) the addition of clothing or accessories, with the addition of clothing often involving overlaying of a second identity on top of the initial normative costume (the disguising of Euripides' relative as a woman in *Thesmophoriazusae* for instance); and, (4) costume changes and exchanges, wherein the costume becomes a vehicle of status (the rejuvenated and better dressed Demos at the end of *Knights* or the repeated exchange of slave and heroic costume by Dionysus and Xanthias at the gates of Hades in *Frogs*).

The subsequent chapters focus on clusters of plays, which taken together demonstrate both Compton-Engle's categories of costume manipulation at work and also the importance of costume manipulation in the creation of meaning in performance. Chapter 2 establishes of the nature of comic costumes, laying out our evidence for them, and then demonstrates the ways in which the comic body can be used on the comic stage, focusing on *Knights* and *Lysistrata*. Chapter 3 continues to focus on normative costumes in Old Comedy, looking at the way everyday Athenian clothing can be used and manipulated on stage to create meaning, with a particular focus on *Wasps*, *Assemblywomen*, and *Wealth*. The section on the use of footwear as a symbol of civic engagement (65–67) is particularly interesting, and there is much of value in this chapter. Chapter 4 explores the use of disguise, especially as it relates to Old Comedy's engagement with tragedy and the performance of gender. It focuses particularly on *Acharnians*, *Thesmophoriazusae*, and *Frogs*. Chapter 5 addresses the costumes of the choruses of Old Comedy. As with the earlier discussion of the actors' costumes, Compton-Engle establishes what the evidence is for the appearance of choral costumes and argues for the importance of their visual impact on the audience. More important for Compton-Engle's overarching argument, however, is her discussion of the ways in which choral costumes are manipulated differently than the costumes of actors. The discussion in this chapter focuses on *Birds*. The brief conclusion touches on the changing nature of comic costumes on the Greek stage in the fourth century. One wishes that this had been expanded into an entire chapter on costume in New Comedy, but we can hope that this will be a future area of research for the author.

My only significant criticism of this book is that I wish that there might have been a bit more material in a number of places. As mentioned above, a chapter concerned with comic costumes in the fourth century would be welcome, as would a chapter on the evidence for costumes in Old Comedy provided by the fragments, perhaps pointing to whether the use of costumes in Aristophanes is indicative of the use of costume in Old Comedy generally, or specific to Aristophanic stagecraft. Compton-Engle does an excellent job laying out the evidence for the use of costumes in Aristophanes and assessing their dramatic significance. She is reluctant, however, to make any claims when the evidence is either unclear or lacking. For example, it is accepted that the phallus is an integral part of the costume of Old Comedy, and there is discussion of the phallus at various points in the book. But Compton-Engle avoids taking a stand on the issue of whether the phallus was a standard part of all costumes in Old Comedy, including female characters and choruses, simply acknowledging that "the phallus may have been worn continuously by actors who would switch between male and female roles within one play" (28). This is not an insignificant question, both in terms of our understanding of something fundamental about the nature of Old Comedy, but also of what was required backstage. Did padded body costumes need to be changed in addition to the outer layers of costume? No certain answer is possible, but I would like to know the informed opinion of (now) the foremost scholar of Aristophanic costuming. Quibbles aside, this is an excellent book which provides a welcome contribution to the growing scholarships of the practicalities of the stage and their significance in performance.

NOTES

1. One can look to Revermann's *Comic Business: Theatricality, Technique, and Performance Contexts in Aristophanic Comedy* (OUP: 2006) for an example of scholarship that questions the "significant action" hypothesis and the primacy of the text.

HALLIE REBECCA MARSHALL
University of British Columbia

Amy Holzapfel. *Art, Vision and Nineteenth-Century Realist Drama: Acts of Seeing*. Routledge Advances in Theatre & Performance. New York: Routledge, 2013. Pp. 227.

Theatre historians have acknowledged the rise of photography as a prominent influence on the search for greater reality onstage in the latter part of the nineteenth and early part of the twentieth centuries. The description "photographic" appears prominently in reviews of Broadway productions as the century turned, usually in admiration for the "reality" presented in terms of dialogue as well as set design. Amy Holzapfel invites us in her study, appropriately, to re-see the major currents of nineteenth century theatrical realism. To this end, she places five major European "realist" playwrights—Scribe, Zola,

Ibsen, Strindberg, and Hauptmann—in the context of concurrent realistic movements in photography and art to illustrate the visual as well as the social elements of their most celebrated and popular works.

Holzapfel introduces her ambitious study by going much further back than the end of the nineteenth century, invoking Euripides' *The Bacchae* to illustrate how "characters lose track of their own seeing bodies" (3). Pentheus, Holzapfel claims, with his fatal desire to be the ultimate spectator witnessing an incomparable show from the best seat possible, is "the progenitor of modern realist theatre" (3). The introduction impressively draws from Diderot's "fourth wall," Nietzsche's views on the immersion of the actor and the audience, Schopenhauer and Goethe's studies of vision, and the works of many painters, photographers, and scientists to give the reader a foundational understanding of what the act of seeing meant to nineteenth-century audiences. Holzapfel further delivers a succinct summary of the criticism of realism that has dominated twentieth- and twenty-first-century discourse roughly since the time of Brecht. It is this criticism that Holzapfel effectively and importantly addresses throughout her study. As Holzapfel clarifies, her goal is not so much to save the genre of realism from naysayers, but rather "to challenge the rhetoric that continues to haunt the way we look back upon and narrowly define nineteenth-century realism" (7). It is a challenge that the book meets with scholarship that expertly combines deep examinations of theatre, art, photography, and the history of science.

In Holzapfel's first chapter, which focuses on Eugène Scribe and the *piece bien faite*, she establishes the pattern of contextualizing the playwright and his plays in the contemporaneous worlds of art, photography, and philosophy. She begins with an analysis of Jean-Baptiste Simeon Chardin's 1734 painting *Blowing Soap Bubbles* as an example of the theatrical use of lighting and attention to detail that marks Scribe's detail-oriented brand of realism, particularly in his classic *The Glass of Water*—a world, as Holzapfel notes, that is "governed by *things*" (23, Holzapfel's emphasis). Through thoughtful and persuasive analysis, Holzapfel makes a compelling case for Scribe as a pioneer of nineteenth-century realism rather than the antithesis of the movement, even allowing for the naturalists' disparaging reactions to Scribe and those most influenced by him. Among the most notable reactions, of course, came from Émile Zola, giving Holzapfel a natural bridge to her next chapter.

As photographers like Gaspard-Félix Tournachon investigated the underbelly of Paris in such photos as *The Sewers,* Zola sought a similar view of the underbelly of the human condition in his novels and plays. Zola's experiments also corresponded closely with the increasing scientific interest in the active, rather than passive, observation of the scientist in the process of experimentation. It is this wave of experimental science, Holzapfel argues, that allowed

Zola to simultaneously expound upon the primacy of artistic temperament while insisting upon "truth and accuracy in art" (54). By explaining the way scientists influenced and created their experiments, Holzapfel makes a compelling case for a different way of understanding Zola's "scientific" realism as not merely a passive reproduction of facts and details, but as an attempt to create a living portrait of his characters' inner conflicts. Holzapfel's reading of *Thérèse Raquin* illuminates the play as the principal example of "Zola's theory of naturalism as an active, interpretive, and paradoxical negotiation between visual objectivity and subjectivity" (77).

For the chapter on Ibsen, Holzapfel introduces his subject through the last known picture taken of the playwright, which was in fact a stereograph—two slightly different images taken together for use in a stereoscope. European studies of the nature of vision and the art of the Pre-Raphaelites frame Holzapfel's examination of a few of Ibsen's notable plays, including *A Doll House, Ghosts,* and *The Wild Duck.* Here, Holzapfel perhaps misses an obvious opportunity to discuss the portrait of General Gabler by omitting *Hedda Gabler* from her study; the theme of watching and being seen would seem to be a natural fit for her study. Nevertheless, the connections between art and photography and Ibsen's ongoing interest in the tension between what we can and cannot (or will not) see remain engaging and provocative. The double vision of Ibsen's final photographic likeness proves a potent symbol for Ibsen's photographic rendering of what he would refer to as the "life-lie."

In the fourth chapter, it is August Strindberg himself who provides many of the chapter's most intriguing photographic studies in his series of self-portraits. Strindberg's definitions of the notion of "self" and his descriptions of such characters as the Captain in *The Father* and the title character of *Miss Julie* reveal the same interest in characters "in a state of continual flux" that emerges in Strindberg's series of photos (131). Holzapfel makes the astute connection between Strindberg's work and that of Sir Francis Galton, who produced composite photographic images of racial and ethnic groups as a physiognomic study (a series of studies that contributed to virulent racist stereotypes). Both men were investigating "the institution of the nuclear family" (132). In the case of *Miss Julie,* Strindberg's emphasis in his directions regarding the face further illustrates his technique of photographic composite to attempt to present a living soul onstage.

Holzapfel's final chapter contextualizes the work of Gerhart Hauptmann, particularly through the work of photographers such as Alfred Stieglitz and painters influenced by the schools of impressionism and naturalism such as Max Liebermann. "Hauptmann was, after all, a painter's dramatist," she writes, and her study allows the reader to read Hauptmann through his "pictorial conception of nature" (167). Analyses of *Before Daybreak* and *The Weavers* bring the study to a fitting climax that brings together the contributing streams of Holzapfel's subjects—the areas of photography, art, theatre, and science: "Our view of the outside world [...] is not fixed, stable, and static but always in flux and in relation to the world beyond our own bodies" (184). Vision as an unstable and subjective action lies at the heart of the study.

Holzapfel's invitation to re-view nineteenth-century realism as a still-vibrant part of theatre history is a welcome reminder of the highly theatrical subjectivity that often gets lost or ignored in descriptions of "photographic" and "scientific" theatre. Her examples of the unsettling instability of seeing and observing throughout the book provide scholars with a different way of appreciating the artistry and imagination of the nineteenth-century realists. The book should rightly inspire continued examinations and re-viewings of an important, and perhaps imperfectly understood, group of theatrical artists.

MICHAEL SCHWARTZ
Indiana University of Pennsylvania

Ellen Ecker Dolgin. *Shaw and the Actresses Franchise League: Staging Equality*. Jefferson, NC: McFarland, 2015. pp. 243. Paperback $55.

As its title promises, this monograph focusses on connections between the plays of George Bernard Shaw, the Actresses Franchise League (AFL), and suffrage movements in England and America in the late nineteenth and early twentieth centuries. The scope and value of the book go beyond the specific references in its title, however. In fact, the book's subheading "Staging Equality" represents the wide-ranging content of the book equally well. Throughout the text, author Ellen Ecker Dolgin offers detailed and sophisticated analysis of the complex interplay between theatre practices and politics of this period; she considers the activities of the suffrage movement as acts of performance, women's bodies in activist protest in relation to their roles at home and on stage. With this focus on embodied activism, viewed through the lens of performance, Dolgin's considerations of the relationship between theatre-making and culture one hundred years ago have profound practical implications for activist-artists today, especially feminists working in a crossovers between stage and street such as those featured in the book. Therefore, while the text is a specific look at Shaw, the actresses and activists of the AFL, and the politics of the historical period in which they worked, it is also an inspiration to artists and scholars using performative methodologies to enact social change today, especially in relation to equality of gender, race, sexuality, class, and other intersecting factors impacting historically disenfranchised groups.

The book is the second by author Ellen Ecker Dolgin to cover subjects relating to drama and suffrage. The impetus for the second book came from nascent threads that emerged in research for her first, *Modernizing Joan of Arc* (2008). In the study of St. Joan as icon of the suffrage movement, Dolgin noted the unlikely linkage of Joan, Hedda Gabler, and Medea: "Glaringly disparate on the surface, these three figures embodied society's response to individuals who dared defy proscribed behaviors for wives, daughters or self-promoting leaders. Startlingly, each of these figures was portrayed onstage or on the streets in the same year, 1907, as Elizabeth Robins's play" (3). Elizabeth Robins's *Votes for Women* was produced as part of the Vedrenne-Barker seasons at the Royal Court Theatre (1904–1907), which also featured the plays of George Bernard Shaw in productions that secured his reputation as a major playwright. Significantly, American actress Elizabeth Robins played the first Hedda Gabler in London in 1891. In 1908, actresses (including Robins) formed the Actresses Franchise League to coordinate activist strategies for women's rights that included theatrical performance, known as "suffrage drama." Dolgin explains, "Each layer I found led me back to one thought: the interconnectedness among the writers, theatre practitioners and the public at large" (5). "The stage became the site for representing pressing social issues as well as radical solutions. What people saw onstage and heard in public speeches applied to them directly and invited them to re-shape their own individual identities and goals" (6). Her book then traces the dialogic relationship amongst theatre artists and practitioners, considering their plays and political practices in tandem.

Chapter 1, "Getting Past the Tableaux," focuses on the tradition of the tableau vivant from the late eighteenth century to the early twentieth century. In Chapter 2, titled "Her Unrecognizable Self: Smashing the Idol of Woman," Dolgin chronicles reception to Ibsen's plays in the period, and plays by Shaw and Wilde, particularly those that respond to *A Doll House*. Chapter 3, "Theatre No Stranger Than Ourselves" covers the transition in theatre in the 1890s, including the New Woman as subject. In Chapter 4, "Moving Mountains in Small Spaces: New Drama ca. 1900–1914," she covers in detail the production of plays by Shaw, Galsworthy, Barker, Robins, and modern interpretations of Euripides in the Royal Court Theatre seasons of 1904–1907. The next two chapters, "Breaking News: Transatlantic Theatrical Activists" and "Tandem Stages: Transatlantic Suffrage Drama," cover the development of the AFL and the suffrage drama that developed on both sides of the Atlantic before the First World War. Chapter 7, "Crossing Aisles and Isles: 1908—World War I," looks at the little theatres in England and America and the development of activist and artistic directions in the early twentieth century. The study culminates powerfully in Chapter 8, "Splintered Souls: 1914–1924," which analyses works from the First World War to the mid–1920s in America and England.

Amongst its several strengths, the book offers a comprehensive survey of plays about women's rights and social roles in the period, with synopses and analyses of works such as *Votes for Women* and *How the Vote Was Won* (1909) by Christopher St. John, along with other lesser known performance events relating to suffrage in this period, such as *Diana of Dobson's* (1908) by Cicely Hamilton. In her close reading of Shaw's plays, conducted in large part through staged readings and discussions, Dolgin draws out previously obscure aspects of his dramaturgy in relation to portrayal of the New Woman and promotion of women's rights. One is particularly struck by the ways theatre served as a connective thread across suffrage activities, connecting the movements in America and England.

Another strength of the book is Dolgin's layered coverage of interconnected subjects, accomplished through topic-based chapter designations, as opposed to a chronological, linear presentation of the history of the period. While, as a reader, I occasionally lost track of threads developed in part over more than one chapter, or referenced across several, the book's nonlinear organization and structure is reflective of the interconnectedness of the feminist aesthetics and politics covered. A synthesizing description of the AFL, its key players and history, might assist in contextualizing the significance to the theatre and activism of the period for readers unfamiliar with this group. However, such concerns for traditional structure and context are minor when weighed against the payoff of the unconventional structure.

The greatest strength of the book derives from the force of its cumulative argument, which is best iterated in the overlapping, topic-based style Dolgin employs. As a director and scholar working frequently with the plays of this period, using staging strategies to promote the fair representation of women on stage and off, I found the presentation of the central argument to be extraordinarily effective and inspiring to my practice. Dolgin contextualizes the significance of the realistic style and Ibsen's and Shaw's focus on central female figures in their plays, within Victorian values and the nineteenth century fascination with static visual picture and sculpture: "the proliferation of references to sculptural qualities in women reflected the determination of the male gaze to freeze actual women into beautiful status or encourage their live counterparts to regard statues or idols as ideals for themselves" (20). Dolgin demonstrates how plays by Shaw and his contemporaries, including suffrage dramas, as well as the formation of the AFL, combine to comprise an elaborate, layered cultural phenomenon that broke the static tableau—brought the picture to life and smashed the statue—through the live activities of women's bodies. Dolgin traces this embodied artistic activism from the tableau vivant to post First World War plays—Edna St. Vincent Millay's *Aria de Capo* (1919) and Shaw's *Heartbreak House* (1920). She explains the use of the harlequin and other commedia characters and tropes in the later plays as part of the overall project of the period: "For Shaw, as for Millay, the old form of commedia [...] frame[s] their social indictments. It is especially effective because the fixed character roles that show no growth have the counterpoint of evolving concepts of gender, class, sexuality, and social justice peeking out of the shadows" (211).

Dolgin ends the final chapter with a brief return to the iconic Frenchwoman who inspired the study. Referencing the last moments of Shaw's *St. Joan* (1923), Dolgin asserts, "Here is Shaw's last masterstroke: Joan's traditional prayer and her glance towards the heavens, reminiscent of so many visual representations of Joan, whether on canvas, in sculpture or onstage. Shaw recognized that Joan's story remains unfinished [...] use of Joan's prayerful plea and prose—a last jab at the melodramatic tableau freeze—turns the theatre into a congregation in search of an answer" (215). Effectively, artfully, this is where Dolgin leaves her readers as well—motivated to contemplate and then enact unfinished progress to equality, begun so well by activist-artists, across streets and stages, over a century ago.

ANN M. SHANAHAN
Loyola University Chicago

Judith Fletcher. *Performing Oaths in Classical Greek Drama*. Cambridge: Cambridge University Press, 2012. Pp. 277. Paperback $34.99.

Religious oaths are not something that we in the contemporary West take particularly seriously in our daily lives. Outside of particularly solemn contexts such as courtrooms and legislative and executive posts, few moderns would consciously invoke a deity as a guarantor of their honesty or commitment. The few fossilized oaths that remain in our vocabulary, such as "I swear" or "as God is my witness," are now little more than verbal intensifiers, designed to add intensity to our statements without any real intention of getting God directly involved in our affairs. This was not, however, the case in ancient Athens. In an environment where legal sanctions were weak and the gods seen as very present and involved in human life, oaths were a serious business. If one invoked a deity's name when making a promise or declaration, one stood at risk of that deity's vengeance if one broke that oath by lying or failing to deliver.

Judith Fletcher's book, *Performing Oaths in Classical Greek Drama* explores how the serious business of oaths is portrayed in ancient Athenian tragedy and comedy. Drawing on speech-act theory and studies of ancient ideologies of gender, Fletcher provides an incisive and often stimulating examination not only of dramatic depictions of oaths, but also how those depictions related to the real-life use of oaths in the politics and daily life of democratic Athens.

The book's cover illustration shows David's painting *The Oath of the Horatii*. Perhaps surprisingly, this eighteenth-century CE French depiction of an oath from Roman legend serves as the perfect illustration for Fletcher's main thesis about oaths in fifth-century BCE Greek drama. The painting shows three young men, the Horatii triplets, extending their right arms to swear an oath before their aged father. At the opposite side of the painting sit the family's female members, weeping and isolated, in a different world from the active and determined males. Fletcher convincingly argues that this same gender-separation is to be found in depictions of oaths in Athenian drama. Oaths are, under normal circumstances, the domain of adult, male citizens. Meanwhile, women and "unmanly" men's oaths often go awry, showing that they lack the proper control of language necessary to serve as a citizen and a political actor. Through a close examination of all the extant Athenian dramatists, Fletcher traces how this gendered ideology of the oath is upheld or challenged in a variety of genres and narratives.

This gendered paradigm of the oath, Fletcher proposes, is found in its most canonical form in the plays of Aeschylus and Sophocles, the subject of the first three chapters of her work. In many of these plays, the successful performance of oaths marks the transition of a young man into full adulthood. In Aeschylus's tragic trilogy *The Oresteia,* the maturation of the hero Orestes is demonstrated in his ability to carry out successfully the oath he swore to avenge his father's murder (45). Likewise, Sophocles' *Trachiniae* and *Philoctetes* both contain instances of young men whose transition to adulthood is marked by their swearing oaths to a father or father-figure, who in turn receives the oaths and recognizes the young men's authority to swear (85–87, 96–98). Oaths not only serve as the gateway into adulthood, but remain a major aspect of the adult, political world. Oaths serve to bind individuals and communities together in friendship as exemplified by the oath of alliance between Orestes and the Athenian people at the end of Aeschylus's *Eumenides* (66–67), or the similar oaths of friendship exchanged between the Athenian king Theseus and the Theban Oedipus at the end of Sophocles' *Oedipus at Colonus* (121–22). By contrast, women's oaths in Sophoclean and Aeschylean drama are depicted as flawed and dangerous. Just as Orestes swore to avenge his father's murderer, so the murderer, his mother Clytemnestra, also swears that her act was a just vengeance for her daughter Iphigeneia's death. But where Orestes' oath is a noble and productive pledge sworn to the Olympian gods. Clytemnestra's is presented as a dark and perverted spell, sworn to destructive underworld powers and sealed with the impious murder of her husband (49–50).

Having established the "proper" form of oaths, Fletcher proceeds in the second half of the book to deal with more perversions and distortions of oaths in the works of two more contrarian writers: the comic poet Aristophanes and the iconoclastic tragedian Euripides. Both writers, she argues, are fascinated by the failure of oaths and oath-makers. Where Sophocles and Aeschylus showed adolescents and adult men proving their moral fitness by successfully using oaths, Euripides' presents the opposite: deformed or deficient men failing miserably in their performance of oaths. So, for example, it seems inevitable that the children of Oedipus in Euripides' *Phoenissae*, products of unnatural incest and laboring under an ancestral curse, will fail to keep their oath of friendship to one another and plunge their city into civil war (130–32). Both the eunuch slave in the tragedy *Orestes* and the satyr Silenus in the satyr-play *Cyclops* likewise swear dishonestly—just as their distorted bodies are far removed from the toned physique of the ideal male citizen, so too are their oaths deformed and deficient (142–46, 146–52).

In the comedies of Aristophanes, oaths are, like everything else, thrown topsy-turvy by the anarchic spirit of comedy. In the *Lysistrata* the rebellious women perform a burlesque of an oath-sacrifice and present their agreement to abstain from sex as a military alliance (228–34). This adoption of activities normally in the male preserve prefigures the women's inversion of traditional power-relations, as they assume authority over the city's men. In the *Clouds* Aristophanes' distortion of the oath goes further: the comic Socrates, having "proven" that the gods who guarantee oaths do not exist, can teach his students to perjure themselves with impunity, confident that their dishonesty will never be subject to divine punishment (164–71).

This summary can, of course, only give the barest skeleton of the book's content. In the course of investigating the Greek dramatic oath, Fletcher deals with a host of other fascinating topics that this issue throws up: the book includes fascinating discussions of topics as diverse as ancient constructions of gender, Olympian theology, and the power of language to shape society. I myself was particularly struck by Fletcher's frequent attempts to link the depictions of oaths in tragedy to the social and political context in which they were first performed. She frequently suggests interesting ways in which the keeping and breaking of oaths in drama reflected Athenian citizens' anxieties about the many oaths that governed their public and private lives in the fifth and fourth centuries BCE (e.g., 99–101, 139–41).

Fletcher's investigation is deeply anchored in the scholarly literature surrounding all the plays she discusses, and engages carefully and thoughtfully with the many debates that the ancient dramas have generated. Indeed, the primary function of most of her investigations is to show how consideration of oaths can reinforce and deepen pre-existing interpretations of the various plays. So, for example, she shows how the traditional interpretation of the *Oresteia* as a movement from tribal vengeance to civic justice is reflected in the use of oaths in the plays, which begin with Clytemnestra's demonic ritual, move through Orestes' more sedate oath of vengeance, and conclude with the oaths of impartial citizen-jurors in Athens (58–59). This approach, though not as immediately thrilling as the generation of an entirely new interpretation, is still a worthy academic contribution. Indeed, a perhaps unintended consequence of the degree of the book's engagement with the scholarship is that it could serve as an excellent resource with which to introduce those new the study of Greek drama to the debates surrounding the various playwrights' works.

Such an introductory function may, however, be somewhat hampered by what amounts to my only major complaint about this book. While it was always a fascinating read, it was not always an easy one. At the level of sentences and paragraphs, the text could be quite convoluted and difficult to follow, and I often found myself having to read passages several times in order to make sense of them. The order of the chapters seemed likewise confused at times, as one chapter on Aristophanes was detached from the others and inserted between two chapters on Euripides, damaging the flow of Fletcher's arguments concerning both authors. All in all, it seemed to me that the book could have done with another round of editing in order to make the prose tighter and more readable. This was especially true of the introductory chapter, which seemed unnecessarily long, and whose connection to the main body of the text was not always clear.

That being said, the book certainly does repay the effort it sometimes required. It deals with a fascinating and under-examined aspect of ancient drama, and definitely enriches the study of all the ancient Greek playwrights. With the caveats mentioned above, I would certainly not hesitate to recommend this to anyone interested in the history and theory of the ancient stage.

DANIEL B. UNRUH
Cambridge University

Index